HISTORY AND LEGENDS OF THE
EUROPEAN WATERWAYS

Other books by Roger Pilkington include:

Twenty volumes of the 'Small Boat ...' series, from *Small Boat through Belgium* (1957) to *Small Boat in the Midi* (1989), Children's adventures from *Jan's Treasure* (1955) to *The Ormering Tide* (1974), *I Sailed on the Mayflower* (1990) and *View from the Shore* (1995)

Scientific or Religious works, including:

In the Beginning
World without End
Heavens Alive
Revelation through Science
Robert Boyle – Father of Chemistry
The Ways of the Sea
Sons and Daughters

HISTORY AND LEGENDS OF THE EUROPEAN WATERWAYS

Roger Pilkington

with sketches by the late
David Knight

The Book Guild Ltd
Sussex, England

The Book Guild Ltd
25 High Street,
Lewes, Sussex

First published 1998
© Roger Pilkington, 1998

Set in Palatino
Typesetting by Acorn Bookwork, Salisbury, Wiltshire

Printed in Great Britain by
Bookcraft (Bath) Ltd, Avon

A catalogue record for this book is
available from the British Library

ISBN 1 85776 219 3

CONTENTS

INTRODUCTION

This book is not about waterways. That is, there are no lists of
names and addresses of departmental engineers, and no infor-
mation as to the number of locks or the height of bridges. It is a
guide to leisurely travelling throughout Western Europe, and if
it is based on rivers and canals that is partly because I like to
explore in that way. Every place mentioned here has been personally visited by myself at some time or other, by water.

The choice of waterways is not fortuitous. The Romans used
them, medieval monarchs extended or improved them, and they
are steeped in history and legend in a way that few landbound
places can be. European civilisation spread along the water-
courses, and from earliest times their castles and keeps, their
abbeys and cathedrals have been redolent of legend in a way
that no motorway city can hope to be. And what would our
Europe be, without its immense treasury of legends?

The earliest transport routes were, of course, the larger rivers:
Rhine and Rhône, Moselle and Meuse; it was by these routes
that the church spread from the Middle East, establishing new
communities and bringing to the local peoples new knowledge
of farming as well as newer ideals. And their history is well
documented, too. We have in Western Europe a heritage such as
no others have.

In theory – but probably not in practice – one can enter the
waterway system at Calais and penetrate in the space of a few
years to Vladivostok. In this book we shall not do so, and we
shall not actually roam in the lands of Eastern Europe which
used to be cut off from the rest by the Iron Curtain. There are
good reasons for this – lack of dredging on the one hand, and
my own increasing age on the other. And languages, too. I
never feel content when I cannot speak the local language and
talk to the inhabitants and hear their tales of the past. Besides,
it seems discourteous to expect people always to understand
English!

The places I have chosen for mention are those which offer a
special interest of history, or of legend. Naturally some of the
large centres of population do just that, but as Paris, Rotterdam
and Frankfurt are well-known, vast, and well-documented in

standard guide-books I have omitted them and left it to the guide-books to provide enough omniscience.

Then there is also the question of what to include. What are the criteria of selection? Firstly, every place mentioned is easily accessible to any boatman who starts out from the shores of England and reaches the continental coast at one of the many ports large or small which have access to a canal or river. All these places are linked to form a wide-spread network of those that seem to me to have a tale worth telling, whether true or fictional. The only exception is Sweden. It is possible to reach Sweden without any long sea voyage at all, and it is a country of such fascinating waterways that it would at least be ungracious to leave it out. Besides, we have a close affinity with that wonderful country. Did not the Vikings, both Swedish and Danish, have a great influence upon the development of Britain?

At the same time I realise that for every family that has the time to travel slowly by boat and see the beauty of an unspoiled Europe, there are many who have not the time, and maybe not the inclination either, but whose interest in the people and the places is every bit as real. So I have tried to keep the motorist in mind, too. After all, there is nothing superior about boating, even if it is probably true that at a speed of five knots one is more likely to take in the wonders of the scenery, and of nature, than at ten times that speed. So I hope that the motorist who wants to dig beneath the surface of our common heritage will find this book a good introduction to the countries that lie to the side of the flyovers and roundabouts.

There is one further limitation. I hope that a certain standard of accuracy is maintained, and if between my writing this book – the result of 20 years of inland voyaging – a canal has been closed, or replaced by another, I hope the reader will forgive me. But I think that as far as can be ascertained, all the routes dealt with here are in navigable condition and can still lead one into a world, whether modern or medieval, which is vanishing beneath the impact of modern technology.

Roger Pilkington.
Grouville in Jersey, and Montouliers in the Midi.

PART 1

HOLLAND, BELGIUM AND
NORTHERN FRANCE

The entrance to the continental waterways is at Bordeaux, Le Havre, or most conveniently at any harbour north of Cap Gris Nez except Blankenberge. Calais, Gravelines, Dunkirk, Nieupoort, Ostend and the Scheldt are all within easy range. And very soon, whichever one chooses, one is in the country of the Flemish weavers, or the great Dutch painters. I have assumed a southern entry here, to lead to the city of Furnes, capital of all that was left to the heroic King Albert when the Germans invaded and destroyed so much of his small country of Belgium in 1914. Indeed, at the lock at Nieupoort, where five waterways meet, there is a splendid equestrian memorial to him, and the name of the nearby street commemorates the lock-keeper who saved the remnant of that country by judicious use of the sluices.

Beyond Furnes we come to two of the most splendid cities of Europe – Bruges and Ghent – before turning northward toward Holland.

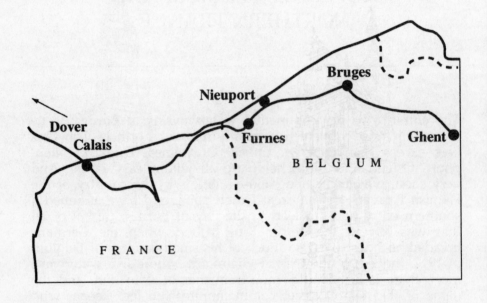

1

Furnes, Bruges and Ghent

Furnes (Veurne)

The Canal de Furnes was completed before Louis XIV was born, and so ranks as one of the oldest in France. It runs from Dunkirk to Nieupoort in Belgium.

3

The only account of this canal I have found is in Commander Moens's *Through France and Belgium by River and Canal in the Steam Yacht 'Ytene'*, published in 1876. Moens yachted in style, with several tons of coal and a crew to stoke and manage the ship, and he and his men had the right attitude to obstructions. On the Canal de Furnes he was stopped by a temporary bridge. He hunted out the burgomaster of Adinkerke, who responded only with unsatisfactory grunts, but would not order the bridgeman to remove the span. However, a barge soon arrived and its crew and Moens's men set about the bridge and demolished it, whilst the bridgeman stood by as quiet as could be.

The successor to this bridge is still there, beyond the quay where the Belgian customs officers, Sam-Browned and genial and portly, and with just a trace of Groucho Marx imparted by their cigars, clamber over the barges to make a formal inspection of the papers of any such strange and unexpected craft.

There is a mysterious beauty in the first view of Furnes, its spires peeping up behind the chestnut trees at the edge of the meadows, and not a detail in that very Flemish picture has changed. Past a white-washed cottage perched on the bank and tilted slightly backward the canal curves quickly toward the town, aims straight for a massive brick bastion, decides at the last moment to double round it instead, and then kinks back in the town moat to join the quiet Canal de Bergues and follow the fortifications round towards the harbour basin.

Furnes, or Veurne, is famous for its annual Procession of Penitents, and one cannot think about this great trudging in black hoods and cowls and habits without wondering that the municipal penitence began as a kind of communal atonement for the alleged sacrilege of a young soldier and not for the frightful fate dealt out to him by the authorities, who had him led round the town and exhibited with his hands enclosed in red-hot gloves of armour before publicly strangling him, burning his body, and pounding the ashes. But that, of course, was in the days of the Inquisition, when one was supposed to be doing the young man a kindly turn by such treatment.

Justice was certainly tough in those times, but it could be strangely sympathetic, too. Punishment by beheading was common, and any transgressor might consider himself lucky if the magistrate merely ordered him to have one of his hands chopped off with a cleaver. Yet in Furnes the second half of the fifteenth century brought the pleasant custom of 'symbolic'

4

execution, and instead of having to sacrifice his own head or hand, a guilty party would be required to provide and sacrifice one in bronze instead. Seven such articles are still to be seen in the town hall, and one can only feel that Pieter de Beert escaped lightly if he had merely to expiate his bold threats to throw the magistrates out of the window by having a sculptor or foundry-man cast him a head in metal.

Like many a Flemish town, Furnes does not perform its curious rites just to attract attention. It is a place where nuns and priests are so much part of the scene that if they were absent one would think the town had met with some disaster. So, too, beside the gilded and pillared doorway of the magnifi-cent town hall a plain white cross now stands against the wall. Across its arms is the plain legend *Gedenk O Mens!* – 'Remember, O Man!' Others scattered through the town recall the burghers with the same direct simplicity to remember – not the wars of 1914–18 or 1939–45, but the season of Easter and the Passion.

The little gabled buildings around the market-place are neat and compact, and each differs just enough from its neighbours to be intriguing. They are low, as though specially designed to give place of honour to the town hall and the Spanish guard house, and they seem to watch each other across the great square as though expecting something to happen. But the only events appear to be that the council has erected the same double gallows type of street light which is such a commonplace disfig-urement in Britain, and has allowed the splendid wide pattern of coloured cobbles and bricks which covered the square like a great tapestry to be scored over with geometrical parking lines in yellow and white. But these things I suppose must be accepted in an age of internal combustion.

It is better to notice instead the stepped gables and striped awnings, the tree-decked remains of great religious houses plun-dered by French revolutionaries, and the splendid belfry tower which stands sentinel over the wide flat plain extending to Ypres, a tower as light and airy as the neighbouring nave of St Walburga's is sober, and as the square tower of old St Nicho-las's church is simple and severe but formidably strong. Had its bells not been stolen by the French revolutionaries, they might still sound gentle and sweet across the wet green meadows and the dikes and canals, as once they did. And they would have tolled across a scorched and muddy and tree-less landscape in 1918 to tell that peace had come at last to Belgium. For Furnes

5

was long the headquarters of brave King Albert in the little corner of his land that remained to him.

And if Furnes survived, that was partly because of the lock-keeper Karel Cogge, in memory of whom the Karel Coggelaan runs down from the main street to the harbour. He was the man who persuaded the Belgian command that by careful operation of the sluices and canals and use of the tides, it would be possible to flood the German lines along the Yser front but keep the Belgian trenches dry. In this he succeeded, and Furnes remained untaken, free, Flemish, and proud. But perpetually penitent.

Bruges

6

The glory of Flanders in medieval times, Bruges is situated at a junction of canals which remind us of its continual struggle to have an outlet to the sea. The earliest was the canal to Damme, a port now silted up and abandoned. Then came the Ostende and Plassendale canals, and later still the Canal de Bruges à Ghent.

Bruges is also proud of the 'Holy Blood'. The story of this famous relic is a strange mixture of legend and tradition and is bound up with the Holy Grail, which is said to have been used at the Last Supper and then employed by Joseph of Arimathea as a receptacle for some of the blood of Christ. At this point the tale branches in a number of directions, according to the nationality of the tellers. English legend would naturally like Joseph to have brought the vessel to England, where its subsequent loss gave good scope for medieval story-telling. Others, however, prefer Joseph to have guarded the relic in Jerusalem. Bruges takes the detail further than most and tells that Diederich, Count of Flanders, took part in the Second Crusade along with a contingent of men from Bruges, and was rewarded for his support by the presentation to him of a few drops of the Holy Blood by the patriarch of Jerusalem. This priceless treasure was carried home by Abbot Leonius of St Berten, and when the victorious crusaders reached Bruges once more in the spring of 1148 the count himself bore the relic into the city.

The Count of Flanders had a little chapel built to house the relic, and this shrine is still to be seen, although it has been much embellished in later centuries, and the actual container for the relic, wrought of gold and silver and studded with gems, dates from the seventeenth. The relic is believed to have remained continually in its chapel under the guard of the Brotherhood of the Holy Blood until the day in 1303 when it was brought out and carried round the city in procession, in thanksgiving for victory in the battle of the Golden Spurs. Ever since, the procession has taken place annually except during times of violence or siege – when the relic has always been hidden by one of the inhabitants, as for instance during the French Revolution, when a priest sealed it up in the wall of his house.

Bruges takes its relic extremely seriously and regards it as something between a patron saint and an insurance policy, or more specifically as a favour from God to protect the people in the midst of their hard struggle to preserve the Catholic faith. 'Neither the history nor the inward life of our City can be rightly interpreted apart from the miraculous Divine pulsa-

7

tion of the Holy Blood.' In 1938 the mayor suggested that a pageant play involving several thousands of the citizens should be performed in veneration of the Holy Blood, and now this remarkable performance is repeated at intervals of five years.

If Bruges seems haunted by the past, the memories which hang over it are not all peaceful ones of nuns and merchants and painters. Flanders is more stained with blood than any other part of the world and, though Ypres has seen terrible destruction, the narrow streets and alleys of Bruges have witnessed violence and massacre on many occasions. As we turn left from the Predikherenrei along the quay of the Groene Rei and over the little bridge towards the centre of the city, we pass through a narrow alley spanned by a gilded corridor window connecting the town hall and the law courts. This alley is the Street of the Blind Donkey, and through the arch is the Bourg, now a square in which the coaches of travel tours lie between the trees, but once the site of the fortress of the Counts of Flanders and the nearby Church of St Donatian.

It was in 1127 that Charles the Good, the Count of Flanders who first set the example of kindliness to the poor, was struck down by one of the proud and jealous family of the Erembalds as he knelt in prayer before the altar in the Church of St Donatian. Flushed with their success, the Erembalds and their supporters rushed through the city, killing as they went, but their triumph was short. The people were roused. Rumour said that a hunchback had been cured and straightened as he went to touch the body of the murdered Charles where it lay before the altar. The Count's friends rallied throughout Flanders and sacked the wealthy homes of the Erembalds, and when allies within Bruges let them through the gates of the city a pitched battle was soon raging in the narrow Street of the Blind Donkey.

Forced to give way before the fury of the Count's avengers, the Erembalds retired fighting to the stronghold of the Bourg and closed the gates, but in spite of their desperate resistance the attackers eventually forced an entrance and drove the survivors back down a passage into the nave of the church of St Donatian. The grim last stand was made in the church tower, and only when the attackers began to batter at its foundations did the 30 survivors of the Erembalds come down and surrender, 'pale and livid and ugly' as a contemporary writer recorded, 'but our citizens wept when they saw those who had once been their leaders led away to prison'.

They may have wept, but their tears did not save the Erembalds. One by one they were led to the top of the tower of St Donatian and thrown down into the square below. Today, the country people sit contentedly on the same spot to wait for the buses which take them out to their villages in the same Flanders which Charles the Good had tried to serve.

When we attend the Play of the Holy Blood we find ourselves sitting close beside the massive monument to Pieter de Coninck and Jan Breidel, the heroes of another fearful fight within the streets. It was in 1302 that trouble broke out between the Leliarts – the nobility of Bruges who supported Philip of Navarre – and the mass of the people. Pieter de Coninck, Dean of the Guild of Weavers, roused the populace against paying taxes to support the lavish entertainment afforded to Philip the Fair of France and his Queen Joanna. Standing in front of the belfry he called for resistance, and he was at once seized and imprisoned in the Bourg, but the sympathetic mob assaulted the stronghold and rescued him. Soon de Coninck, together with Jan Breidel, the Dean of the Butchers, and 5,000 Flemish patriots were installed at Damme, planning the liberation of their land from French rule.

The signal for action came when de Chatillon, the French Governor of Flanders, entered Bruges with 2,000 knights to put down any trace of insurrection. News was carried to Damme, and in the early dawn de Coninck was at the Porte St Croix and Breidel at the Dammepoort. Silently the burghers still within the city armed themselves, and when the Flemings entered the streets the French were taken by surprise – and probably in the middle of a hangover.

In the streets and at the town gates furious Flemings shouted *'Schildt ende Vriendt'* – Shield and Friend – and by forcing others to repeat these guttural Flemish words they immediately identified the Frenchmen and killed them on the spot. Throughout the morning of the terrible Bruges Matins the disordered French knights faced the pikes of the burghers, the stones hurled from the roofs by the women and children, or the clubs of the apprentices of the Guild of Butchers, but by evening they had been slain to the last man and only de Chatillon and his chancellor escaped in disguise through the alleys and over the cobbles slippery with the blood of the French knights.

De Chatillon reached Paris, and Philip the Fair at once raised an army of 40,000 to sack Bruges and teach the Flemings a lesson. The burghers of every Flemish town marched to meet

9

them. From Bruges and Ghent and Ypres and Furnes, even from Maastricht, the townsmen marched in their own guilds, with de Coninck and Breidel at their head. They camped in the marshes before Courtrai on the banks of the River Lys or Leie. Cutting down the brushwood, they covered the dykes and the quagmires, and when the French nobles charged, their horses sank floundering in the morass. De Chatillon was killed, and his chancellor was clubbed to death. The French commander, the Comte d'Artois, was wrenched off his horse by a monk who had run from his cell to join the fight. Twenty thousand Frenchmen were killed, for the loss, it is said, of only one hundred Flemings, and the Battle of the Golden Spurs – so called from the gilt spurs torn from the bodies of the French knights and carried home as trophies – went down in history as the first occasion when a revolutionary people's army defied and thoroughly defeated the trained might of a great military power.

The cobbles of the Bruges quaysides, too, have witnessed other scenes besides the lading of the rich cargoes of cloth or barrels of wine and kegs of butter, and the Quai Vert is still haunted by the shape of a Spanish soldier who could find no rest for his soul among the horrible memories of the crimes he had committed in the name of the Inquisition. Even the quiet idyll of the Minnewater beside the Begijnhof stirs memories of violence and horror, for the swans which preen themselves under the willows or sail slowly down the medieval canal to solicit scraps from the tourists in the little trip launches are not just there by chance. They belong to the city, and they still remind the burghers of the year 1488, when their forefathers rose against the great Maximilian of Austria himself, confined him within the city and dragged his favourite and supporter Pieter Langhals into the market place, to suffer torture as the first man to try out the rack which he had invented, and which he had intended to use to enforce the will of his master.

In an orgy of revenge, Langhals was tortured, stripped and executed in the market square below the belfry, but when once more the burghers of Bruges had to submit to the vast power of the Holy Roman Empire in an uneasy peace, Maximilian ordered the city to keep swans on her waters, that these graceful birds with their long necks might ever remind the citizens of his favourite and executive Pieter Langhals – Peter Long-Neck.

It is after dark that Bruges is at its loveliest, for in the glow of the lamps the memories of bloodshed and torture seem to fade into the darkness beyond.

10

Ghent (Gand)

Ghent lies on the Upper Scheldt (Escaut), the River Lys, the Canal de Bruges à Ghent, and the Terneuzen Ship Canal. As a port, Ghent has always shared with Bruges the disadvantage of not being on the sea. At least it stands on a navigable river, but little of its commerce reaches it by way of the estuary because at low water the water can be very low indeed. For centuries the city has used other routes to the coast, and as one after another the chosen outlets became silted up, closed by wars, blocked by international treaty or choked with weed, some new channel had to be constructed. The Bruges–Ghent canal is one of these, but it was no longer sufficient for the traffic when once Ghent began to enter upon a new prosperity. A shorter and more direct cut to the sea was needed, and the energetic mayor Lieven Bauwens, who developed the cotton industry of the city, had the old sixteenth-century canal to Terneuzen enlarged to form a proper ship canal. Since then it has been widened and deepened on more than one occasion.

Ghent likes to describe itself as the 'Manchester of Europe', but even this piece of self-abasement does not keep people away from it. As a Lancastrian, I can see that both cities have a connection with the fabric trade, and each has a ship canal, but further than that the similarity is not obvious. Manchester has nothing to compare with what is to be seen on every hand in Ghent, a city where buildings from the thirteenth century onwards jostle each other in competition to be admired. The burghers are proud of its riches, and rightly so, for there can be few façades in the world to equal the row of guild houses and the other buildings which have to do with ships and boatmen, the splendid line of gables which faces across the Graslei quay to the black water of the Lys. It is a view which never tires, one that at each visit seems to be even more intriguing and mysteriously beautiful than before.

Then there is the cathedral itself, with the incredible microscopic detail of the *Adoration of the Mystic Lamb*, and the orchestra of angels familiar from every book on the history of painting. In contrast to this splendour, the side streets wandering back from the shadow of St Bavon's lead away by quiet and curiously timeless *béguinages*, where the French Revolution might never have been and where nuns come and go, pensive but not too downcast, through the grand portals put up by generations of founders and benefactors. Turn another corner, and

11

the Castle of the Counts frowns grimly from fathoms of mud and congealed filth in a stagnant backwater, and to remind one of the days now happily gone, a circle of white cobbles not far away marks where the municipal cauldron of oil was kept at the boil when there were Anabaptists or witches or any other unpopular people to be done away with as hideously as possible. And always, soaring over all, is the tower of Ghent's famous belfry, set right in the centre of the town and topped by a gilded dragon defiant and just a little spiteful.

In the base of the belfry there is now an ingenious scale model of the medieval town upon which a sort of miniature *son et lumière* is performed to recall the days of the great local patriot, Jakob van Artevelde, who brought prosperity to his city and was slain for his pains by an ungrateful crowd. It is surprising how many buildings are recognisable as having survived the six centuries since that time, but even more astonishing is to discover that the only change in the waterways has been the addition of the present connection with the sea, and the excavation of the new ring canal and the docks. For even in the fourteenth century, Ghent was a port with contacts throughout Europe and a centre of inland navigation.

Ghent is a large and modern city, but the outlook across its high-pitched tiled roofs from the top of the great tower of St Baaf's cathedral shows that tucked away behind the busy streets there are still courtyards of great charm where the Begijns and the nuns come and go in slow peaceful downcast walk between the trees and round their little formal gardens, gay with Ghent begonias. And down below, in the cathedral itself, is the incomparable polyptych of the van Eyck brothers.

The *Mystic Lamb* has had some strange adventures. Under Austrian rule the picture was locked up because the Emperor was offended by the nude figures of Adam and Eve. A few years later the whole thing was seized during the French Revolution, but instead of being destroyed it was taken to the Louvre until the battle of Waterloo ensured its restoration to its native city. Some of the panels, however, were sold privately, and later they were bought up by German galleries and were on view in Berlin until 1919, when a special provision of the Treaty of Versailles provided for their return to Ghent. Adam and Eve had meanwhile been once more considered rather risqué for an ecclesiastical picture and had been banished to the Musée Royal at Brussels. Their places were temporarily taken by a couple more adequately clothed, but the original pair were eventually restored to Ghent again and during the 1920s the complete poly-ptych remained reunited in St Baaf's. Unfortunately, however, this state of affairs did not last. Somebody stole the bottom left-hand panel and tried to ransom it anonymously for a million francs. Very properly the demand was refused, and nothing more was heard of the panel until some weeks later, when a highly respected burgher was making a speech, in the course of which he had a sudden stroke. Just before he died he made the astonishing revelation that it was he who had stolen the van Eyck panel, his business having run into debt; but unfortunately death overtook him before he had finished his confession and explained where he had hidden it. The panel must certainly be in existence, but it has never yet been found, and a very compe-tent reproduction has had to take its place.

The sombre Castle of the Counts of Flanders still stands in the surrounding waters of the Lys. It is a grim edifice, complete with torture chambers and a guillotine introduced into city life with the French Revolution, but at night its forbidding appear-ance changes to one of great beauty in the skilful floodlighting, the outer curtain wall rising majestically out of its own reflection in the still water whilst the massive keep looms cold and powerful within.

Nearby is the lovely Butchers' Hall with its long row of step-gabled windows, and the magnificent Graslei or Quai aux Herbes, an unspoilt row of medieval buildings and guild houses which is one of the greatest glories of Europe. At night the buildings stand out so faintly in a bluish-grey gleam that one can hardly be sure that it is not just the cold glow of a full moon which is falling on them. There is the house of the Corp-oration of Free Boatmen, of 1531, the Guild of Masons from a few years earlier, the House of the Grain Measurers, built in the seventeenth century, and the tiny house of the toll collector next door to the Spijker, the granary which even in the twelfth century was storing the grain which the city exacted as a toll of one third upon the cargoes passing through her waterways. And up in the night sky the three great towers of St Nicholas, St Baaf and the City Belfry stand out in the glow of the lighting, the smooth golden balls and the gilded dragon on the Belfry's spire shining gay and confident over the city.

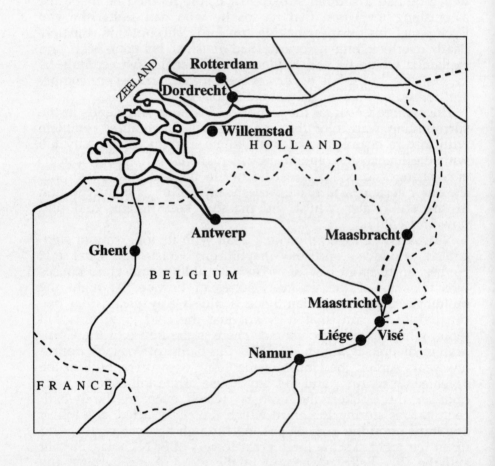

2

Zieriksee, Willemstad, Dordrecht and the Vliet

Already we are in a countryside with canals in almost every direction. In heading northward I have assumed leaving Ghent by the ship canal to Terneuzen on the Scheldt. This is a busy route, leading to Flushing, Antwerp, and particularly to the South Beveland Canal, a short link across to the main area of Zeeland. The places I have selected as interesting are Zieriksee, Willemstad and Dordrecht. The last of these was the centre of clandestine printing of English books at the time of the persecution of Protestants under James I. The entrance to the Wollwevershaven, a good place for overnighting, is seen in the *View of Dordrecht* by Albert Cuyp, in the Kenwood Gallery on Hampstead Heath. The view has not changed much since those days.

Zieriksee

With old dikes, newer dikes, and now the huge barriers of the Delta Plan, Zeeland is an area won from the ever-menacing sea by sheer digging. Indeed, diking and mending breaches in the banks has always been a matter of life and death for the people of the Netherlands, so much so that it was always vital that no petty and private squabbles should interfere with the communal struggle against the water. Long ago, the instant that work on the dikes was necessary a state of dike-peace was announced, and anyone who imperilled the general safety by starting to fight was promptly sentenced to death. Refusal to work on the dike was also a capital crime, and to encourage the others such an individual was sometimes skewered alive on a pole which was stuck in the gap to be filled. Those who, from sheer infirmity or loss of limbs, were unable to tackle the diking were sometimes turned out of the land, and a strange law provided that if a man were unequal to the task of closing a breach in the part of the dike under his care he had to put out his spade and leave

15

it there. This implied that if any other man could dig and fill the breach he might do so, and if he should succeed in closing the breach he automatically took the land, farm, livestock and all.

Zierikzee, the main but small town on the Zeeland island of Schouwen, is perhaps named after some half-legendary Zierik or Sigerik who first established a community upon the particular *ee* or creek which is still represented by the old harbour. Throughout much of medieval times there was a small town on ground slightly higher than the surrounding marshes, but Schouwen itself had still not been diked, and the monks of St Baaf's at Ghent grazed their sheep in the watery meadows and sought fish and fowl in the marshes. Perhaps it was they who built the mounds of refuge, a few of which can still be made out on the island. Or maybe it was the Zeelanders of longer ago, people who eked out a strange and watery existence in the intervals between ferrying the departed spirits on their final journey.

At St Baaf's in Ghent the body of the Irish monk was buried to whom the cathedral of Zierikzee was later to be dedicated. Little is known of St Lieven, and some Dutch authorities are convinced that he did not exist – whether he had a body or not. They think his name is mixed up with *Onze Lieve Vrouw*. But I prefer to think that he was one of those energetic Irish monks who evangelised the tough places of Europe, that he really was martyred in Flanders about 657, and that he had previously preached to the wild fisherpeople and boatmen of Schouwen. His area of apostleship was certainly a watery one, even more so than it is today, and perhaps that is why he became a patron saint of sailors in this corner of Europe. The cathedral dedicated to him was to have had the highest tower in the world, and had it been completed to its original dimensions only the Eiffel Tower and a few of the larger skyscrapers would even today overtop it. But it proved easier to plan a tower of such size than to build it, and after 80 years the work came to a halt with the tower at its present massive proportions. People say that the building work was stopped after a fearful night of storm and flood when so many ships were sunk that 500 women of the town were widowed before morning broke, and the master mason also was drowned. Perhaps this is yet another fiction, but it could well be that some unusual disaster took away the enthusiasm for building and also dried up the flow of money.

Schouwen has often had trouble with its dikes, but if the floods have breached them none can say that this is necessarily the fault of the dikemen and engineers. Once a fisherman sailed

16

out and inadvertently caught a mermaid, but heartlessly he would not let her go. Her merman husband broke the surface and cried out in anger that the people of Schouwen would forever have cause to lament that they had stolen his beloved, but no doubt they did not believe him. Perhaps the merman is still bent upon the ruin of the islanders, for in the storm of 1953, when the Zeeland dikes were breached in many places, such a gap was torn at Schelphook that it was only closed by the efforts of the largest repair fleet the world has ever seen. A ring dike more than two and a half miles long had to be built to stop the rush of tide through the gap, which had by then scoured a channel a third of a mile in width and up to 20 fathoms deep.

The materials were brought up in a fleet of nearly three hundred barges, and what with the tugs and draglines, bulldozers and railway locomotives needed to shift the mud and sand and stone, the repair of Schouwen's dike cost several times the entire value of the island. Yet the Dutch can never allow themselves to think in ledger fashion about their sea defences. If they were always to abandon an area because the diking was too costly, there would be little of Holland left except for Limburg and the low hills around Arnhem. And this the dikemen have always known. Andreas Vierlingh, the great dikemaster of the sixteenth century, had warned that to maintain Schouwen would cost ten to twenty times its worth – but only, he said, because a parsimonious attitude to diking had persisted and the people (who in those days had to foot the bills) had tried to hold out the scouring waters of the delta with inadequate banks improperly maintained.

Zierikzee was the central town of Zeeland, even if Middelburg might be the capital, and it was an important prize for the Spaniards to capture. If Duiveland and Schouwen could be taken, the Spanish command realised, then Zeeland and southern Holland could be sundered and dealt with separately. The mercenaries under Mondragon were sent to wade up to their necks in the swift waters of the estuary, and they forced a way across the Zijpe narrows to Duiveland. The island was occupied, then all of Schouwen except Zierikzee itself. Although sympathisers had the gates of the city open to receive the Spanish troops, the garrison and the Protestant minister with his church council refused to capitulate so easily, and breaching the dikes, they left the Spaniards on the bank-tops outside the town and themselves within the walls.

William of Orange determined to attempt the relief of the loyal town, and a fleet was made ready under the fearless Louis Boissot, hero of the courageous relief of Leiden. After an unsuccessful skirmish, Boissot decided to combine a powerful attack by sea with a sortie from within the walls. He sent instructions to the defenders by pigeon, but unfortunately the bird came into the hands of the Spaniards. Mondragon – whose name is still perpetuated in one of the restaurants in the town – promptly blocked the harbour, protecting it with old hulks chained together, and with a shoal of stones and piles. Boissot brought his fleet sailing in, and leading the onslaught in his own flagship, the *Gouden Leeuw* (or *Golden Lion*) he took her straight for the obstruction, charging down upon it before the wind. But for once his audacious technique of conquest by ramming did not succeed. Instead, his ship stuck fast in the wreckage, whilst the Spaniards poured fire upon her from a safe distance. The remainder of the ships were beaten back, and as night fell only the flagship was there, left high and dry by the ebbing tide, an easy target for open assault in the morning.

Boissot knew very well that his ship was lost, and that the dawn of the new day could only lead to capture for himself and his men. He must also have had no illusions about the fate which would be theirs if they fell into the hands of the Spaniards, so under cover of darkness he leapt into the water, together with the 300 men of his ship. Some swam to safety, others were shot in the harbour channel, or drowned. Boissot himself was seen some time afterwards, still swimming and sustained by a broken spar, but before help could reach him from the other vessels his strength was at last exhausted, and the fearless sailor-commander was drowned.

The old harbour of Zierikzee is inside the town, reached through a bascule bridge which spans the gap between two defending towers of very different style, the step-gabled Noordhavenpoort and the beautiful Zuidhavenpoort with its four little corner turrets.

Willemstad

On the Hollandsch Diep, just round the point beyond Dintelsas and on the extreme tip of Nord Brabant, lies the attractive little town of Willemstad. Little of it is visible from the water except the sails of a windmill projecting into the air, for Willemstad lies

hidden not only by the dyke but by the massive fortifications which surround the town.

Willemstad is no longer a fortress, but it still preserves its geometrical structure intact. It was built in 1583 by William the Silent in the form of a seven-pointed star, and at each point the high walls broaden out into a massive bastion. Their names – Holland, Zeeland, Utrecht, Friesland, Overijssel, Gelderland and Groningen – recall some of the estates of the Netherlands which at that time had rallied to his cause and revolted forever against the cruelties of the Spanish monarchy and the papacy. Outside the walls a moat 40 yards broad surrounds the town and follows the same geometrical outline, and this in turn is enclosed in a lower outer wall, defended on its exposed side for most of its length by a second, somewhat narrower, water obstacle. Beyond this the rich fields and small holdings and orchards of fruit stretch inland to the horizon.

Because of its elaborate array of walls and moats Willemstad is compact within its boundary. Today the walls are edged with rows of trees, and from the walks beneath them one can look

19

far out over the prosperous land of Brabant behind the town, or northwards across the channels to the dimness of the distant smoke lying over Rotterdam. Or one can look inwards across the orange-tiled roofs of the little houses to the Prinsenhof, the pretty country residence built by Prince Maurice early in the seventeenth century.

The fortifications are cut in two places only; on the landward side by the Landpoort – now a mere bridge instead of a gateway – and on the water side by the Waterpoort, through which the harbour cut passes into the shipping channel beyond. Beside the Landpoort the fortress wall at either side of the road is provided with a vertical slot, and the same arrangement is found on the corner of the town hall and on the hotel which faces it across the top of the main street. Into these grooves massive boards can be lowered to keep out the dreaded invader – not in this case the Spaniards, but the rising waters of a flood – and as an extra precaution the entire street and market place along the line of the town hall and hotel is raised into a formidable hump. This ridge forms a barrier high enough to protect the town from all but very exceptional floods, and it can be raised still further by setting emergency boarding along the top.

The great moat, originally dug to keep attackers at bay, has another very practical use, too. It is connected by way of culverts with the inner end of the harbour, and during the flood of 1953 careful judgment of when to open and close the sluices enabled the people of Willemstad to maintain their town in a relatively dry condition. Only two of the townspeople lost their lives, whereas 60 were drowned in Numansdorp, the ferry terminal on the opposite shore of the Hollandsch Diep, and across the fields beyond the Landpoort 60 more were lost in the farmsteads and cottages swept away by the water which streamed from the broken sea wall to flood the country as far back as the second line of dyke four miles further inland.

Had it not been for the stout ramparts of William the Silent the fate of Willemstad might well have been disastrous, but the walls which were built to withstand an army were well able to hold out against the water, and the only weak place in the defences was at the boards capping the hump of ridge between the town hall and the hotel above the harbour quay. Here the driven water succeeded in forcing an entry close against the hotel, and it ran down the reverse side of the hump in such strength that it washed away the corner of a house in the main street and began slowly to rise against the doors and walls of the lower-lying houses beyond. But on the ebb tide the streets were drained through the sluices into the moat, and this reservoir could in turn release its surplus water out through the harbour, so that at the end of two days Willemstad was almost the only piece of dry ground amid a watery waste which extended for miles in every direction and remained inundated for months.

Dordrecht

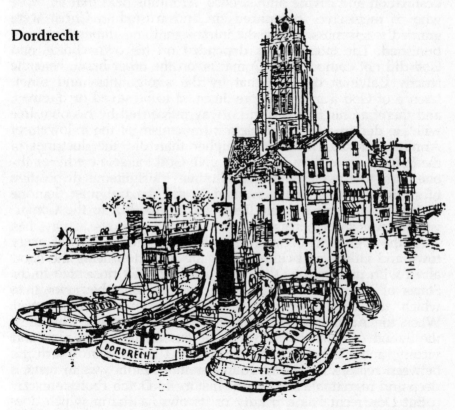

At the junction of the Kil and the Merwede or Rhine, Dordrecht is a great centre of shipping, but it also has its own claims to historical fame. It was here that the meeting of representatives was held which founded the Dutch nation. It was at Dordrecht, too, that the brothers Jan and Cornelius de Witt lived, those two great patriots who were later to be dragged out by a crowd worked up to fever heat by the crafty allegations of pamphleteers, and torn to pieces. Here, in some unrecorded alley, stood the printer's shop where the tracts of Barrow were running through the press when Johnson came from Middelburg to

21

destroy them, and here was held in 1618 the great Synod of Dort (the alternative name for Dordrecht), at which the long and bitter disputation between the supporters of Arminius and Gomarus was fought out.

This dispute, which began on matters of theology between two professors at the University of Leiden – Hermans (or Arminius) and Gomar (or Gomarus) – was centred around pre-destination and divine omniscience. Arminius held that all those who of themselves renounced sin and trusted in Christ were granted forgiveness, whilst the intransigent and impenitent were punished. The fate of man depended on his own choice, and God did not compel him. Gomarus, on the other hand, held the strictly Calvinist doctrine that by the almightiness and omni-science of God a man was pre-destined to be saved or damned, and therefore his fate was in no way influenced by his own free will. He declared that the tolerant humanism of the followers of Arminius elevated man even higher than did the doctrines of the Papacy, since they refused to give God the sole credit for the one thing that mattered above all other – 'a righteous disposition of spirit'. The Arminians wanted to see the Calvinist doctrine and books reformed in the light of criticism, but to the Gomar-ists this was sheer heresy.

As the argument became more bitter, the dispute split every town and village and church from top to bottom, and it became allied with politics too. The Arminians formally presented to the States of Holland a 'remonstrance' setting out their views, to which the Gomarists replied with a 'counter-remonstrance'. When the Arminians were finally expelled from the Church at the Synod of Dort the forces of intolerance had won a notable victory, and the heat of feeling involved in the wordy struggle between remonstrants and counter-remonstrants was to leave a deep and regrettable scar on the history of Dutch Protestantism.

But Dordrecht has a beauty of its own, a charm which does not depend upon historical memories. Nor are the simple stateli-ness of the Groote Kerk and the renaissance elegance of the doorways of the merchants' houses along the quays of the basins its chief ingredient. Without the shipping the town would lose nearly all of its extraordinary fascination, for it is at Dor-drecht that the Rhine first meets the highways of the sea. Openings in its quaysides lead through to basins of great beauty, in which row upon row of tall-funnelled steam tugs and their more racy diesel descendants lie moored between tall white-capped piles, whilst outside in the river the water is heaved into a seething turmoil by the wash of heavy traffic and the thrust of the deep-set screws of further battalions of tugs. For though at first sight the Nieuwe Haven might appear to be a pool in which these stately craft are laid up for retirement, they are there only for a brief respite from the heavy duty of shepherding the cargoes of the fairways beyond. And, appropriately enough, the doors of the houses on the quays and in the alleys beside the tidal creeks running through the town bear little brass plates announcing the occupation of the inmates. Skipper, tugmaster, tugowner, charterer, ships agent, towing agent, chandler, fuel agent, pilot, master engineer and shipwright – the men of Dordrecht are men of the water.

The Vliet

This canal leads from the lake of de Kaag through toward the docks of Rotterdam. It is of interest to the English or American reader, as it is the route by which the Pilgrim Fathers set out on their desperate venture.

The shortest route by water from Amsterdam to Rotterdam is by the Vliet, which skirts Leiden and Delft on its way. It is a waterway of modest scenery that is pleasant rather than remarkable, with here and there a housing estate or a graceful mansion standing back from the water. The Vliet carries little traffic, but perhaps that is because it is beginning to feel old, for it is a waterway ancient enough to have been mentioned by Tacitus. In its original form it was built before AD 50, and a Roman canal ship was actually found in the mud when the canal was dredged out and enlarged for modern craft of modest size.

Yet even more than the Romans, it is the Congregationalists of whom one thinks when steering down the almost straight course of the canal towards Delft, and it does not take much imagination to see the convoy of three horse-drawn craft moving at walking pace on the first stage of that remarkable journey. The boats were piled at the bows with the bundles of belongings of those of the Leiden party who had elected to emigrate for the second time within 15 years. There were bundles and boxes of private belongings, and particularly of cloth, for many of those who were leaving had worked in the cloth mills of Leiden. There were quantities of gin, too, and beer, and part of a printing press, and some tools. One family had a library of books, and one of the deacons had a few bottles of medicine.

Indeed, the travellers were taking whatever might be useful in a land devoid of all civilisation, besides the many gifts showered upon them by the friends who were accompanying them in the canal craft to take leave of them at the dockside.

Somehow a picture has become established which portrays the Pilgrim Fathers as a band of decidedly grim and elderly men, pious and determined, but morose, puritanical, and dull. In fact, a few of them were indeed fathers in a parental sense, but nearly half of those who sailed away from Leiden to board the *Speedwell* at Rotterdam docks were teenagers or even younger. With them there travelled in the canal craft the less adventurous of the Leiden congregation, those who had chosen when the matter was put to the vote to stay in Holland and risk the Spaniards rather than Red Indians who, if the tales of sailors could be believed, would delight in 'fleaing some alive with the shells of fishes, cutting of the members and joynts of others by peesmeale, and broiling on the coles, eate the collops of their flesh in their sight whilst they live'. Finally, there had come to Leiden for the canal trip to Rotterdam the members of other churches in Amsterdam.

And so the little flotilla moved along the Vliet, waving to the Dutch who had so befriended the men and women and children driven out of their homes in England at the whim of King James I. Slowly the countryside of dikes and mills and farms drifted past them, and now and again the drovers of the ships would slap their horses or blow loud and long on their horns to bring the bridgekeepers to raise the bascules. From time to time they would meet a market boat, or a water ship taking the brown and peaty water to the brewery to give a strong colour and a healthy tang to the beer. Then the horses would leave off pulling, the tow-ropes would slacken and sink, and the oncoming craft would glide over them.

And what famous names there were among those who were leaving for ever – the Brewsters (though the father had gone on ahead to organise stores in England), William Bradford, Samuel Fuller, Edward Winslow. In one of the ships was John Robinson, too, who next morning knelt upon the edge of the wharf, and 'with watrie cheeks commended them with most fervente praiers to the Lord and his blessing', as William Bradford recorded.

It was on a July evening in 1620 that the emigrants passed along the Vliet. Within less than a year half of them were dead of exposure, of malnutrition, or of disease. But the rest survived in the settlement they had begun to build on the coast of Massachusetts, and fulfilled beyond all expectations 'the great hope and inward zeall they had of laying some good foundation, or at least to make some way thereunto, for propagating and advancing the gospell of the kingdom of Christ in those remote parts of the world.'

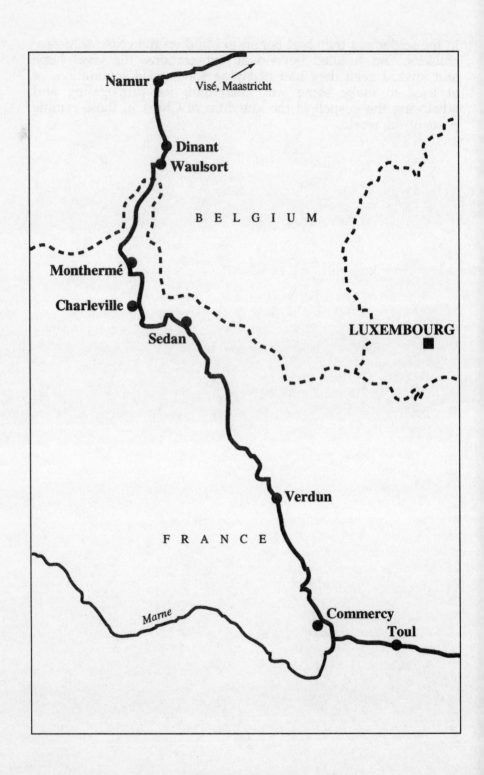

Namur

Visé, Maastricht

Dinant
Waulsort

B E L G I U M

Monthermé

Charleville

Sedan

LUXEMBOURG

Verdun

F R A N C E

Marne

Commercy
Toul

3

Maastricht, Visé, Huy, the Meuse Gorge, Laifour and Chateâu Regnault, Revin, Verdun and Commercy

A particularly beautiful route toward the south is that of the valley of the Meuse, passing through the Ardennes. It is most easily reached by way of the Albert Canal through Belgium. It is of course a war-torn landscape, but that part of it which is in Belgium (as far, that is, as Givet) is Belgium's most attractive scenery. Beyond that point the Ardennes gorge is wilder, and the legends crowd in upon us. It is in particular the scene for many of the great deeds of Bayard, the magical horse whose influence spread even as far as Bayard's Leap in the North of England.

Maastricht

On the Meuse in Holland, immediately below the Belgian frontier, but also accessible from the Albert Canal the mere name of Maastricht reminds one of the EEC, and the undertakings optimistically made there. But conferences have to take place somewhere, and it is not the fault of Maastricht if it has, in some places, an unfortunate reputation. More properly, its name should remind us that its existence goes back at least as far as the Romans, who established there a *trajectum* or crossing of the Maas. Indeed, Maastricht considers itself to be the oldest city of the Netherlands.

With its Romanesque cathedral of St Servaas, and the austere façade of the basilica of Our Lady, its bastions of ring upon ring of walls one inside another, and part of the city moat converted into the Maastricht-Liege canal, the city certainly has an air of having weathered many a stormy century, but its atmosphere is not entirely that of a Dutch town. Maastricht is indeed very different from Utrecht or Haarlem, Delft or Gouda, and belongs more properly to the Limburg area, much of which was

27

included within the boundaries of Belgium by the political map-makers of the nineteenth century, and the city still seems to recall the days when the powerful prince-bishops of Liège were enthroned in the basilica as lords of the land, and when princes and emperors struggled bloodily for possession of the city which commanded the lowest point at which the Meuse was crossed by a bridge.

In contrast to the rest of the Netherlands, Maastricht has always been a stronghold of Roman Catholicism, and although the city gallantly supported the insurrection against the Span-iards throughout months of ruthless suppression and cruelty, rape and burning at the hands of the Duke of Alva's mercen-aries, it somehow retains a flavour of a Catholicism more appro-priate to Mediterranean lands. The statue known as the *Sterre der Zee*, the Star of the Sea, is the focus of a particular veneration of the Virgin which is said to date from the fourth century, even if the particular reason for it has been lost in obscurity.

The Star is no astronomical body, but a Madonna-and-child statue, carved and painted perhaps as a decoration for a patri-cian house several centuries earlier, but which eventually came to be lodged in a chapel of its own in the basilica of Our Lady. And this sweetly simple, yet really very beautiful, carving has become an object of local pride and devotion and also, it seems, of miraculous awe, for there are attributed to it certain special curative powers. The local records tell of a great gathering on Easter Monday in 1556, at which an eight-year-old girl, para-lysed and dumb, was healed, and every year the statue was carried through the streets for days on end at the head of a crowd of barefooted penitents and pilgrims from far and near. Whenever danger threatened, the statue was hidden – in the tannery mill, in religious houses or wherever a place of tempor-ary safety could be found for it. Across the river to Wijk, over the hill to Slavante, or upstream to Visé the image was smuggled, and legend told that the morning lark still sang at Slavante over the spot where it once lay hidden, whilst in Visé the wife of the barge-skipper who carried it to safety up the river was miraculously raised from her death-bed. It was not until the year 1684, however, that the image of the Virgin, holding out a pear towards the clutching hand of the infant Jesus, received its inappropriate name of *Sterre der Zee* when the Count of St Pieter was shipwrecked at sea and was saved from drowning when he called upon the name of Our Lady of Maas-tricht.

Standing at the back of the group of pilgrims which is to be found at any hour of the day kneeling before the statue, one can only admire the intense devotion of those who come to visit the shrine. But what is so thoroughly out of keeping with what one knows of Holland is the collection not just of votive tablets which crowds the wall, but of little silver arms and legs and even abdominal organs hung there in testimony to the curative powers of the statue. Yet in spite of this, the scene has nothing of that fearful sense of paganism which so easily nauseates the visitor to a sanctuary in Spain or in the South of France.

An excursion of exceptional interest is to the Hill of Sint Pieter, just at the edge of the town. One cannot enter without a guide, for the cavities hewn out of the soft stone from Roman times onward extend right through into Belgium, and the maze of passages formed by leaving pillars of stone to support the roof is not one which can be easily followed. Stone was quarried there in Roman times, since when it has been used for buildings as far away as the United States. Soft enough to cut with a saw, the stone hardens on contact with the normal drier environment.

During the Second World War the passages were charted by the Resistance, and were used as an escape route for Allied airmen. But what is more extraordinary is the impulse which has led people not just to carve their names, but to reproduce life-size replicas of such paintings as Rembrandt's *Night Watch* on the flat surfaces. And if one may be surprised to meet a cyclist underground, he will be a mushroom farmer about his business.

Visé (Wezet)

The Albert Canal runs high above the Meuse, following the edge of the cavity-riddled hills towards Liège. The river itself is the frontier for several miles, but then Holland cuts sharply away and the Meuse is Belgian from shore to shore. The little town of Visé, or Wezet, clusters neatly on the further bank at the foot of the plateau across the stream. It is a favourite place with fisher-men: and no wonder, for in the Berwinne stream which runs behind the town a young man is said to have caught a fish which, if not necessarily of immense size, was certainly of an unusual species. If one can believe the local people – and I have no authority to say one should not do so – there was once a young man named Jean, strong in muscle but just a little weak

29

in the head. He was useful on his father's smallholding, and a handy lad to assist with lumbering, but usually he looked after the pigs whilst his brother, Pierre, and his father did the jobs requiring more intellect.

One day Jean decided to go fishing, and having dug some good fat worms he made his way to the brook, baited his line, and cast. All morning he sat in that doleful way that fisherman will, a curious blend of hope and disappointment, and when at last he felt a bite and pulled his line he drew out a very under-sized perch. Taking it from the hook, he cursed it in a casual and grumbling kind of way, and threw it back. Then he changed his pitch to another part of the bank.

He floated his line, and again the worm was taken. A fish remarkably like the first was on the hook. Once more Jean threw the fish back and moved his beat some way up the stream. When he caught the useless creature a third time he was so enraged that he held the little fish in his hand and stormed at it. 'Stupid damned fish,' he cursed. 'Go to the devil. '

He had raised his hand to fling the fish back into the stream – for he was not the kind of cruel lad who would have left it on land – when he was astonished to hear the fish answer back. Presumably it addressed him in Walloon.

'If you knew what I was worth to you, you would never curse me and order me to the devil,' the perch reproached him in a rather fishy voice. 'Listen to me and I will tell you what to do. '

Open-mouthed – for he was not used to being addressed by fish – Jean stared at the perch and listened. The fish asked to be put on the bank to die. Jean was then to cut the body into four portions and bestow the pieces around his father's cottage, one inside and three outside the house itself.

That night Jean did as he was told, and when he arose in the early morning he found the piece of fish he had put in the chimney corner was transmuted into a gleaming sword. The other pieces had become a fine stallion, and two enormous hunting dogs.

Thankful for these gifts, Jean took them with him when he went out with the herd of swine. Thus he continued for a while, the dogs helping to watch over the pigs and to make very short work of any imprudent wolves which emerged from the forest to attack them. Meanwhile Jean himself would charge across the clearing on his noble horse, cutting down thistles until he was a swordsman expert beyond compare, one who could swing his

30

blade over his head and split a tree trunk with a single blow of his unbreakable weapon.

The reader will have already suspected that the good little fish had not thus equipped Jean without some special purpose in view. Sure enough, the opportunity soon came, in terrible if not altogether unexpected form. A most hideous and fearful beast with seven heads emerged from the forest of the Ardennes, and proceeded to terrorise the people into providing it with one human victim per week, selected by a lottery. If there was the slightest delay it would open its seven mouths and send seven tongues of flame to scorch everything within reach.

Various heroic knights endeavoured to slay the creature, but always it got them first. Then came the awful day when the bingo fell upon the angelic, beautiful, pure and altogether typical daughter of the King. And this King, as any good father might do, at once promised her hand in marriage to the man who would save her.

Jean went to the palace, where the court people naturally laughed at him, but the King was ready to let him try his arm against the beast. Besides, there were no rivals. All the best knights had already died in the attempt and had been eaten up. Only their bones and armour remained in a heap as a horrid reminder.

The princess was very pleased to see even a peasant come to save her from disappearing down seven throats, and she gave him a tender kiss of encouragement. He was just trying to find words to thank her, when a horrible grumbling noise broke in upon them, and the monster rushed in from its den, with fourteen foaming jaws – for no previous hero had succeeded in severing even one of the necks.

The creature darted at Jean, who flung himself into the attack, slicing and chopping with his sharp sword. As each head was cut from its neck and felled to the ground the beast belched more fire and fumes, but always Jean would catch the adoring and fearful, if terrified and limp, look in the beautiful eyes of the princess. Thus encouraged, and aided by the agility of his horse and the flank tactics of his two dogs, Jean continued his attack and victory was his. With the last of his strength he had delivered the final slash to the seventh neck, and the struggle was over. By this time the princess had already swooned, but the moment Jean had cut the bonds which held her to the monster's feeding tree she recovered sufficiently to say she wanted to be married at once. Jean snatched her to his saddle and galloped to court. The chaplain was sent for hurriedly, and that was that.

The couple should then have been ready to live happily ever after, but while the princess was attiring herself for the night, Jean noticed a bright light somewhere up in the hills. He asked his bride what it might be, and she told him it was a castle haunted by evil spirits. Filled with curiosity, he waited until she was asleep, then stole out of bed and made his way to the castle.

Unfortunately, the princess had made a mistake. It was not evil spirits but a particularly tough collection of brigands that lived in the castle, and they easily set upon Jean and disarmed him. And that also would have been the end of the tale had it not been for Jean's brother, who set off with the horse and the dogs to rescue him. The dogs burst in the gate of the castle and flung themselves upon the wicked men. The two brothers disarmed them, handcuffed them and hauled them off to the King's court, where the villains were branded with red-hot irons and extradited. Jean had the princess as intended, Pierre received the castle of the brigands. The princess had many children, as all the best princesses did.

Since the day Jean delivered the neighbourhood from the terrible seven-headed man-eating monster, Visé has been a quiet and peaceful place. And, as far as I am aware, no other fisherman angling in the Berwinne or the Meuse itself has hooked a fish half as interesting as the little perch which asked to be put on land and quartered by Jean, the simple-minded.

Huy

On the river Meuse, upstream of Liege, Huy has a remarkable pilgrimage chapel, Notre Dame de la Sarte. This chapel has for more than a century been put under the care of a community of Dominicans, and it contains a chocolate-box Madonna decked out with clothes very much like those of her counterpart at Hasselt. She has a crown and a sceptre and an infant with an orb, and she stands in a baroque niche very full in the figure and just a little like something out of *Alice*. Yet if one were to take away the clothes one would find a truly beautiful mother and child already clothed in folds of carved garments, the mother sitting quite simply with the child perched on her knee. It is the tricking-out of a sitting figure as a standing one that very naturally adds to the circumference; and as though to try

to make her look thinner, she has been given a huge gilt key.
The child is also endeavouring to support with his free hand
another key as long as himself. Perhaps, one day the fashion
will change and the poor Notre-Dame-de-la-Compassion will be
allowed to sit as naturally as any other mother might, instead of
having to support such a volume of trumpery.

The statue has a curious history, told by the white friars.
According to the town records, there was long ago a chapel on
the hill which, in the struggle between the Dutch and the Spaniards, was ruined. It is probable that the zealous Hollanders
threw down anything which reeked to their reforming noses of
graven imagery, and so the poor little Madonna was bereft of
house and home. Huy itself was repeatedly sacked and
pillaged by any army that came that way – as most armies did
– and eventually only one wall of the chapel remained. As for
the Madonna, she had become a toy – and perhaps an Aunt

Sally – for any children of the town who strayed as far as La Sarte.

In 1621 a young girl named Anne Hardy took pity on it. She had been to fetch wood in the forest, and seeing the Madonna, she decided to take the statue home and care for it. She undid her bundle and wrapped the figure inside the sticks; then, finding herself unable to lift it off the ground, she summoned a man to help her. A woman also came to assist, but the three of them together could not move the faggots from the ground. Surprised, and rather frightened, Anne told what she had done. So the Madonna was taken out again, and the bundle at once resumed its proper specific gravity.

Now such a tale would cause a considerable upturn, but the clerics of the great collegiate church in the town below were not to be stampeded. They appointed a commission, held a public inquiry, and their interrogations are there for all to read. A score of wonderful happenings were attested – and all the while the poor little Madonna was left out in the rain at the foot of the ruined wall of her chapel.

The inquiry lasted – as inquiries do – for three years. Then the chapter was convinced that a place of pilgrimage could be established, and it persuaded the town to make available the land where the monastery now stands.

All went well until the year 1656, when the valley of the Meuse lay hot and dry under the most scorching summer weather within memory. Crops were dying, and there was no pasture for the stock. The chapter and city council resolved together to solicit super-natural aid for rain-making, and thus it came about that on the particular day in August when the memories of the local patron saints, Domitian and Mengold, were traditionally venerated, the statue was brought down in state from La Sarte. To the accompaniment of peals of bells and salvos of cannon she was implored for a whole day on end, and then taken back in procession to her newly built chapel at La Sarte. She had only just passed the portal when the wind came as a prelude to a downpour.

The cheers at the success of the enterprise gave way to scepticism when, on the following day, the sun beat down with undiminished vigour – for no doubt there were those who suspected, even in those times, that gunfire might precipitate clouds as effectively as processions. But the rain soon returned, in quantity, and the country was saved. Notre-Dame-de-la-Compassion was now sure of a permanent place in the regard of the people.

Soon the tale of La Sarte was attracting pilgrims from as far away as Flanders and Brabant, and the statue was the centre of invocations for every conceivable benefit, even for the appointment of good emperors. Then came Louis XIV with his wars, and Huy was once again a place for sacking and pillage. The French commander gave the order to blow up the fortress which overtopped the town, and at the announcement that this would be done forthwith the people living within range of the demolition fled for their lives. Indeed, their departure was so hurried that nobody remembered the statue, which was at that time reposing in the noble collegiate church, right at the foot of the fortress rock. The French sappers lit the fuses, there was a tremendous rumbling report, and half of Huy was crushed under the torrent of falling masonry. But not the great church, in which the statue was still calmly sitting in its niche.

This new achievement consolidated her victory, and the wooden Madonna reigned supreme until the French Revolution. Then Huy was 'incorporated', and the collegiate church put up for compulsory public auction. The night before the sale four local people hatched a plot, and broke into the church through one of the stained-glass windows. Swiftly they loosed the statue, made off with it, and hid it in the back of a baking-oven. When fleeing they unfortunately dropped the cloak of the infant Jesus, and this caused the French to discover the theft and trace it to the right part of the town. Yet so well was the statue hidden that it was not discovered. The hiding place was changed more than once, but after nine years the iconoclasm had died down, the French were on the decline, and the Madonna could at last be brought out into the open. She was taken back to her sanctuary, and there she is still to be seen, rather overdressed but with a quietly confident face beneath the crown awarded her by one of the Popes. And now, as ever, she has her faithful admirers who will travel to Huy, in sheer adoration.

The Meuse Gorge

From the Écluse des Quatre-Cheminees upward the Meuse is given the undignified name of Canal de l'Est, Branche Nord; but it is the Meuse just the same, and the 50 miles of winding gorge between Givet and Charleville must be one of the finest stretches of navigable river in the world. It is even too remote and wild to have been beset with a chain of robber castles and forts, and only the ruins of the chateâu of Hierges can be glimpsed for a moment, before reaching Aubrives.

The destruction of this stronghold was the final act in one of those terrible tales of medieval times. Gontran, the Count of Hierges, was a worthy man, kind to his tenants, generous to the poor, a friend of pilgrims, and in fact blessed with all the attributes which would single him out as one for whom the Devil was secretly hotting up the cauldron. Gontran had a fair daughter, Isabelle, a wondrous beauty fairer by far than any other maiden along the Meuse. She embroidered and cared for the sick, and was virtuous in every way. Courted by all, she very rightly had no thoughts for any other than Gilbert of Orchimont, the most gallant, knightly, modest, charming and thoroughly respectable young lord far and near. A troth was plighted, and the young lovers swore eternal fidelity. Everyone was delighted – everyone that is, except for two. The individuals were the Lord of Pélémont and a knight named Ravenaud, and if the latter of these was a bad man his friend the Lord of Pélémont was not a man at all, for although he lived in a fine castle overlooking the loop of Meuse now cut off by the canal tunnel at Ham, above the lock of Trois Fontaines, he was the Devil, who just happened to find it a handy form of disguise to be taken as a *seigneur*.

The engagement of Isabelle and Gilbert was drawing near its end when Ravenaud presented himself at Hierges in the guise of one returned from the Crusades. Gontran put him up for the night, and next morning the stranger gave Isabelle a wonderful ruby necklace, with his compliments. In fact – though he did not reveal this – it had been made in the private workshops of his friend the Lord of Pélémont, in return for the familiar promise of the customer's soul. Every ruby contained a drop of the blood of the damned, and the lady who wore it would burn with desire for none other than Ravenaud.

And so, of course, she did. When everyone from far and near had assembled for her wedding, Isabelle announced that she had decided to marry Ravenaud instead. Gilbert, pale, sad, and jilted, bade her a sorrowful farewell and went off to slaughter the Moslems, vowing that he would always think only of her.

After a reasonable delay for a new period of engagement Ravenaud and Isabelle were duly married, but on the bridal night Isabelle removed her necklace. Suddenly she beheld in front of her a man so vile, unworthy, lustful, lecherous, deceitful, hideous and cruel, that she let out a scream. There was a struggle as Ravenaud endeavoured to fasten the rubies round her neck again, but she snatched them and hurled them out of the window. Ravenaud's magic disguise was gone forever.

Yet Isabelle, being a virtuous and honest girl, accepted her lot and bore in suffering silence the years of increasing horror and callousness and vice. Even when the husband told her of his diabolic bargain it added little to the load of misery she bore, and if she remained alive it was because she held in her memory the face and lips and eyes of Gilbert of Orchimont. But the news was more than her father could stand. Poor worthy Gontran, he collapsed and died of shock when he heard it.

Then began a regular reign of terror, for the Lord of Pélémont called nearly every night, bringing with him the most disreputable comrades. Based at Hierges, these men, with Ravenaud at their head, would sally out for a night of slaughter and pillage and rape and brigandage before returning to the castle to carouse. So things went on for several years, but one night there was a loud report on the hillside at the loop of the Meuse, and in the morning the castle at Pélémont was found to have vanished. In its place was a great cavity which can be seen to this day, and which strangely resembles a slate quarry.

When he heard about Pélémont disintegrating without a trace Ravenaud was thoroughly scared – as well he might have been, for his time was not far off. One night the expected sulphurous glow filled his chamber. The Devil had come for him.

But Ravenaud was not one to give himself up without a struggle. He leaped out of bed and, fleeing through the passages of the castle of Hierges with the Devil at his heels, he succeeded in reaching his wife's bedroom and snatching her crucifix. The Devil swore, and departed with an odour of brimstone. He would get hold of Ravenaud by some other means. Meanwhile he quietly removed his recalcitrant servant's quality of invulnerability, as Ravenaud realised very well soon afterwards, when the tenants from the nearby village of Vireux-Molhain revolted and one of them wounded him with an arrow. In panic he stocked the castle of Hierges with provisions, fearing a siege.

The attack came very soon, and it will be no surprise that Isabelle sighed and sobbed with delight as she saw from her window that the forces of the nobles of the Meuse valley were led by a sun-bronzed warrior fresh from war in the Middle East. Gilbert of Orchimont had returned, and he was riding to deliver her from the friend of the fiend.

A whole day of ferocious onslaught made no impression on

37

the stout walls of Hierges, and as night fell the attackers were obliged to pitch camp in a ring roundabout. It so happened that during the night watches some of the men of the Count of Agimont, who were encamped near the walls, saw a strange reddish sparkle among the bushes. It proved to be a black goat (or, more accurately, the Devil in the guise of such an animal), with a necklace of rubies caught round its horns. Lured by the jewels the men gave chase, and the goat led them on, only to disappear through a crevice in the rocks. Adventurously the soldiers followed the creature into the hillside, and when the red glow suddenly vanished they halted in the blackness, struck a light, and discovered that they were in an underground passage. Gilbert was at once informed and, taking a troop of men with him, he followed the passage to its end, and burst out into the interior of the castle.

The defenders, who were few enough, fled. Ravenaud, fleeing through the hall of the castle, found his wife praying in her room. He ran her through with his sword just before the faithful Gilbert could overtake him and strike off his head with a single blow of a sharp and trusty blade that had mown down Mussulmen by the hundred.

Tenderly he raised the body of Isabelle in time for her to beg and receive his pardon, and the renewed vow of his eternal devotion. Then she expired in his arms.

Next day the walls of the castle were broken down, and there they have remained across the centuries, at the edge of the quiet hamlet of Hierges, where the wooded hills fall gently to the orchards on the starboard hand, across the river from the lone lock cottage. As for the site of the Devil's own castle of Pélémont, the splendid loop of the Meuse on which it was situated has now appropriately been provided with a nuclear station instead; and if the villagers think that it has been constructed by the same lord and master, who can blame them? Besides, they might be right.

Laifour and Chateâu Regnault

One day when out riding, Roger the Proud struck with his sword a serf who was foolhardy enough not to flee from his path, and the man was seriously enough wounded to be deformed for the rest of his life. And though Roger cared nothing for what he had done, a more thorough knowledge of the legends of chivalry and retribution would surely have prevented his being so surprised when one night soon afterwards he had a terrible vision in which he learned that, in punishment for the deed, he must change his name to Roger the Cruel. That was all – except that one more offence would cause every item of his possessions to return whence it came and there would only be left to him his steed and his trusty sword, with which he would have to start life afresh.

Next morning the proud and rather shaken knight was disconcerted to find that wherever his name had been boldly carved or scribed in the wood and stonework of his castle an invisible hand had somehow erased the word 'Proud' and cut 'Cruel' in its place. Repentant – or at least thoroughly scared – Roger promptly gave himself over to a life of charity and sobriety, and it was not until he was old and white-haired that he knocked down a child when out hunting, and was unwise enough to ride on without stopping.

That same night, the legend tells, the blow fell. The carpets rolled themselves up and became airborne for Spain and Persia, soaring against the moonlit sky like migrants bound for Africa at the first hint of autumn. Then the timbers of his bed came apart and sped though the windows toward their native forests, whilst the trout leapt the hills like flying fish to the swift Semois in which they had been reared. Soon nothing was left but his own horse and sword, and the castle itself. Yet even as he lay trembling on the bare stone floor the chateâu itself began to rock and crumble, and dashing out of the deserted courtyard – the watchmen having already been spirited home to the villages of their birth – Roger leapt upon his charger and followed behind the trundling mass of stones as they loosened themselves and rolled down to splash into the waters of the Meuse, where to this day they remain. As he sat on his horse, sword in hand, the ground opened beneath him and Roger the Cruel vanished from the face of the earth, buried in the hillside opposite Laifour, and if any should doubt that such things could indeed come to pass in the forest of the Ardennes, then they have but to look up from the river and see the red water from the knight's tears tricking down between the oaks and the birches, stained with the rusting of the long-buried sword.

The horse is still there too, and now and again when a barge chugs heavily round the bend towards the Écluse de la Commune in the early mist, ready for the first opening of the lock at six-thirty in the morning, its steersman may hear a whinnying from somewhere on the screes above him, and just occasionally he may be fortunate enough to see the dim shape of a haggard old charger, ruefully picking at the little knots of coarse grass which grow in the crevices and on the ledges, up beside the ruddy trickle of water. At least, that is what they say in the hamlets down the valley, and surely they should know.

Yet if the Meuse valley is sprinkled with the legends of somewhat traditional misdeeds of knights and ladies, it is also the scene of much of the stirring action in that great treasure handed down from the Middle Ages, the *chanson de geste* of Renaut and his incomparable horse Bayard. Not even the exploits recounted of Odin's steed so caught the imagination of people throughout Western Europe as did the spirited deeds of the bay charger which could put to flight the armies of Charlemagne or leap through the air with the four sons of Aymon on his back, and yet was so gently sympathetic and understanding that when, during the seige of Montauban, the two little children of Renaut were in danger of death from starvation, he bit open one of his veins every day and filled a stable bucket with his blood to nourish them. And so strong was he that, even when the last drop of his blood had been drained, he was able to lead the fugitives all the way from Gascony to Dortmund.

The song of the Four Sons of Aymon is the work not of a single *trouvère* but of at least three, and embellished with the additions of many an itinerant *jongleur* who repeated the tale at court or at the lists, or to the common people in the market place. It tells the famous story of how the white-bearded Charlemagne swore to revenge the death of one of his sons at the hands of a member of Aymon's family, and how, when he was moved to grant a pardon to all except the actual perpetrator, Renaut quarrelled with the Emperor's nephew over a game of chess and split his skull from crown to chin with a single blow of the chessboard.

Hunted by the entire host of Charlemagne's realms and by their own sorrowing father Aymon, who was bound by an oath of loyalty to the Emperor, Renaut and his brothers reached the safety of the Ardennes on Bayard's back and there, at the junction of the Meuse and Semois, built an impregnable castle with the aid of Renaut's fairy god-mother Oriande, whose delicate little subjects worked overtime through the hours of darkness to trim the stones and build the walls. There they lived in peace and security for seven years before news reached Char-

40

lemagne of their whereabouts and he set out with his host to attack them, and after their brilliant seizure of his supply train they might have held out for many more years in their fortress on the hillside had they not been betrayed by the crafty Hervis, who sought admission as a friend and secretly opened the gates by night. With the castle in flames, it was once again the noble Bayard who carried the four young men to hide in the forest.

And a fine quartet the brothers were. Allart, the eldest, was serious and scholarly enough to speak Latin; Renaut, the leader and hero, 15 feet tall, was noble in thought and deed as no man before him, utterly fearless yet humble; next came Guichart, a straightforward, trusty fellow, strong in arm and a good swordsman; and Richard, the youngest of the family, was another giant, ready always to slash with his sword and send flying the heads and arms of a score of attackers, yet endearingly adolescent in his inability to face the rigours of winter or starvation with the reserves of strength which his elder brothers could bring to bear.

It was only after many years of siege and marching in Dordogne and Paris, in the Ardennes and in Westphalia, that Charlemagne grew tired of the feud and was willing to grant peace to the four exiles, on the sole condition that Bayard should be surrendered. Defiantly Renaut refused, but the noble horse himself whispered in his master's ear that he wished to be surrendered, so that future generations would treasure the memory of his last great deed. In tears his master let the faithful animal depart, then set out himself disconsolate for the Holy Land.

Great was the delight of Charlemagne when at last he had the chance to revenge himself upon the bay horse which had been responsible for the death in battle of hundreds of thousands of the noblest and highest throughout his territories, and he had the animal dragged to the bridge of Liège, there to be flung unresisting into the water, with a heavy millstone tied around his neck.

The soldiers and men-at-arms, the knights, the great barons such as Ogier the Dane and the Archbishop Turpin, all but Charlemagne himself wept that such a fate should be meted out to the loyal Bayard, but their sorrow was short-lived. Soon a stirring could be seen in the water, and there reappeared first the ears, then the nostrils and the whole head of Renaut's steed. Lifting a hoof he shattered the millstone to fragments, swam to the bank, shook himself, and set off along the valley at a gentle trot, pursued by an army of horsemen whose sympathy was quickly turned to rivalry when the Emperor offered a reward of 10,000 gold pieces to the man who should recapture the famous steed.

At Anseremme a sheer cliff fell to the stream and barred the way of escape, but if the horsemen thundering down the valley thought that Bayard was finally in their power they were soon disillusioned. With a disdainful glance over his shoulder at the horde bearing down upon him, Bayard leapt right over the cliff and disappeared forever into the forest of the Ardennes from which he had come. And if anyone should doubt it, there on the tall needle of the Rocher Bayard which drops straight to the waters of the Meuse, a solitary hoof-mark shows where Bayard tapped it with one of his fore-feet as he skimmed the summit, to vanish from human view but to be remembered, just as he had wished to be, in a tale passed down through the centuries, and still told today.

At Château-Regnault there stands above the river and silhouetted against the sky a tall, stately ridge with four sharp and rocky points, the Rocks of the Quatre Fils Aymon, the very spot where, in the song of the minstrels, the great castle of Montessor had withstood the siege of an army drawn from every corner of the Emperor's dominions. And on the crest of the hill behind, there is a massive sculpture of Bayard, proud and haughty, with Aymon and his four sons standing at his flanks.

As for Renaut, after his voyage to the Holy Land he felt that he had killed so many men during his lifetime that in his declining years he would devote himself to a more constructive task. Incognito, he presented himself at Cologne, where work upon the cathedral was in progress, and seeing four labourers struggling with a heavy stone he tapped them on the shoulders and suggested that they had better let him handle it alone. He swung the block to his shoulder, carried it across to the scaffolding, and set it in its proper place.

The foreman at once took the hefty newcomer on to the payroll, and for a while he worked valiantly, carrying hods of mortar for the masons. It was not long, however, before some of the workmen realised that if the work were to proceed at such a pace the job would soon be completed and they themselves would be paid off. Creeping up to where he slept between the stones on the site, they fell upon Renaut and murdered him. So the hero died, probably the first victim of restrictive practices of organised labour, but his name survives in those churches of the Rhineland which are dedicated to St Reinhold.

42

Revin

Revin, where a tunnel cuts off the bend of the Meuse which almost encircles the town, owed its former freedom to the fact that in the eighth century its abbey sheltered the Prince of Colimé, a natural son of Pepin le Bref. The prince invested the place with the right to be considered a free sovereign territory, and this status – which persisted down to the time of Louis XV – had its advantages both for the Revinois and for merchants and shippers from elsewhere. Netherlands traders would ship goods from neighbouring towns either to Revin or to its sister-towns of Fumay and Fépin which enjoyed similar liberties, and would then reload them into other boats with certificates guaranteeing the wares to be of local origin and therefore duty-free.

Yet sovereign status did not guarantee a peaceful existence, and along the waterfront of Revin the balconied houses of Spanish design still recall the occupation by the Spaniards in 1591. The French monarchs, too, were also inclined to raid the territories which provided their enemies with convenient salients through which to invade the country. Nevertheless, the free status was real enough to be of benefit to refugees, and upon the revocation of the Edict of Nantes many Protestant fugitives escaped to settle in the safety of these Meuse townships.

Immediately above Revin the stream makes a double bend around the foot the 1,300-foot Mont Malgré Tout, and the Écluse des Dames de Meuse leads out into a long cut flanked by tall pines. Behind them the shallow river sparkles and bubbles over the rocks below the weir, and where the stream rejoins the navigation channel it runs past one of the most glorious sights of the Meuse, the Ladies of the Meuse themselves. Tall and stately, the cliffs tumble hundreds of feet to the water's edge, densely wooded and clothed in the brilliant green of early summer. So beautiful are they that it is hard to believe that these are no ordinary cliffs eroded over the centuries by the springtime flood-water sweeping down the river and dashing against the tilted beds of schist, but – if we believe the legend – the bent backs of three noble yet ignoble young ladies, rooted for ever to the spot with their heads turned away from the scene of their disgrace and their shoulders bowed in shame.

Hodierne, Berthe and Iges, the three proud daughters of the high and mighty seigneur of Rethel, were wooed respectively by Héribrand, Geoffroy and Vauthier, the valiant sons of the equally high and mighty seigneur of Hierges. Just as their court-

43

ships were in progress and each of the young men was about to acquire a wife and two twice-over-sisters-in-law, Peter the Hermit came to stump the country, calling upon the nobility, the men at arms, the villagers and fishermen of the Ardennes to leave home and join the crusade against the Infidel. Dutifully the brothers rallied to the standard of Godefroy de Bouillon, but they found time to marry their sweethearts before setting out for the Holy Land. No doubt they did so in confidence that their brides would await their return in prayer and in embroidery and other demure occupations, and for many months these expectations were fulfilled. The castle of Hierges, lapped by the waters of the Meuse, echoed to the sighs and sobs of the virtuous trio. No more balls, no more hunting and gaiety, but a chaste life of sorrowful waiting descended upon the château. Even an itinerant singer who tried to restore the colour to the cheeks of the noble girls by his ballads was driven from the door.

Hasty wartime marriages, however, were as brittle then as they are in our own day, and if at first absence makes the hearts of the ladies grow fonder, there was a limit to their faithful longing. One day there arrived on horseback the three wicked knights without whom the story would have been incomplete, handsome and rich young men but wily and smooth of tongue. No doubt they too should have been fighting the Saracens, but they explained to the ladies that by a curious coincidence they each happened to suffer from a debilitating weakness of the sword-arm, and as they hated to see virtuous ladies so disconsolate they had come to cheer, with music and song and genial company, the sorrowing brides of the noble and valiant Héribrand, Geoffroy and Vauthier, so unfortunately detained abroad on business. Soft words and a good dose of strong liquor soon wore the ladies down, and the remainder of that part of the tale needs no elaboration. Next day the knights departed on horseback in search of other pining wives of crusaders, and they had the decency to tip each of the ladies of Hierges a hundred gold marks for their services.

But what were the weird cries which had so disturbed the three wives during this shameful night? They were those of three gyr falcons which had come to alight on the towers of Hierges to deposit there three great red jewels – an avian hint that the husbands had fallen in the battle for the tower of David.

According to the tale, the actual retribution was swift. In spite of their Eve-like protestations that it was the water-nymphs of the river who had beguiled them and led them into temptation,

Hodierne, Berthe and Iges were wafted from the castle and planted away beyond the river to stand there for ever, bowed under the weight of their guilt and weeping endlessly in humiliation. Today the water of their tears still trickles down to swell the grey stream of the river below, and in the evening, when the sun sets across the forest to the westward, one may yet see on their faces the flickering glow which some say is from the flames of the burning camps of the Infidel in the east, though others are sure that it is the reflection of the flames of Hell itself.

Verdun

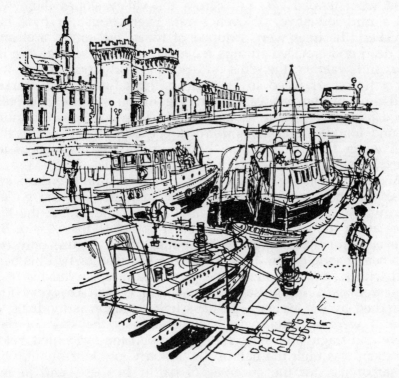

A short way downstream of the city of Verdun is the lock of Consenvoye, for summer campers an excellent site between the lock and the weir-stream of the river itself. The bather knows it as a place of deep and clean water, with meadows where one can bask in the sun and perhaps awake to find a cow sandpapering one's chest with its rough and rasping tongue. For children Consenvoye means a sandy beach below the weir, and

45

the wonderful scent of juicy grass-stems crushed underfoot. To the bargemaster it is the one really badly designed lock on all the Meuse, the wrong length, wrong width, and with awkward sloping sides which grind and bump at the hull. But to the historian, Consenvoye is the locality where the German forces crossed the river to drive past the stronghold of Verdun in the direction of Paris. At great cost they were stopped, and for four years the battle of Meuse raged along the great arc of front which swayed to and fro within a few miles of the city.

For nearly a year the opposing armies mined and tunnelled under the hills to dynamite each other and bury whole platoons or companies of men in the limestone soil. Then the bombardment was stepped up, and across the valley slopes there was not a bird left alive, or even a rat. Every house or byre had vanished, the trees were stripped of twigs and limbs, and only the dead and creviced stumps remained to show where once the oaks and walnuts, the elms and poplars had stood. There was not a flower or weed to be seen, nothing but a pock-marked landscape of churned earth with fragments of wire and steel, bloodstained rags and broken bones. It was a good hunting ground for kites and carrion crows – except that they too had their wings torn off and their bodies crushed by the concussion of explosives and the searing of hot flying steel.

About 160,000 men have their graves around Verdun, and these are those whose remains were identified by the patient men whose task it was to turn and re-turn the soil of the hillsides along the valley to recover such bodies as they could. But of every four slaughtered in the battle of the Meuse only one was neatly shot, or run through with a bayonet, or had his head cleft with a spade, or met some other death which left his body preserved as a recognisable corpse. Three men of every four who died by the Meuse – perhaps half a million individuals, or more – were so utterly destroyed that only the stain of their brave and tragic little lives remained upon the tormented fields. For them was built the hall of the 'ossuary' of Douaumont, with 46 sarcophagi for the 46 areas of battle. In these, and in two huge vaults, were placed the sad bits and pieces of human bones and teeth, a colossal monument to the fantastic folly which gripped the minds of the most civilised countries of the world. At night a huge lantern of red and white turns on the top of the tower to remind people for ever, but somehow the very idea that this slaughter took place is unreal.

The lad and his girl hiking with rucksacks or canoeing down

46

the sweet summer stream cannot really believe that this thing happened. It belongs to another age, as relevant to them as that of the Neanderthalers. Those elderly, grey-whiskered men in berets and macintoshes examining the monuments – yes, of course, one knows they are the veterans. They come, faded and with lumbago, in special buses. They fought here, on these hills, and somehow they escaped with their lives. They are thoughtful and sombre, but even they can hardly believe that it happened. The memory of these same hillsides as they were 80 years back is more like a bad dream. Then there were no monuments, no trees and fields and fences, nothing but madness blended with heroism.

The hills are rough with the chalky topsoil flung up from the shell pits, but woods of conifers cover the crests where the worst carnage took place, and in the valley the meadows and fields of crops grow much as they might elsewhere. But there is an uneasiness about the valley, a sense of tragedy which others have noticed and is not a thing of my imagining. The canal is pretty, the banks such a blaze of poppy and scabious, thyme and campanula and toadflax that one might be in a garden. But it is a memorial garden just the same, and even if none of the vast monuments and boneyards are close enough to the canal to be identified as anything more than a column or a glint of white, the death of all these men has somehow left an indelible stain upon the quiet valley of the Meuse.

As for the city of Verdun itself, it is of course a place of memorials, and generals cast in bronze or hewn in stone. Yet already the battle is too distant in time. Schoolchildren may still be brought there to learn of French heroism, but they are bored, more interested in the motorcars and the shop windows. And personally, I think it right that the young should be more interested in the future than in the past, and perhaps many of those men whose femurs and vertebrae lie packed in the giant containers of Douaumont would rather that it were so. They had believed that they were dying for a new Europe and a new world, but now a new generation visits Verdun, one that does not hate, is not too easily roused by patriotic slogans, yet has no illusions that life will be all nylons and hairdos. And that may well be a far, far better memorial to the half a million men torn asunder than all the flags and lions rampant on the ruins of Verdun's forts.

As for the city of Verdun, its name is so inseparable from the First World War that it is difficult to imagine that it can have existed independently of it. But the place is older by far, for once it was Verodunum, the beautiful citadel, and thither came the energetic St Saintin to break down the idols and plant the chapel named after his successor, St Vanne. Thus began the great ecclesiastical city on the hill above the river, clearly marked off from the dwellings of the mere merchants along the river. The upper city was one day to have a great episcopal palace, the lay town a rich collection of beautiful little houses. But the battle of the Meuse reduced these to ruin, and those that were rebuilt were knocked down again 20 years later. The dreadful They-Shall-Not-Pass memorial, in the worst taste of the 1920s, proved too solid for the bombardments of the Second World War, but many other things were lost for ever, though the body of the massive Porte Chaussée was left solid and medieval and severe, but stately in is protection of the bridgehead.

The tremendous battle is not the only thing of horror tied to Verdun, even if its earlier role in history is less well known. It would be pleasant to relate that in the Middle Ages Verdun was a shining example of humanity, but this is not the case. The old town of merchants was a flourishing centre of the slave trade. Ships ploughed up the river from Dordecht, bringing captives from Frisia and Germany and from Britain. Others came over land, by road, tramping the hundreds of miles in fetters. At Verdun they were sold to a community of Jewish merchants who had on their books plenty of orders from good customers, and particularly from the Caliphs of Cordova and Baghdad. The slaves were sorted, forwarded in smaller craft to the portage and then transmitted down the Rhône towards their destinations. There were girls, always needed in harems. There were young boys, too, who fetched a good price. But the speciality of Verdun was the trade in eunuchs for the caliphal palaces. Castration was a flourishing trade at Verdun, for some of the Moorish or eastern rulers needed safe eunuchs by the thousand.

It is an uncomfortable comment upon the attitude of Christians at that time but perhaps a more reassuring sidelight on the changing outlook of human communities, that the Church had only one objection to this traffic. It was that the eunuchs were transported to the lands of the enemies of the faith where their souls would inevitably be consigned to perdition. It was therefore hoped that Christian slave-dealers would undertake their work responsibly, and not sell their wares outside the Christian boundaries.

Commercy

On the Canal de l'Est, Branche Sud, Commercy is the last town of any size as one ascends the Meuse, and it is a place of mild industry. It also has the distinction of making madeleines. To judge by the number of madeleine factories and pastry-bakeries throughout the town, there can be very little time for very much else. But considering the display of madeleines in the shop windows, the fabrication of this delicacy must be energetically pursued.

In fact Commercy has a Brotherhood of the Companions of the Madeleine, dedicated to making the Commercy creation better known and more widely consumed. Its brethren have very grand red-and-blue capes and wear on the end of a gold or silver chain a madeleine of bronze. The society has grave and impressive ceremonies at the installation of its officers, and the brethren take part in two festivals, the June Feast of the Madeleine, and the July Feast of St Madeleine – that is, St Mary Magdalene. The first of these is the more pastry-cooked of the two, and is the occasion when the Master and Wardens of the Madeleine are enthroned.

The town tells two different stories about madeleines and their origin. They are both linked to the magnificent monarch Stanislas Leczinski of Poland, the same who was driven out by Peter the Great and so became Duke of Lorraine and made Nancy one of the most beautiful cities in all France. Stanislas took over the palace begun at Commercy by the Duke of Vaudémont and developed it into his own favourite residence. But with the Revolution the glory of Stanislas departed and the palace came to be barracks, police station and anything else the town might need. The German army took it over, and during the battle of 1944 a fuel tanker was struck by a shell and exploded inside the court. The great building was burned, and for 20 years only a pillared sandstone façade as ruined as a Roman temple stood high above the river, but it was rebuilt and the splendid carved heads of proudly snorting horses were once again staring out imperiously from the stable wings.

According to the lesser story, King Stanislas came in from the hunt and ordered his cook to produce some dessert for his guests. The good woman strove to excel herself, and produced the delicacy which ever since has been known by her name. The difficulty about this tale is that one would not expect a man of such eighteenth-century splendour as Stanislas to have a female cook. Besides, the other tale is more romantic, and if some serious local historian has satisfactorily proved that madeleines were made at Commercy before Stanislas Leczinski came to Lorraine, we can ignore this piece of interfering erudition and join the madeleine makers in asserting that it was in the year 1755 that Stanislas was giving one of his famous open-air parties in his domain of Vaudémont, between the Upper Meuse and the Moselle. Lunch was about to be served in a pavilion among the woods when a chamberlain came to Stanislas to say that the chief of commissariat wished to have a word with his royal master.

The chief butler was thereupon shown into the presence and revealed the fearful tragedy which had taken place in the kitchen quarters. The chief pastry-cook had quarrelled with the prime scullery boy and had walked out, incensed. He had taken the cakes with him. There was no sweet for the dinner.

Stanislas, proud of the reputation of his table and no doubt fond of his cakes also, was dumbfounded. The local account adds that if he had not worn a wig he would certainly have torn at his hair, so perplexed was he at the news. But the situation was saved by the major-domo, who ran to the rescue bringing with him a beautiful girl with rosy cheeks. She was an under-potato-peeler or something of the sort, but her grandmother had a very good line in cakes and she herself knew how to make them. She told Stanislas that she would produce better cakes than the lately departed chief pastry cook.

The king told his dwarf to delay the meal and draw out the interval between the courses by means of some well-chosen tumbling tricks and clownings. A game or two of draughts also helped, and when at last the guests were allowed to reach the dessert course the girl had done her work. Tired, but with rosy cheeks – though with a dash of flour in places – she was summoned to appear before Stanislas and be congratulated upon the best cakelets he had ever eaten. The king asked her what she called them. But the girl did not call them anything at all. They were just 'what grandma bakes' as far as she was concerned.

The king commanded – as only such a personage could – that the delicacy would be known by the name of the girl herself, Madeleine, the potato-peeler from Commercy. She herself was to be promoted to the position of royal pastrycook in chief and would receive a royal pension when, at the end of many years of pastry-cookery, she should retire.

And thus it came about, according to the royal pleasure of Stanislas Leczinski, ex-King of Poland, Duke of Lorraine, and father-in-law of Louis XV. Madeleine was happy in her work, but she was also prudent and preserved the secret recipe of her grandmother for her descendants alone – who, one must assume, were numerous enough to give rise to all the establishments which now flourish in Commercy.

4

Nancy, Soissons and the Armistice Clearing

Beyond the Ardennes the scenery is quietly pastoral, and after reaching the Canal de la Marne au Rhin the route turns southward at Toul to become the Canal de l'Est, Branche Sud, leading to the Saône and the Rhône. It has few towns of any consequence, but Nancy is a place of great and little-known beauty. Alternatively, one can continue eastward from Nancy and over (or through, as it involves two tunnels) the Vosges to Strasbourg. This way leads down the inclined plane at Arzviller, which bypasses a descent of 17 locks, and enters the Rhineland plain of vineyard villages and German language. It is probably the most scenic route to the south, as well as to Switzerland.

Nancy

The former capital of Lorraine, Nancy lies on the Canal de la Marne au Rhin. At Frouard there is a lock connecting with the River Moselle. The long pound from Liverdun to Nancy is a pleasant one, no longer rural but attractive. For the first few miles the canal is separated from the Moselle only by the railway, and when at Frouard the river suddenly turns away northward it is almost at once replaced by the Meurthe. This stream is not pretty at this point along its course, but that does not matter. If the Meurthe is rather shabby and little more than a receptacle for factory refuse, the canal pound is oily but interesting. For mile after mile it winds along the hillside above the river, cutting past shipyards and slips and dry-docks and skirting Champigneulles and Maxéville to run under the windows of smart new blocks of flats, sweep round by rundown and shabby tenements, hurry past a sorry village of shacks, or pass a neat port basin where tugs and barges lie waiting for something to happen, and engineers are busy with the machinery of maintenance craft.

53

Along the edge of the waterway dozens of barges lie empty, or retired, or just being painted for another year of voyaging. Dogs sit on the hatches, children bathe fearlessly in the soupy water, and an old bargemaster sits half-asleep beside his dangling line and float. Ashore, greyed old pensioners sit on chairs outside their canalside cottages.

Five miles beyond Frouard, Nancy begins to crowd in upon the canal, but over beyond the bustle and the rattle of machinery in the factories along the banks there is a view of wooded hills, and in the nearer distance the copper domes of the capital of the Dukes of Lorraine. One basin follows another, and beyond a succession of bridges the waterway broadens into the wide expanse of the Port Ste Catherine and Port St Georges, where the barges lie eight or ten deep along the quays, waiting for their turn beneath the cranes. The port area of Nancy is practical rather than aristocratic, but it is not very far from the centre of one of the most beautiful cities in the country.

Yet even for France Nancy is exceptional, and particularly in its relation to the river. Perhaps this is because it is relatively new, for although set in a countryside through which flowed the Roman trade with the Mediterranean, Nancy was not even a minor settlement in Roman times. It was founded by the Dukes of Lorraine, and was endowed with its present splendour by Stanislas Leczinski, ex-King of Poland. There were many Dukes before him, but as the great benefactor of the city he so remodelled it that Nancy is inseparable from his memory. In fact it is because he created a city of such beauty that Stanislas is remembered at all.

But even the elegant Duke Stanislas somehow failed to think of developing the city along the river Meurthe, and Nancy still has the rare distinction of leaving a sizeable river to pass outside it, very much in the way that Oxford has relegated the Thames to the gasworks and slaughterhouse area. In the case of Nancy the river is even further from the city, and the Meurthe is allowed only to touch the suburbs of St Max and Malzéville which once served as a somewhat limited port area for the passenger trade to Nancy. Nowadays there is a proper port with room for scores of barges, but this is on the canal and not on the river. The Dukes of Lorraine seem always to have been water-shy, and this is a pity – for Stanislas and his master craftsmen could have worked wonders with the rather humdrum Meurthe and might have made it a great ornament in which to mirror their splendid buildings.

The Place Stanislas in Nancy is so splendid that one can hardly believe that any city council could have had the vulgarity to destroy its appearance. Yet this is precisely what has been done, for not content with allowing the splendid buildings of the Place de la Carrière to be defaced with the familiar scrap iron of tottering television aerials, they have permitted the whole great spaciousness of the Place Stanislas beneath the balcony of the City Hall to be turned into a car park. By day and by night poor Stanislas himself stands in the centre on his pedestal, looking out over what can still be seen of the beautiful eighteenth-century iron grilles, flinging out his hand in a wide gesture as though to display to visitors the horrid rows of Citröens, Peugeots and Renaults which crowd up to his feet. Once he was the father-in-law of Louis XV and a great patron of the arts, but today he has become a motor salesman dressed for comic opera.

Whatever the *échevins* may have done to ruin the square, Nancy has not altogether lost its pride. Every night in the summer season it shows itself to visitors by floodlighting its best buildings and the trees of the Pépinière park, and by staging an

55

ingenious kind of *son-et-lumière* inside the City Hall itself. This building is later than the age of Stanislas, but it has as fine a staircase as anyone could wish to have in a palace, and at the foot of it begins the ingenious performance which leads the visitors on from one room to the next while synchronised electronic devices take care of their architectural education. It is all very well done, and the performance does not last long enough to become boring. Besides, it would be worth suffering considerable quantities of taped omniscience for that chance to step out on the balcony and look across the lamp-lit square to the house of the Ducal Intendant (now the Grand Hotel), and the former Bishop's Palace, and the Medical College now metamorphosed into an Arts Museum, and over the fountains of Neptune and of Amphitrite. Straight across the square and beyond the statue of Duke Stanislas the street named after the architect Héré runs from a triumphal arch to the Place de la Carrière, where Héré himself ingeniously put new fronts on the buildings and gave the final touch to the vista with his elegant Government House. Many people think the Place Stanislas to be without exception the finest square in Europe. Certainly it could be, if one had the opportunity to see it uncluttered by the hundreds of vehicles of an age entirely opposed to every principle of the men who built it.

Stanislas and his queen were not so grand and remote that they could not enjoy a curious festival which persisted in Nancy until inevitably the Revolution arrived to put down all gaiety. It was an elaborate Valentine festival, and on the proper day all newly-weds of Nancy, rich and poor alike, were obliged to leave the city and collect a fagot – though to save them trouble, there would always be country people immediately outside the gates with a stock of fagots to sell. Ribbon vendors had also set up their stalls, and so had travellers in pruning-knives, for each couple had to trim their stick with ribbons and the bridegroom had to acquire a woodman's knife to hang from his jacket button.

The couples took their decorated fagots to the ducal palace and then to the City Hall, where they themselves were given certain privileges. No doubt all this was the survival of some ancient fertility rite, but the real sport came in the evening when the couples danced at the palace whilst spectators threw peas under their feet to trip them up. Then came a great dinner at the City Hall, with wine and fireworks and a bonfire, and the married couples would come to the balcony overlooking the

56

Place Stanislas and call out the names of such other young men and women as they thought should be married, supplying them all with possible partners. Those thus selected had to set about a formal courting within the week; if they declined, a bonfire was lit in front of their houses and they had to wait another year. Unless, of course, they preferred to make their own matches without assistance.

Soissons

France is a country of waterways, and along all the mostly rural network there are two places which appear to me of great historical interest. One is Soissons, on the River Aisne; the other is not far away from there, just outside Compiègne. Neither are very likely to be on a through route selected by a yachtsman, but perhaps those travelling by car might find them well worth a detour. On the Aisne, Soissons has a war memorial of exceptional interest, for it not only commemorates the First World War but covers all the wars in which the town has been involved. One relief shows the incident of the Soissons chalice.

Clovis (or Chlodwig), King of Franks, had been converted by his Christian wife Clothilde, and Remigius, the Bishop of Reims, had to arrange a special piscine to cope with the baptism by total immersion of thousands of Clovis's troops.

The Frankish warriors had a way of robbing monasteries, and now the monks saw their chance. They told Clovis that some particularly fine communion vessels had been taken from them, and they asked him to be so kind as to recover them if he could. Clovis told them not to worry. It was the custom at the end of a campaign for the booty to be set out on view and for each warrior to take his share. He would keep his eyes open, and having the first choice he would select as his share the items the monks described to him, and hand them back.

When the day of distribution arrived, Clovis was as good as his word and picked out the various items on display at Soissons, including a particularly fine chalice the monks were desirous to recover. That was all he would take, he said modestly. It was now the turn of the others. But this did not please a rough and tough Frankish warrior, who stepped forward and demanded to know by what right young Clovis should be allowed to help himself to what ever he wished. And without waiting for a reply he raised his mighty two-edged sword above his head and brought it down with such force upon the chalice that he sliced it in two.

Clovis apparently said nothing. He had not sufficient power to risk being involved in a trial of strength with the Frank, so he appeared to disregard the matter. But he was only biding his time. He had his chance on the occasion when the victorious warriors were drawn up for his inspection, and like a modern general he walked along the line, making a remark here and there until he came to the tough who had worsted him.

Disgraceful, he said. Dirty equipment, lack of polish on the sword and buckler. And as for the shield, filthy was hardly the word for it. He thereupon snatched it and flung it on the ground in front of the infuriated warrior, who with an oath bent down to pick it up.

And that was his mistake, for as he did so Clovis swiftly drew his own mighty blade, raised it above his head, and brought it down so violently that – according to the Merovingian records – he cleft the man neatly in two from the crown of his head to the groin. Then he replaced his sword in its sheath.

'That's what he did to the chalice,' he remarked as he moved on down the line.

The Armistice Clearing

The Aisne is an unusual river. So lacking is it in factories that its water runs clean as a trout brook, so clear and fresh that one can see the weed rooted on the bottom and flicking its mane in the current. It is also a gentle river of backwaters and weir streams, and of peaceful cottages with lawns and flowerbeds sloping towards the willows at the water's edge. Four miles up from Compiègne the river turns to flow close against the forest, and only a short way from the bridge of Le Francport is a wide clearing edged with cypresses, and crossed by walks which lead toward three curious and flat memorials. The first, inscribed 'Marshal Foch', is a flat tombstone lying between the lines of a railway track. In the middle of the formal glade is a broad and flat memorial recalling the event which took place there, and at the further side a second tomb-like stone is set between another pair of rails. This one is marked 'The German Plenipotentiaries'. These are not graves, but the two slabs mark where two railway coaches lay in the drizzle of early November 1918.

It is natural that this place should have become a national

shrine, even that people should queue to peer into peep-shows of blood-thirsty pictures of the slaughter of those four years of the First World War – for there is a curious streak in human nature which draws men and women to their television screens if a battle is to be acted out and there is a chance of seeing death and destruction. Yet I think it a pity that highly charged emotions should have cleared this area of forest and added pomp, and memorials, and government grass to a setting which by its own dismal nature was more appropriate as the scene for the final act of those four appalling years. Could the clearing only have been kept as it was it might have proved infinitely more moving, though even now the Wagon-Lit dining-car housed in a museum of its own is something which can cause a catch in the throat and bring tears to the eyes of some who in 1918 were not yet born.

Only when one looks away from the neat lawns and flower-beds and the orderly rows of trees to peer instead through the windows of this elderly dining-car does the thing suddenly become real. In fact it is not the original piece of rolling-stock at all, for Hitler's curious bent for the theatrical led him to use it in 1940 for the capitulation of the French themselves, thus reversing the roles of 22 years earlier. It was then taken to Berlin and put on show, and there it was blown to pieces in an air raid. Yet this does not matter, for one contemporary restaurant-car is much the same as another. There it stands, with the table set out as it was in 1918, with blotting-paper and ink, and little cards to show who sat where during those days of fateful meetings.

There were no Americans present, no Canadians, Greeks or Japanese, not even a representative of Belgium. The British were there, but only represented by a trio of men of trifling importance who could not compare in stature with Foch. One was 'Sir Wemyss' (Sir Rosslyn Wemyss, First Lord of the Admiralty), and with him were a rear-admiral and a naval captain. It was Foch who gave the orders.

The Germans arrived just as day broke. They had travelled in a railway coach which had belonged to Napoleon III, plushy and aristocratic but with its windows boarded. They had no idea where they were. Four hours earlier their train had left Tergnier junction, and when at last it stopped and the shields were taken off the windows they saw nothing but a woodland dripping in the misty rain, and a little way from them a second short train with a Wagon-Lit dining-car, to which a duckboard track led from beside their carriage. The two railway tracks were in fact short spurs laid from the Aisne valley line as sites for mobile artillery. There was nothing else in sight except for the pair of wheezing locomotives and the caped and helmeted figures of armed police dimly outlined in the grey of the woodland dawn.

It was 8 November. Foch summoned the plenipotentiaries to his car, and his aide General Weygand read out the terms. 'The Germans were depressed and dismayed' says the official account. 'The English admiral played with his monocle.' Foch refused to stop the fighting until the terms had been accepted, and Captain von Hellsdorff was sent off to Spa to obtain the Kaiser's approval. He found the Emperor gone forever. Meanwhile, Foch ordered the attack to be pressed as hard as possible.

On 11 November the Germans attended again, with instructions from Hindenburg. The meeting began just after two in the morning, with the French guns pounding away in the darkness along the length of the Western Front. Three hours afterwards, the armistice was signed. It stipulated that the war would cease six hours later, at eleven o'clock. There had only been 30 minutes of this uneasy peace when the locomotive on the one spur began to chuff and puff as it backed its train through the leafless birches toward the main line. In the wagon with the monogram and crown of Napoleon III the German mission was on its way back down the Aisne valley, heading for Tergnier junction.

PART II

THE RHINE

The Rhine has for 2,000 years been the main transport route of Western Europe. Day and night the ships of the riparian nations and Belgium are pounding up and down its length, carrying fuel and raw materials to Holland, France, Luxembourg (via the Moselle), Germany, and Switzerland. The Lower Rhine is treated here as the section of river from the Dutch frontier as far as Cologne. It is the seat of much of German industry.

The International Commission for the Rhine (on which, oddly enough, Britain is represented) is responsible for overseeing maintenance, and regulating the traffic.

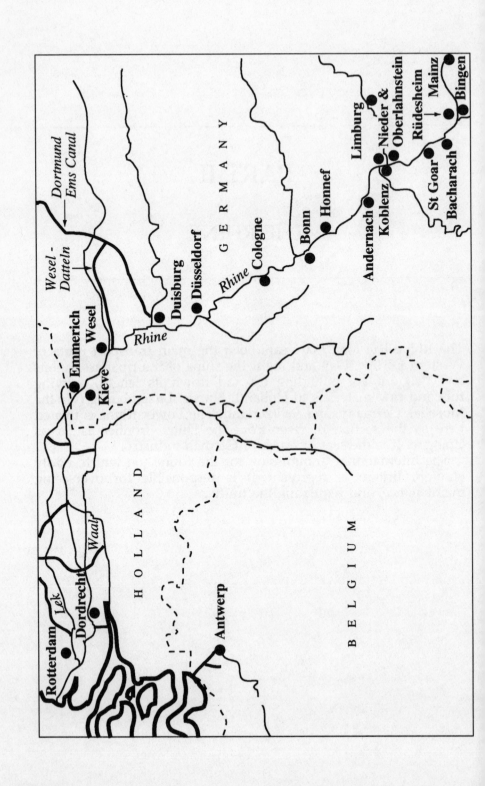

5

The Lower Rhine: Cleves, Emmerich, Speyer, Karlsruhe,
Duisburg and Düsseldorf

Cleves (Kleve)

Cleves lies at the end of the short Spoy Canal, leading off the
Rhine just below the Dutch frontier and at once returning into
Germany.

Presumably it was somewhere along this watercourse, at the
nearest point of the original river bank to the city of Cleves, that
there once came into view the mysterious craft propelled not by
200 diesel horses but by a single swan which held the tow-line
round its neck. It came, as Wagner reminds us, in answer to the
urgent call for help which the beautiful young widow Elsa gave
by raising to her lips the rosary from which dangled a tiny bell
of silver, and in its stern sat a golden-haired and blue-eyed
young man in shining silver armour, a rescuer as striking and
unusual in his own appearance as in his original method of
avian-powered water transport.

In his chronicle, written about 1500, Gerd von Schuren
describes the stranger as standing upright in the little craft and
holding a golden sword in his right hand. A hunting-horn hung
from his belt, and upon his fingers a ring of great value
sparkled in the light. His shield was red and bore a silver heart-
shaped device with eight golden sceptres and white lilies,
bunched together with a jewelled golden clasp. I am not certain
what the College of Heralds would have made of such an
emblem, but at least we have it on good authority that the
young man was none other than the knight Lohengrin, guardian
of the Holy Grail. Or was he? For already the tale is becoming
confused, and there seems no doubt that the tale of the swan-
hauled knight was originally located upon Nijmegen; or perhaps
it began in earliest medieval times without any precise location.
However, by the eleventh century it was Lohengrin wooing Elsa
at Nijmegen, and some little while later Beatrix being courted by

Helyas at Cleves, to which castle he brought his own coat of arms.

Elsa (or should it not be Beatrix?) was Duchess of Cleves, and a less operatic version of the tale presents her not as a widow but as the heiress of her father Count Dietrich of Teisterbart, a noble and worthy lord in Carolingian times. His sons had all been slain in one campaign or another, and that was how it had come about that when the old count died his daughter was richly endowed with lands and property which included the city of Cleves. But it matters little which account we accept, for the point is that Beatrix was very rich and she was also very beautiful, so it was only natural that when her adored husband (or father) died, one of his vassals – the wicked, covetous, dark-haired and brown-eyed Telramund – claimed the Duchy of Cleves for himself, ingeniously pointing out to Beatrix that the only way of remaining duchess would be to marry him. And being a very tough young man, he openly declared that he would fight in single combat any knight who wished to take up the challenge on her behalf.

In vain did Beatrix (or was it Elsa?) appeal to those within her realm. None was courageous enough to risk being cleft to the navel by Telramund's mighty sword, and so the day came when the whole population of Cleves, some of whom had the decency at least to weep, gathered before the castle to watch her led off as an unwilling bride. Some hundreds of knights were present, but in the days of chivalry it was not considered chivalrous to rise in a mass and chop down even the most atrocious bully.

So Telramund came out, defiantly repeating his challenge three times over. Nobody stirred, except for a few women who wailed bitterly. It was then that Elsa remembered that on her rosary there hung the magic bell which could be heard to the ends of the earth when danger threatened, and she had no sooner tinkled it than the swan-drawn craft appeared. The hero landed, perhaps near the jetty of the Cleves sailing-club, and, dismissing the swan (which sailed gracefully away, towing the empty boat behind it), he took up the villain's challenge.

Fierce and long was the fight before Telramund fell, run through by Lohengrin's sword. The people cheered, the knights rattled in their armour. Here was a fine young fellow indeed, they agreed. As for Elsa, she knelt before her deliverer, but he raised her up and asked her if she would marry him. It would have been unchivalrous and against nature for her to refuse.

Soon the pair were passionately in love, and only one little

66

cloud lay on their horizon – the fact that Elsa had to promise never to ask her deliverer who he was, whence he came, or how he had learned such an unusual method of navigation. All went well until their family of three sons reached adolescence – for even in medieval and legendary days children sooner or later began to be worried by those difficult childhood problems of the where-did-I-come-from-Mummy kind. Alas, their unfortunate mother had always to parry their inquiries, being unable to explain their father's antecedents or why it was that she herself had always to refer to him as 'You, dear', or 'Darling', or 'the Duke your father'.

Gradually the sons grew up, and all three became counts. No doubt they ruled their domains justly, but as they were unable to say who their father was gossip began to spread. Somewhat sensitive about being considered bastards – even if quite pleasant bastards – the young men demanded of their mother that she should tell them the secret. She did not do so, but in turn she asked Lohengrin whether he would not wish to explain to his sons their strange and noble origin.

Lohengrin made no reply, but after a last long kiss on the lips of his beloved Beatrix he rose from his bed, put on his armour and, leaving the Schwanenburg's portal, he strode sorrowfully down to the river bank and blew on his silver horn. Fearful and silent, the people watched as once again the swan came gliding round the bend, the boat trailing astern. Lohengrin (or Helyas) gave his eldest son the mighty sword and to the youngest his silver horn. Then he blessed them and stepped aboard. He never looked back as the swan turned and began to draw him away down the river until he had passed out of sight.

Thus Lohengrin returned to the Graalsburg, to continue his faithful watch over the Holy Grail. As for the sons, they ruled their lands in contentment, now that their illustrious parentage could be revealed, and they became the ancestors of many noble and battle-hardened knights of the Rhineland. The stately swan vanished except from the Cleves weathervane and the coats of armour of many a noble, until Wagner's youthful and schizo-phrenic patron, Ludwig II of Bavaria, tried out swan-powered navigation for himself at his castle of Neuschwanstein in Bavaria and got into trouble with his family when the water came through the ceiling of one of the better bedrooms.

Yet so great was the sorrow of the knight's true love and spouse that even now Beatrix-Elsa of Brabant haunts the rooms of the Schwanenburg, converted though they may be into the local government offices and museum.

Cleves was almost annihilated during the Second World War. It has been rebuilt in good market-town style, and is still crowned by the splendid mass of the Schwanenburg, which towers so high above the houses and market that from its upper windows one can see far across the plain to the Rhine. And it is impossible to look down into the mellowed courtyard without thinking not just of Beatrix but of Anna, daughter of the Duke of Cleves, a young girl destined to become the victim of power politics.

King Henry of England had decided to take as his fourth wife the 16 year-old Christine of Denmark, a lovely girl who even at that early age was already a widow. She happened also to be a niece of the Emperor Charles V, so the marriage would have been a wise one diplomatically, at least from Henry's point of view. But the Pope, still furious over the treatment of Katherine of Aragon, neatly stopped the king's intended fourth marriage by excommunicating the bridegroom, who therefore had no choice but to turn to the protestant stable instead. Anna was eligible; she had money, and her brother-in-law was the powerful Duke of Saxony. Chancellor Cromwell made up his mind to induce Henry to marry her.

Somehow the news had gone about that Anna was not in the top class of European beauties, so King Henry commissioned Hans Holbein to go over and paint her portrait (which is now in the Louvre), and it seems probable that the artist at least did his best with a somewhat unpromising subject. Certainly the king was prepared to go forward, and he must have been relieved when a message was at last received from Calais to say that Anna and her retinue were there, awaiting better weather for the crossing. The letter was written by the Earl of Southampton, who went on to describe her excellent presence and exemplary table manners, and finished by praising her outstanding beauty which, he said, was every bit as great as it was reputed to be.

Whether Southampton was trying to court favour or was merely myopic in vision may never be known, but when Henry advanced to meet his bride upon her arrival at Greenwich he received something of a shock. Having told Cromwell what he thought about being saddled with a Flemish mare who could speak no word of either English or French, the monarch at once set about planning his freedom. It was not too difficult to assemble 19 bishops and nearly 200 other clergy who could be induced to sign the divorce order. As for Anna, she became the king's 'adopted sister', and lived her life under such comfortable conditions as would not directly antagonise her important Protestant connections abroad.

Emmerich

Emmerich is a pleasant place, a town with a water-front of cafés and skipper pubs, of chandlers and agents, average adjusters and chart suppliers. The air resounds to hoots and toots and the sound of heavy motors throbbing, and along the promenade there sit or walk such very old or very young people as like to come to Emmerich for no other reason than to watch the ships.

Throughout the centuries travellers by water have stopped at Emmerich. It may have been to clear the customs, or to change ships and (in the old days) tow-horses. Or just because of weather which made further voyaging difficult or dangerous.

'I stopped at Emmerich and spent three pence on a good meal,' wrote Albert Dürer, whose diary was remarkably commonplace and domestic. 'I also drew there a goldsmith's apprentice, Peter Federmacher from Antwerp, and did a woman's portrait. The reason for our stopping was a great storm wind. I further spent five pence and changed one guilder for food. I also drew the landlord.'

There is a pleasant tale to the effect that Dürer was once up a ladder, sketching on the wall of a church the outline of a mural which his patron, the Emperor Maximilian, wished him to execute. As he reached over to one side the ladder began to slip, and quickly Maximilian ordered one of his attending nobles to go and hold it fast. The courtier hesitated to undertake such a common task, so Maximilian brushed him aside and himself stood holding the ladder.

'Idiot!' he exclaimed. 'Can you not see that art is of much greater worth than noble birth? You fool – I can any day raise a hundred simple peasants to ranks of knighthood and nobility, but where among you is there a single noble that I can make into such an artist as this Albrecht Dürer, whom you have grudged even the simplest service?'

Speyer

A cathedral city on the Rhine, Speyer is extremely ancient. It even has a Jew's bath, which is known to have been in use

more than 600 years ago, and may well be older. It was part of
the layout of a whole synagogue complex, and it consists of a
bathing-place excavated down to below the level of the Rhine in
the ground, with a stone staircase leading down into the water.
This was to fulfil the Old Testament injunction that women had
to be purified after menstruation by washing in running water.
Of course it all depends on what one means by 'running', but at
Speyer the almost imperceptible flow of the ground water was
evidently taken to be adequate for the hygienic principle

involved. Complete with washing facilities and changing rooms, it reminds one of the smaller bathing places in Bath, and in its medieval elegance it is certainly a reminder that the Jewish community of Speyer must have been important, and therefore that the city was a rich one. And so it was. Its cathedral was for centuries the largest in Germany, and it was started by the Emperor Konrad II in thanksgiving for his coronation in 1027.

Konrad wished to provide a burial place for the Emperors of his own (the Salian) dynasty, and the cathedral he envisaged was not only to be as glorious as the imperial line itself, but larger and finer than any other building in all Europe. There may have been a variety of reasons for selecting the river bend at Speyer as the site for his dream, but certainly he would have been influenced by the fact that a church had already stood on that hill for 400 years, a church built by the Merovingian King Dagobert.

So vast was Speyer's cathedral that it was only finished in the time of Konrad's grandson, but while it was still incomplete its founder was himself buried there. In fact he died in Utrecht, and his body was placed on a barge and hauled all the way up-river by men plodding along the shore. In every church then in existence, the bells tolled as the funeral boat crept up the river.

'Brülez le Palatinat' was the order given by Louis XIV, and so fearfully did his soldiery carry it out that even the Sun King's own chaplain long refused to give him absolution for his manifold sins and wickedness. At Speyer the French not only plundered the houses but broke into the cathedral and tore open the graves of the Emperors and their families, but because the men never realised that there was more than one layer of tombs the earliest Emperors escaped. Yet it must have been a gruesome scene as the soldiers – if we can believe Victor Hugo – rummaged through the coffins, snatched any jewels or objects of gold, seized the rings from the bony fingers and, when nothing was left but dust and bone and shreds of royal shrouds, swept the remains into a hole in the floor. 'Drunken corporals rolled the skulls of nine emperors into a hole, with their feet' he wrote. A guide to Speyer goes further and speaks of the soldiery 'playing ninepins with the heads of Barbarossa's wife and children, of Henry V and Rudolf of Habsburg'.

Worse than the lack of respect and the greed shown by the soldiery was their blind fury of destructiveness. Orders were given to destroy the entire cathedral, and with the firing of the building the first four arches of the nave fell in, to lie derelict for nearly a century. They had been completed just in time for the French to storm the town again and, once in possession, to attempt in good atheistic ardour to raze the cathedral to the ground. Fortunately the walls were too solid, and the Revolutionaries had to be content with declaring it a quarry and instituting a system of penalties for any citizens who should try to obtain stone elsewhere. Yet the difficulty of taking down a cathedral is that one has to begin at the top, and not everyone is willing to climb so many spiral steps to fetch down a stone. The cathedral suffered little damage, and was spared any further destruction by the defeat of the French at Waterloo. After its sufferings during the destruction of most of Speyer in the Second World War, it has been magnificently restored, and by its sheer vast emptiness gives at once a sense of awe and reverence which the bones of emperors could never provide.

In front of the west portal is a curiosity in the form of a vast sandstone bowl known as the Domnapf. Long ago it was the custom that this should be filled with wine at the installation of a new bishop, and the townspeople set about drinking the health of the new prelate until the dish was empty. More curious still, it was an asylum, corresponding to the more usual sanctuary at the steps of the altar. If a person fleeing from justice could reach the bowl and climb up into it, he was to go free.

Karlsruhe

Karlsruhe, on the Rhine between Strasbourg and Speyer did not just happen. It was founded by one of the species of the lesser margrave, and the story tells how he happened to be dissatisfied with his palace at Durlach – or, more correctly, with the people of that small town – and had in mind to transfer the margravial residence to a less restricting situation, to some spot which would give him the opportunity to realise to the full the architectural ambitions which very properly stirred in his aristocratic and baroque heart. Riding out from his castle for a day of hunting in the Hardtwald forest he happened to become separated from his retinue, and, sitting down upon the stump of an oak-tree, he went to sleep.

It is usual in such tales for the margrave to be awakened by a hermit, a white stag, a beautiful but languishing maiden or the devil in a frock-coat, but for some reason none of these apparitions visited him. He slept very soundly indeed, and when at last his hunting companions found him he opened his eyes and declared that never before in all his life had he slept so peacefully. This, therefore, would be the spot on which his new demesne should be established, and because he had rested so sweetly he, the Margrave Karl Wilhelm, would call it *Karls Ruhe*, or Charles's Rest. A church would be built over the stump in commemoration of his afternoon nap, and there he would eventually be buried.

The new château was indeed built, and so was the church in the crypt of which Karl Wilhelm was in due time laid to rest. It has long since vanished, but in the nineteenth century the Archduke Ludwig Wilhelm, in whose territory the margravial district was then incorporated, had a pyramid erected in Egyptian style – though on a more prudently economical scale – as a vault for Karl Wilhelm's remains. This curious and exotic monument still stands at the tram-stop in the centre of the city, and as the last resting place of Karl Wilhelm it is in fact *Karls-Ruhe*.

Whether or not he fell asleep when hunting, the Margrave Karl Wilhelm did in fact found Karlsruhe in the year 1715, when he chose to replace his palace at Durlach, which had been destroyed in the War of the Spanish Succession. Wishing it to be the centre of a new settlement, he issued far and wide a proclamation that any who chose to move thither would be given freedom from taxes for several years, and would also receive a free building site and timber. This unusually handsome offer attracted people from many lands, and a new town was quickly established.

Karl Wilhelm lived in the right era to be a man of the Baroque, and this meant very much more than just being inclined towards flamboyant ornamentation. It involved a detailed geometrical plan for the community, and in place of the humility of the individual in comparison with the height and sober majesty of Gothic construction, there was a deliberate cultivation of breadth and splendour, of light and air. Freedom of expression was permitted in the finer detail of architecture, but only in so far as it did not interfere with the proportions of the whole grand plan of the margravial or episcopal, or royal patron. Breadths and lengths of streets, lawns, rivers and ornamental canals, even the shape and position of trees and hedges, everything within the orbit of the Baroque patron had to conform to his basic plan, and if necessary any hills or other unfortunately intrusive features of the landscape would be removed. The patron of the age of Baroque would stand no nonsense from nature, whatever licence he might allow to his own interior decorators, and those who came to settle within the framework of the scheme were obliged to adopt certain prescribed dimensions for their houses. Window sizes, the height and proportions of doors and arches and gables, all were ordained according to the masterplan, and compared with more recent town-planning the effect was often extremely satisfying.

But the patron was more than a town planner. He himself was the centre of all things bright and beautiful, and though his chubby angels might spiral up to heaven on the pillars of the church, the patron's own residence was the thing to which the eye of the visitor – and of the townsman, too – was ingeniously and subtly to be drawn. Not that the subtlety was particularly marked at Karlsruhe, for Karl Wilhelm's planning put his splendid residence at the centre of a compass rose of radiating streets and forest rides, no less than 32 of which converged upon the mansion. It is these which have determined the layout of the inner part of the city ever since.

Duisburg

Smoke – white, grey, green or black, purple and orange – rises so dense from the tall stacks of the foundries and furnace halls that the sun seems to have given up the attempt to break through. The Rhine is iridescent in hues compounded of reflections and mill effluents, topped with a shimmer of the interference colours caused by the thin film of oil and diesel fuel heaving on the waves thrown up by the unceasing traffic. The air may be slightly irritating to the nasal membranes, but the bustle and clang of Duisburg's heavy industry have always appealed to me as a child, even if an ageing one, of the industrial area of South-West Lancashire.

None has written better of Duisburg than the anonymous author of the local brochure put out some years ago for the benefit of any English-speaking tourists who might be lured to the city. 'This town has no idylls, is by no means elegant for making you a mirage of something not being there,' he confidently declares. 'Maybe Duisburg gets publicity by facts otherwise generally being typical to prevent somebody from starting a visit there, for example: smoke and noise, cold steel, soot,

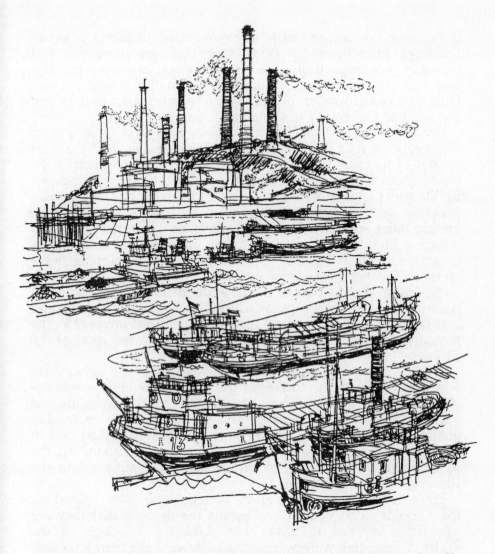

fabric walls and its work. Grey everyday, complication of traffic and not understanding power, this world even gets its own dynamic vitality. Everywhere interesting, you don't need a guide.

'Duisburg is a working town, where the motors of the ships are crewing oily water of the large Lower Rhine to white spray. Blast furnaces pricked off let become night to bright red day. Herein is situated its character. Duisburg cannot cash itself [*Ne peut pas se cacher?*] because all its chemneys are smoking.

'People is unable to mark surely, how many millionaires are

living here. No one can name the number of managers who call Duisburg their home. In every case they are numerous and herewith, not respectfully, we are at the top of money-making. The last one takes a great part of life in this town, because Duisburg has grown up out of coal, iron, steel, ship motors and the spirit of Duisburg's undertainers.'

Duisburg is, in fact, the main iron and steel producer of Europe, and with its 20 miles of Rhine quays and the vast sprawl of its dock basins it is the largest inland harbour in the world. And this brings problems too, for the rate of cut-down by the great river is as much as an inch and a half every year. Multiply that by half a century, and the quaysides should be getting taller and taller as the river bottom is scoured away and dumped in the North Sea. And yet industry has come to its own rescue, for at Ruhrort – where most of the shipping lies – so much has been excavated beneath the town that it is sinking at the right speed. Thanks to the industry of the indefatigable coal-miners, the whole place, docks, railways, quaysides and fuel tanks sink down into the ground at just the correct rate, the subsidence almost exactly matching the drop in the level of the Rhine.

I doubt if water-nymphs disport themselves in the rather dirty water, but beneath the surface of the ground the little people are still as active a ever. Their importance to the metallurgical industry is usually overlooked, and yet in one way or another goblins good and spirits mischievous have played a vital part in developing the immense complex of industry surrounding the River Ruhr, which pours its café-au-lait-tinted stream into the Rhine at Duisburg-Ruhrort.

From earliest times the miners underground were helped by the Kobolds, who were by no means the demons that they are sometimes reputed to have been. Like the Knockers of the Welsh mines, they were well-disposed toward the men who tunnelled into their domains, and they would try to help them. Better versed in geology than the human miners, the Kobolds would warn of imminent roof-falls, and they had sharp noses for carbon monoxide, too. Provided one was nice to these little men of the mines, and occasionally shared a sandwich or a few pfennigs with them, their goodwill could be relied upon. For example, if a miner should strike upon a seam of hard, resistant rock, he could call up a Kobold, who would set to work with his little pick and hack away furiously until he had demolished it.

Sometimes the miners and the little men would work together in harmony for years, but sooner or later the partnership was sure to be spoiled by some foolish young miner deciding to play tricks upon his willing helper, by holding back his pay, or scattering dried peas on the floor to trip him up. The Kobold would not be amused. He would turn the coal to stone, and the copper ore into a much harder material – Kobolded stone, or Cobalt. Then, with a cry of impish laughter, he would leave forever.

Similar to the Kobolds were the Nickels, impish little fellows who had the unfortunate tendency to be impish just for the fun of it. They would play tricks on the miners of Duisburg copper by bewitching the copper in such a way that they changed its chemical properties. Maybe they were really trying to help, because the magical ore they produced was actually far more valuable than mere copper, although the miners did not realise this. The men were angry when their baskets turned out to be full of ore which was different; *'Kupfernickel'*, or copper that had been wizarded by the Nickels. Nor were they any more pleased when the Kobolds revenged themselves for some real or imagined slight by cobolding the ore in the seam. Nowadays many an industrial magnate in the Ruhr is thankful that these two kinds of sprites are touchy enough to tamper with the copper. Both of the bewitched forms – nickel and cobalt – are very well worth the mining.

Duisburg has another claim to fame, which dates from long before its undertainers became so active, for it was thither that Gerhard Kremer fled to take advantage of the freedom of worship guaranteed to Protestants in 1552. From that year until his death Kremer lived in Duisburg, in the employ of the Duke of Cleves. Primarily a mathematician, he constructed mathematical instruments, and it was his interest in the globe that was to lead to his lasting fame as a cartographer.

Until that time ship's captains had been dogged by the difficulty of navigating with charts on which a line of constant bearing (a rhumb-line, as sailors called it) was not straight but spiralled toward the Pole – as in fact it does in nature. The problem was to make a straight course actually appear straight on a chart, and by distorting the scale progressively with increasing latitude, Kremer produced the system of charting still in use today. Being so successful a map-maker he put his own name (which meant merchant) into a suitably classical form as 'Mercator'.

Mercator's projection was such an invaluable discovery that, largely on the strength of it, his patron obtained charters from the Pope and the Emperor for a university. Yet the worthy Duke never managed to get his enterprise launched, and it was a century before the University of Duisburg came to birth. But by then it was too late. Professors and students were too easily lured away by the reputations of the universities in the nearby Netherlands, and after 163 years of not very distinguished academic effort Duisburg's university closed its doors. The future of the city was not to be associated with famous professional names. Its entrepreneurs were to be more practically tied to the earth and the water.

Düsseldorf

At Kaiserswerth the distant outline of Düsseldorf is already in sight, a sign that one can draw in for the night at one of the very best yacht harbours on all the Rhine. Modern Düsseldorf is renowned as a town of wealth and economic miracles, but once the place was no more than a village (or *dorf*) on the banks of the Düssel brook. Today that stream stinks of effluent, but once its beauty moved deeply the spirit of a young man who was something of a mystic. He lived in the seventeenth century.

Close by where the modern autobahn cuts a swathe through the woodland above cliffs which echo to the dynamiting gangs of the hungry Mannesmann works, the Düssel still cuts through a quiet gorge at the foot of limestone crags green with scrub of alder and oak, beech, and a few conifers. It was there that the restless young man would climb to look out across the land where it fell away to the Rhine a few miles distant. When a storm swept in from the west, in the thunder and lightning, the violence of wind and rain, the grandeur of the cliff and the stillness of the forest, the young visionary saw only the might and wonder and goodness and majesty of God in his creation. I like to think that he stood there fearless and soaked to the skin as the words of his great hymn took shape in his mind. '*Lobe den Herrn* ... ' We still sing it in our churches, splendidly translated. 'Praise to the Lord, the Almighty, the king of creation.' Certainly it is known that he stood on that crag above the brook one Whitsunday, weak with tuberculosis, as another storm broke over the land which now is merely an industrial sprawl.

'That is my Father,' he cried as the thunder pealed and the rain beat upon his face. 'My Father with His fiery chariot and

78

horses. I rejoice – for though the mountains may quake and the hills fall, His covenant is unbreakable, His mercy endures for ever!'

Three days later Joachim Neander collapsed and died. Yet he and that craggy bend in the Düssel brook had become so intimately linked that the place came to be known as Neander's valley, the Neanderthal. And there, two centuries later, a quarry-man came upon some bones in a narrow cave, the first known remains of an earlier type of man, a side-branch from the sprouting shoot that was already expanding as *Homo sapiens*, our own species.

The bones were shown to the owner of the quarry, who at once informed J. C. Fuhlrott, a secondary school teacher of Elberfeld who was already known for his researches. Fuhlrott realised at once that the remains could only belong to a more ancient type of human, but when he dared to put forward this theory he was attacked from all sides. Some said the bones were those of a man distorted with rickets, others that the individual had been a malformed idiot. And, as Russians were feared and mysterious beings, it was seriously suggested that the remains were those of a Cossack who had crept into the cave to hide there during the campaign of 1813–14. The scientist Virchow also set himself in vigorous opposition to Fuhlrott, but eventually finds in other caves – particularly in the south of France – confirmed the theory that the individual who had lived by the banks of the Düssel 50,000 years ago was indeed a more primitive type of man than our own.

As we look at the model of his low-browed form in the local museum, one can wonder what Joachim Neander would have thought about the place of that simple hominid in the divine scheme which so filled him with awe and praise. For in Neander's day nothing was known of evolution. Darwin's *The Origin of Species* was published three years after the bones were found, two centuries after Joachim Neander.

Darwin was bitterly opposed by a small and vocal minority of clerics. He still is by a few. Over the years I have discovered that nobody ever sends me rude letters when I write about waterways and boats, but the mere mention of affinity with the rest of the creatures which enjoy this earth and tear each other to pieces upon it is enough to make some people very angry. They like to feel that God keeps a sort of toy-shop and turns out fluffy bunnies and (at a price) humans, all ready equipped for the business of living and working, boating and loving and dying; and if I write back to them and say please will they tell me what they think about mongoloids or hydrocephalics they get angrier still – though they do not answer the question.

Neander's vision was immense and glorious. So was Darwin's and he liberated the human spirit and imagination forever from the small-minded notion of special creation. Nowadays we can be aware of the immense span of time against which life has developed on our little planet (amongst many others, we must assume) and at an ever-increasing rate; onward and upward, from nucleo-proteins in the primeval sea to single cells, then to larger forms endowed with movement. The invention of nerve conduction opened a whole new dimension. Bones and closed-circuit blood-flow emancipated creatures from the water. Up to the trees, and down again, erect on two feet and with the hands free to work tools – and mischief, too. Mutation, selection, the weakest to the wall under God's incredibly daring scheme. A century ago it certainly seemed an impious idea, but now we can accept it as just such a revelation as would have stirred Neander himself.

Neanderthal man ate, loved – or at least mated – and died. I doubt if he ever wondered about God in creation. Behind that low receding forehead, above the massive eyebrow ridges, there was nothing comparable with our own awareness. When the thunder rolled in from the Rhine our simpler cousin was perhaps just a bit frightened, but only as a dog is. He did not understand. Comprehension was beyond him. It belonged to the new species which soon was to supplant him, and hold the future precariously in its neat, prehensile hands.

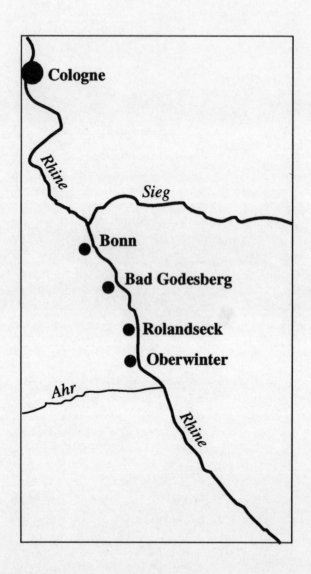

6

The Middle Rhine: Cologne, Bonn, the Drachenfels, the Siebengebirge and Rolandsbogen

The Middle Rhine comprises the section from Cologne (Köln) to the mouth of the River Lahn at Niederlahnstein. It includes the area of the Seven Mountains, and the seat of the Government of the Federal Republic at Bonn. The Seven Mountains are well worth a visit (there is a mountain railway), and it is here that the land of legends really begins, with the story of Roland.

Cologne (Köln)

It was Robert Louis Stevenson who, after a voyage through the canals of Belgium and France by canoe, rashly plunged into the purchase of a French canal barge with the unsurpassable name of *The Eleven Thousand Virgins of Cologne*, commemorating the legend of one of the most surprising inland voyages, when Ursula and her eleven thousand chaste companions drew in to the wharves of that city with a convoy of shipping which would have made even the modern tow-trains of Franz Haniel of Duisburg or Damco of Rotterdam appear insignificant.

Ursula is very much the heroine saint of the Rhine, and particularly of Cologne, and her story tells that she was a Cornish girl of such beauty that her fame even penetrated to Brittany, to the camp of the rough English warrior Conan. This mighty man had subdued the country, but he was now faced with the demotic problem of finding wives for his entire army so that Brittany might be repopulated, and besides this he naturally desired the beauteous and famous Ursula for his own consort. A deputation was sent across the channel to arrange both these matters with her father Dioneth, and an agreement was reached that within three years Ursula and ten high-born and very acceptable friends of hers would come to Brittany, each of them with a retinue of a thousand maidens. The only condition was that before then Conan was to adopt the Christian faith. The girls were not so much as consulted, for in those days young ladies very properly did what they were told.

When at last Ursula set sail with her eleven thousand and ten companions, the ships were blown out of their course by a storm, and running before the wind they passed up the Channel and onward as far as the delta of the Low Countries, where they turned in and sailed all the way up the Rhine to Cologne. Here the news reached Ursula that Conan was not willing to honour his part of the bargain, and so she set out at the head of her party and led them on foot across the Alps to ask the Pope for his advice. Returning towards Cologne, they had almost reached the city when they happened to cross the path of the army of the Huns, who massacred the eleven thousand and the ten, leaving only their leader alive. When Ursula refused to become the wife of Attila, he shot her dead with an arrow.

It is generally believed that the number eleven thousand comes from a misconstruing of the abbreviation XI.M.V. in early records, this being rendered as eleven *Milia Virgines* instead of *Martyres Virgines*. And how far the connection with England is in any way historical is unknown, quite apart from the minor parts played by Attila and – in some versions – by St Peter. Indeed, the truth about Ursula will probably never be known, even in its haziest outlines, but that may well be an advantage, for a Europe robbed of its embroideries of heroes and heroines, of mighty men and chivalrous knights and of maidens whose beauty is beyond description, might be as dull as an overspill town or a modern garden suburb – clean, well organised, pretty in the springtime, and plain enough to drive its inhabitants to the psychiatrist's couch.

The alleged remains of the Three Kings of the Nativity, brought to Cologne by Archbishop Reinhold in the twelfth century, may still bring pilgrims in their thousands to the city, but there can be no doubt that its real treasure is something very different, coming not from Byzantium but from the hand of one or possibly two of the finest craftsmen that the Roman occupation could provide. For if most of the beauty which once was to be found in Cologne was to vanish in the dust and rubble heaps of the fearful bombardment dealt out to the city in the Second World War, that same tragedy brought to light an astonishing survival from the days of imperial Colonia Agrippina.

In 1941 the destruction wrought by an air raid, which was only the faintest shadow of those which were to follow, caused the city authorities to excavate a deep shelter between the cathedral and the river bank, in ground which for centuries had not been disturbed. The diggers and shovels were set to work, and quickly they came upon the remains of the foundations of medieval and baroque buildings. Beneath these, spread over three or four acres running down towards the river, there came to light the walls of a Roman palace, perhaps belonging to the provincial governor. Most of these remains were chewed away by the jaws of the excavating machines, for the palace had been sacked by the German tribes and burned to the ground. But in the dining hall the ashes of the conflagration, mixed with broken tiles, had formed an excellent protective covering for the magnificent Dionysos mosaic, and its thirty one separate pictures in coloured marbles and glass had been preserved until the need for a deep bunker brought them to light. Carefully bedded down under timber and concrete, it survived the bombardment by very virtue of the fact that it was down in the bomb-proof shelter. North of the Alps, the Dionysos mosaic has no serious rival. Its satyrs – one of whom is feeding his little son with grapes – its parrots and panther, peacock and mallard, its still-life with a basket of juicy cherries all shine as gaily as they did when the nobility of Cologne reclined on their couches long ago, glancing out across the loaded tables to where the rowers of a Roman wine-freighter from Noviomagus on the Moselle were turning their craft to sidle it across the current towards the quay, where the wholesaler was awaiting the arrival of the latest vintage.

Bonn

To most people Bonn is Beethoven, and at least there is a real charm about the modest house in which he was born. Besides, it is a pleasant change to visit a German town which has so close and personal a connection with some other great man that it is quite ready to forget that Goethe may have spent a night in the place. Queen Elizabeth I herself cannot compare with Goethe for having every lunch, dinner, bed and breakfast he ever took commemorated by a plaque or mentioned in the local guide-book.

The interest is historical. Except in Africa, where new countries have a tendency to arise like bubbles on the skin of a rice pudding, the birth of a new state is something of a rarity, so it is impossible to chug past the particularly uninteresting water-

The Oscar Huber, last of the paddle-tugs

front of Bonn itself without remembering that it was there that, on 1 September 1948, the Bundesrepublik came into existence. To prevent any possible jokes, the skeleton of a mammoth at the entrance to the museum was decently hidden by brown-paper and potted palms, but otherwise the stuffed or unfleshed animals and birds of the zoological department looked on, dumb and sightless, as the pale Konrad Adenauer set the great nation he loved and served so well on course again as a parliamentary democracy. Exactly ten terrible years had passed since Adolf Hitler had been in Bonn for another event of immense political importance, the meeting which Neville Chamberlain believed would surely establish 'peace in our time'.

Godesberg is only half an hour upstream. Beside the shore to starboard is the white and rather faded mass of the Hotel

Dreesen, with the wash of the upstream traffic breaking on the groynes at its foot. On the left of the side which faces the river the first-floor room with the balcony is No 118, the famous room in which the British Prime Minister stayed, waiting for the summons to cross the Rhine and attend at the Hotel Petersberg among the woods of the Seven Mountains and there meet the Führer face to face. As for the Hotel Dreesen, there is nothing very special about its appearance, and probably the room itself would be ordinary enough had it not been thus thrown into the glare of the limelight of history. As a German said, 'The room is often used for conferences, some of which are indeed successful.' And others only apparently so.

In fact, none of the riverside towns above Cologne is particularly notable until Bonn comes into view, a city which has somehow managed to sit on the very edge of the Rhine itself and yet has forgotten to equip itself with a harbour or quay of any description. Some of the government offices are raised on legs so that at least the bureaucracy can flourish unimpaired in times of exceptional flood, but that seems to be the only thought which the central government casts in the direction of the Rhine.

Upstream of the town and its row of villas and hotels a very picturesque half-timbered inn stands among the limes at Plittersdorf, its terrace looking over the water. This is the Schaumburger Hof, a place of some distinction in British history for it was there that Victoria sat at a stone table beneath the trees and 'exchanged her first words of love' with the handsome young Albert of Coburg-Gotha, a student at Bonn University. Later she was to ride out to the inn and renew those early memories when she visited Bonn for the unveiling of the Beethoven memorial.

The Drachenfels

The Drachenfels – Dragon Cliff – is undoubtedly one of the great sights of the Rhine, and I suspect that the quarrying which nearly demolished it went far to improving its outline by giving it an almost sheer face on the side towards the river. The view downstream from Unkel or Oberwinter toward the crag topped by a crumbled castle keep is one of breathtaking beauty, especially in the early morning, when a silky shining mist of the palest blue lies over the river and the faint outline of the volcanic hills protrudes mysteriously from the sea as though they were the mountains of Tahiti. There is something age-old about the shape of these wooded hills, and their sheer insularity hints that men have lived there for a very long time indeed.

Some believe the Drachenfels to have been the scene of Siegfried's adventure, but this is doubtful. There were many dragons in Germany during the era of such beasts, and that of the Seven Mountains met its death in a different way. The event occurred during the lifetime of Maternus, one of the three men sent by St Peter as apostles to the Rhineland and the one who died in Alsace while on his way there – an event which so distressed his colleagues that they had to return to Rome and fetch St Peter's staff with which to revive him. After this – if we quickly pass over a few centuries – Maternus reached Trier and later became the first Bishop of Cologne. But his success was confined to the left side of the Rhine, to the province of Gaul and the lands to the north. Across the river the terrible German pagans were still intransigent.

Worst still, these horrible heathens would raid across the river to take prisoners. One such capture was a girl of such rare beauty that the toughest of the chieftains each sought to have her as his own. Horsrik was an old warrior whose club had already smashed in countless skulls. Rinbold was younger and fearless. He was also handsome, so it is already possible to guess which of the two is to win the prize. That, however, would be to miss out the bit about the dragon, for when the two warriors raised their weapons to have at each other, the venerable priest of Odin stepped forward and held the men apart. It was foolish to lose one or possibly both of the leaders for the sake of an argument about a Christian beauty, he said. She would be sacrificed at sunrise next morning to the insatiable dragon who lived in a hole on the cliff and terrorised the area. This decision was greeted with applause, though Dr Ruland, when he set down the story, added for the sake of his readers that 'Rinbold, the proud young chieftain, looked sorrowfully at her angel-like face.'

So, next morning, the girl was garlanded and garnished in a way likely to appeal to the monster's appetite and then tied to the tree to which the dragon fodder was customarily attached. The people retired to a safe distance, and then, as the first rays of sunlight came over the forest to light the maiden's golden hair, the scaly beast emerged with bloodshot eyes and flaming breath, and licked its steaming lips at the sight of such a dish. Just as it raised itself upon its tail to strike, the girl pulled out her golden crucifix and held it aloft, an act which had such a dramatic effect upon the dragon that he reared, pitched over backwards, and was precipitated into the Rhine far below. As the cords loosed themselves from her body, two strong arms seized her – but only gently, for Rinbold was at heart a good man, as befits such a tale. He and the old high priest were the first two to be converted. They were quickly joined by thousands more. Even Dr Ruland does not tell us what became of Horsrik, but being a rather horrible old man I expect he remained perverse and obdurate until the end of his days.

The Siebengebirge (the Seven Mountains)

It is said that long, long ago the Rhine flowed through at least two great lakes besides the Bodensee. One of these covered the land upstream of where the city of Bonn was later to be built, and when in early summer the Alpine snows thawed to send a flood of water down the river, the lake would rise and flow over the fertile land on either side. The people who lived there were very concerned at such a state of affairs, and as the hydraulic problems involved were outside their own competence they sent an embassy to the land of the giants, asking them to

89

give an estimate for cutting a channel through the rocks at the northern end.

A bargain was made, and a gang of seven navvies from the country of the giants came to the Rhineland and dug a cleft. The water streamed through the gap – no doubt to the great embarrassment of those who lived further downstream – and a proper river-sized channel was quickly eroded. Soon the lake had gone, and only a plain remained, except that to one side of the channel the seven mounds of rocky rubble were ranged, the spoil which the seven giants had shovelled. Cartographers call these heaps the Siebengebirge or Seven Mountains. Those who live in the neighbourhood say that the hills will not necessarily be there for ever. Giants are tidy-minded folk, and they are likely one day to return and clear up the debris of their digging.

The Seven Mountains are in fact thirty in number; but the name is fair enough, for from a distance only the seven highest peaks can be distinguished. The whole group is a collection of volcanic hills, some of which have yielded the stone for such distinguished buildings as Cologne Cathedral. Naturally, the quarrying was undertaken where suitable stone was close enough to the river for easy shipping, and as a result the Drachenfels was so heavily preyed upon that in 1788 the one side of the castle at the top of the rock was no longer supported and crashed into the void below. The Emperor Frederick William III later stepped in and bought the top of the mountain, together with what little of the castle still remained. Otherwise it would certainly not be there today to provide one of the finest outlooks in all the Rhine valley. At the back of these hills are the remains of Heisterbach abbey, where a monk is said once to have had a curious adventure. I have often wondered whether the tale might not be true, and that this good brother broke through the sound barrier of time, that elusive line which perhaps all of us will one day cross in another way.

Brother Petrus Forschegrund was reading in 2 Peter 3. *'Ein Tag vor dem Herrn ist wie tausend Jahre,'* he read. 'One day is with the Lord as a thousand years, and a thousand years as one day.' The verse puzzled Brother Petrus, and he wandered into the woods to meditate upon it, listening as he did so to the romantically stirring song of the nightingales. As dusk drew in he returned to Heisterbach and was surprised to find a porter on duty who did not know him. Led before the prior – who had also changed during his absence – Petrus gave his name. They looked him up in the register and found that it was 300 years since he had walked out to meditate and had disappeared. Sad to relate, the discovery that the text from 2 Peter was correct was too much for the monk, and he died.

If we look at the history and pre-history of the world as revealed by geology and radio-carbon dating, it is obvious that the importance, the events of each hour or day have continually increased. The world of 1970 or 1980 is as different from that of 1900 as 1900 was from the year 800, when Charlemagne was crowned at Aachen. Further back, it took hundreds of millions of years for the single-celled aquatic creatures to be replaced by even the simplest ones complex enough to live on land. And before that came the long ages of silent hit-and-miss amino-acid formation in the primeval soup of the sea.

Long ages? Only if looked at from our own parochial and shipboard view-point of Greenwich Mean Time. For in fact, time has been accelerating. Teilhard de Chardin was well aware of this, and as a scientist he was naturally inclined to extend the curve of the graph and see where it led. Of course it did not lead to the billions of years of slow roasting or slow cooling of a decaying planet but to a time measured within only thousands of our year-units when humanity would, as it were, take off spiritually into a new level of existence, a spiritual state as much above the present one as our own civilisation is beyond the cave life of Aurignac and the herd-hunting of Solutré. Perhaps he is right.

Nowadays, I hope, we are no longer so scared by time. We accept its elusiveness, we are aware that it cannot conceivably be a straight line. And if any of us should, like that monk of Heisterbach, be tempted to meditate on the Bible as we read it, I doubt if we should need to wander in the woods to convince ourselves of the truth of the text from 2 Peter.

Yet it might still come as a shock to us to realise that we ourselves have to live by the 24-hour day, and if one day this year is equal to a hundred a century ago, we have that much more to achieve in the same unit of local time. Once, things were run by evolution (or by God, if one prefers the term). Since *Homo sapiens* there as been a change to a partnership of ever-increasing closeness, and of ever greater urgency as the time-graph becomes more and more vertical until finally ...

Finally, what? Perhaps the moment when, like Brother Petrus, we pass into a dimension of which we yet know only such little as the visionaries have brought back to us from their travels beyond the barrier of time – a frontier which still bounds our physical existence in a niche of evolutionary current.

But to return to the legend of the monk of Heisterbach, this pensive fellow had, it seems, spent no less than 300 years fascinated by the song of a bird in the woods. Obviously such a thing could not be allowed to occur again, and St Bernard of Clairvaux, already known for his successful banishment of nightingales from the monastery garden of Himmerode to an island in the Moselle, where the rather more kindly nuns of the convent of Stuben willingly received them, was called to rid Heisterbach's woods of the menace. He ordered the nightingales to pack up, and he banished them to the Nachtigallental or Nightingale Valley above Königswinter, to which they return happily each summer from their winter quarters.

Rolandsbogen

The trouble with the romantic Rhine is just that. It *is* romantic – so much so that it manages to crowd into the relatively short stretch of its middle reaches as much legend and history, chivalry and dastardy, true love and bastardy, noble devotion and blind hatred as the rest of Europe put together. Sweeping down upon the current, any steersman who is not completely insensitive to the past has to divide his attention between rocks, the signals of upcoming ships, and the tales of the heroes and heroines, villains and haughty adventuresses who inhabited – and perhaps still haunt – the ruined towers and keeps on either hand. And these castles come so thick and fast that he has scarcely identified one crag-bound watch-tower or keep before the next is already on the beam. And of all the Rhineland tales, none is more tragically romantic than that of the arch set on the hillside across the river from the Seven Hills.

This arch is the Rolandsbogen (Roland's Arch), and the slight bend of the river above which it stands is the setting for one of the greatest and saddest tales of the era of medieval chivalry, a story sung by minstrels in the great halls of many a castle, a tale which varied much with the years and the particular troubadours who sang it, but which was probably one of the most favoured themes of all. For the Song of Roland was perhaps even better known than the great epic of the Four Sons of Aymon. Certainly the ballad was sung on the invasion beach when the Normans landed in England, and it fell to the minstrel Taillefer to bolster their morale by striking up the tale of Roland the mighty, the fearless and chivalrous, the knight who with his handful of companions stationed himself in the Pyrenean pass to hold at bay the hordes of Islam while Charlemagne's army, badly mauled in the battle, withdrew to the safety of the Frankish lands. One by one the men were slain, then Roland himself, and only with his dying breath did he blow one single blast upon the great horn Oliphant. Yet it was a blast so penetrating that Charlemagne heard it across France. It caused him to stop, rally his men, and march all the way back again to slash and rip and slaughter those pagan hordes who had slain his twelve noblest and most chivalrous knights.

However, in the Rhineland the version sung by minstrels to the tough knights in their craggy nests was different. Roland blew his horn, yes; but so great was his natural strength, so powerful his blood, that although he had been left by the Moors for dead in the gorge of Roncevalles he regained consciousness, bound his own wounds, and set out in great pain to limp and struggle homeward, bound for the Drachenfels and the castle in which lived the lovely Hildegund, to whom he had sworn eternal devotion. The journey took him some years, as well it might, but at last he came to Königswinter and dragged himself up the long path which led to the Drachenburg.

Yet all this was in vain. As Hildegund's own ageing father explained to the travel-worn and emaciated knight, her lover had long since been reported as slain and the girl in her sorrow had vowed that she could never look upon another man but would enter a convent. She had got her to a nunnery, right there in the Rhine, on the Nonnenwerth (Nun's Island). See, down there in the trees, where the river curves round the foot of the hill and splits into three separate channels – that is where she is to live her days, in sadness perhaps, but in devotion and charity and prayer.

The news is, of course, terrible to Roland, a blow so fearful indeed that from the sheer shock the wounds caused by the Moorish swords and lances in the pass of Roncevalles re-open and his blood flows out. He is carried into the Drachenburg and, though weak from the haemorrhage, he eventually recovers enough to make his way down to the river and have himself ferried across. He orders a small and simple castle dwelling to be built, and built quickly, right on that shoulder of bluff where he might look down upon the grounds of the convent in the stream. There is to be a bay window where he can sit, weak from his wounds and wanderings, his only wish to watch for

93

the form of the fair Hildegund as she passes every day from the refectory to the chapel.

A more ordinary mortal might devise some means to rescue Hildegund from the convent and whisk her away to Rome to seek release from her vow. But not Roland. He is the flower of chivalry, of acceptance of fate. He will never love another, but nor will he break into the new life of his love. For the rest of his days he will live only for those brief recurring moments when the veiled figures cross the courtyard in the spring sunshine, in the falling autumn leaves or in the powdery snow of a crisp winter's day when the Rhine itself is near to freezing.

And so the years go by. Roland's bodily wounds will never heal. Nor will the wound to his noble heart. It is as though his own life is dripping away as he strains to catch the singing of the choir borne up to him on the breeze. One of the voices is Hildegund's, and now and again he thinks he can distinguish it. And of course Hildegund has long since heard of the knight who has built the tower in order to be near her. Little by little the unbounded spiritual joy which was to attend her in the nunnery ebbs away. One day, heartbroken, she dies. Her companions bury her in the convent.

Roland hears the bell tolling for a funeral. He knows whose it is, for as the sisters file across the court there is only one missing, his Hildegund. He sits at the window, motionless as the chanting wells up from among the trees. The nuns file back to their cells. Roland sits there still, his head rested on his hands. It is dark when his one servant comes into the room to summon him to his evening meal.

But the knight does not answer. The servant steps forward and touches him on the shoulder, only to find that he does not look up. The only thing for which Roland has desperately clung to life itself has gone, and his great and broken heart has simply stopped. There at the bay window overlooking the Nonnenwerth he has quietly died, to be with Hildegund eternally as he had vowed.

The arch is easily visible from the river, and it is sad to know that, quite apart from the fact that the noble knight was himself a legendary and almost Homeric character, the castle ruin at Rolandseck really has nothing to do with Roland, the hero of Roncevalles, for it was not built until three centuries after that famous battle. But it may well be that another knight named Roland loved a girl who had retired to the Nonnenwerth at the foot of the crag. The castle itself eventually decayed, and in 1839

94

even the famous arch was destroyed in a violent storm. However, the poet Freiligrath happened to notice its absence when he was travelling by post-chaise down the valley, and he wrote such vigorous verses of appeal in a Cologne newspaper that money to rebuild the arch poured in and the Rolandsbogen was soon restored to the condition in which it stands today.

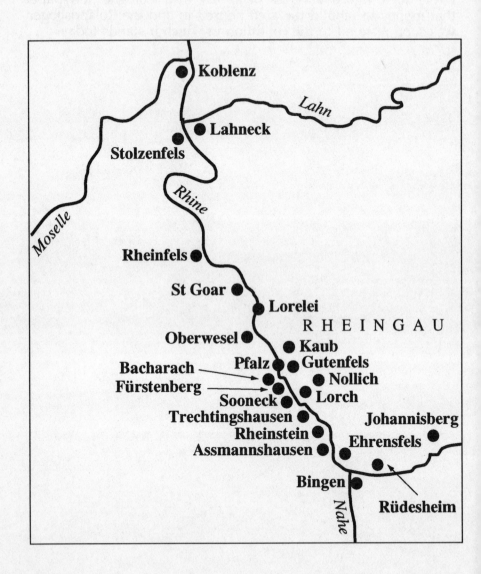

The Rhine Gorge: Stolzenfels, Boppard, Rheinfels and St Goar, Lorch, Trechtingshausen, the Mouse Tower, the Pfalzgrafenstein, the Lorelei, Assmannshausen and Rüdesheim

The Rhine Gorge extends from Koblenz up to Bingen and Rüdesheim. One has the impression from the water that the river is flanked by high mountains, but in fact the gorge is a cleft cut through the table-land by erosion. Almost every corner has a castle standing in a well-fortified and virtually impregnable position, and these were originally erected in the Middle Ages as armed positions from which raids could be carried out upon the shipping, demanding 'tolls' for passage. There were several dozen before a ship reached the Netherlands, and so much money was lost to shippers by this noble brigandage that the Rhine towns, led by Strasbourg, combined sometimes to shoot their way through with floating forts manned by arquebusiers. But the castles have left behind them the richest treasury of legends and tales of love and heroism that is to be found anywhere. Some of the castles are now signal stations, as it is impossible for up-going traffic to see round the corner ahead, and for down-going shipping to be able to stop if not warned.

Stolzenfels

History records that one of the less warlike of the Electors of Trier installed in the Stolzenfels an alchemical laboratory where he sought to transform metals into pure gold. 'It would not have been time and labour cast away, had he instead sought to do the same with his spiritual subjects,' an English visitor once wrote, but in fact the search for the Philosopher's Stone was not always a matter of sheer greed. In the centuries before Robert Boyle it was believed that the physical state of affairs here on

earth was a sort of mirror or cipher of the arrangements in the
spiritual realm. If by grace base men could be made pure, so
surely in the world of chemistry the dirty, sinful metals (we still
call them *base* metals, even in the most exalted scientific circles)
could be transformed to the shining purity of gold. If only one
could discover the reagent to perform this change, then automatically one would understand more about the operation of
divine grace. And if one happened to make a fortune on the
side – well, what was wrong with that?

It may have been this same alchemist, I think, who gave rise
to a curious story about Frundsberg, the tax collector at Stolzenfels. It is said that Frundsberg's accumulating wealth soon drew
the attention of another man, an Italian adventurer named
Leonardo, who called at the Stolzenfels and found little difficulty in persuading Frundsberg that he was an alchemist who
was within an ace of discovering the Philosopher's Stone. If
Frundsberg ploughed his wealth back into alchemical research –
which, the man pointed out, was unfortunately rather expensive
– he would not just be rich but fabulously so.

Leonardo was soon installed in a laboratory at Stolzenfels, and
(just as he had said) the experiments proved extremely costly.
Frundsberg soon ran through his own cut of the toll-money and
had to begin falsifying the Electors' account books. His daughter
Gertraud tried to dissuade him, but failed to do so. Nevertheless, she constituted a threat to Leonardo's business, so he
decided that he would have to silence her. When it was
announced that the Elector was coming to Stolzenfels to collect
the toll-monies there was considerable and very reasonable
alarm, but Leonardo persuaded the poor girl that the only thing
lacking to bring the alchemical reactions to a successful conclusion was the life-blood of a pure virgin. Moved by love for her

father, and perhaps by an idea that the greasy Italian might after all be telling the truth, Gertraud agreed to offer herself.

And so at dead of night Gertraud presented herself at the laboratory. On the table was a bowl for the blood and a dagger. Leonardo told her to strip and wrap herself in a sheet before lying on the table, and the man then carried out some mumbo-jumbo, burning in a flame some wood from the Lebanon. Then he ripped the sheet from his victim, seized the dagger, and would have stabbed the maiden through the heart if his raised hand had not suddenly been gripped by a hand even stronger than his own. No, it was not that of Frundsberg, nor even of the Elector of Trier. The rescuer was young Reinhard of Westerburg, captain of the Stolzenfels guard, who had noticed Gertraud's distraught appearance and had trailed her on tiptoe as she went to the laboratory. It need hardly be added that for a long while he had loved her devotedly from a distance.

Reinhard struck the Italian such a blow on the chin that he went down unconscious. Then he stood with eyes averted while Gertraud wrapped herself in the sheet again, after which the girl told him all that had happened and Reinhard confessed his love for her. He also added that he would have Leonardo handed over to the Archbishop-Elector of Trier, who was due the next day and was always accompanied by a very experienced hangman.

At this Leonardo, whose amnesia was no longer genuine but only a pretence, leapt to his feet and rushed from the laboratory, uttering horrible oaths. He fled for his life, but as it happened to be the middle of the night he unfortunately ran over the edge of the cliff and fractured his skull beyond repair. Gertraud and Reinhard helped cook the books and put the funds in order, and when the Elector arrived he was delighted to find things in such excellent order. A few days later he personally conducted the wedding of Gertraud Frundsberg to Reinhard von Westerburg before returning to Trier with the takings of the Stolzenfels toll.

Boppard

Little of Boppard's castle survives, and it is preserved mainly in the tale of Konrad of Boppard, a pleasant young man but perhaps rather too easily led by others. He was engaged to a girl named Maria, but when the lads twitted him for being willing to give up his independence and become a stay-at-home newly-wed he had second thoughts about the matter and wrote Maria a note to say that he wished to break it off.

Some time later he was out hunting when he was confronted by a young knight in black armour and closed vizor, who addressed him through the slits in the metal to the effect that he had better get ready to be killed. The insult he had given to Maria was now to be avenged by her own brother.

The fight did not last long, and I am sorry to say that Konrad of Boppard was the victor. However, he had the courtesy to open the helmet of his severely wounded opponent and there beheld the pale face not of Maria's brother, but of the girl herself. A few minutes later she was dying – happy, she whispered with her fading breath, to have fallen at his hand alone.

Poor Konrad was filled with remorse, as he certainly should have been. He spent all his money on building a convent (the Marienburg) in her name, and it was to become one of the richest along the Rhine valley. As for himself, at first he joined the Templars, but as his spirit could find no peace he eventually set off for the Holy Land to join the army of gallant warriors, disappointed lovers, conscience-stricken deceivers and impetuous murderers whose only fulfilment lay in cleaving Infidels in half until they themselves fell to a well-aimed spear or the slash of a heavy scimitar.

Until it was destroyed by the marauding Swedes Boppard also had a monastery, which was founded by the Franciscan Bernard of Siena. Locally it was alleged that he reached the Rhine at Kamp and asked to be carried over in the ferry. The ferryman insisted on the usual small fee, but Bernard took the rule of poverty so literally that he had no coin of any kind to offer. Too bad, said the waterman. No cash, no carriage.

But Bernard, it seems, was a resourceful man. Casting his habit on the water he stood on it and, holding up the corners to form a sail, he sped across the river before a following wind. The people of Boppard streamed out to see such a sight, and no wonder, for Bernard made the crossing faster than the ferry.

Boppard to starboard, then Bornhofen to port, and high above it the twin crags with the castles of Sterrenberg and Liebenstein. Probably there is little truth in the tales of the brothers who lived in these keeps, but it would be unwise to look too far into such medieval legends in case the cold light of a reasoning and scientific age should rob them of their character. Better by far to go along with local tradition – which is not always at fault –

100

and assert boldly that there were indeed two brothers, and a sister too. Their father left his fortune to be divided equally among the three of them, and the brothers set about distributing the money. Their sister happened unfortunately to be blind, so the two young men adopted the ruse of sharing out the rents and incomings with a shovel, carefully turning it over and using the back whenever it was their sister's turn. Poor girl, she was fleeced of most of her fortune, but even the portion allotted to her she used to found a convent in Bornhofen.

Happy in their deceit, the two brothers decided one day that on the next morning they would go hunting together. The first one up was to rouse the other. The Sterrenberg brother was first to awake, and seeing the shutters on his brother's room in the Liebenstein still closed he decided to knock him up with a bolt from his crossbow. He pulled back the string, aimed, and pulled the trigger. And just at that moment the tardier brother himself threw open the shutters and was killed instantly as the bolt struck him over the heart. The one who had fired the shot was so overcome with remorse that he went to the Holy Land, either to forget or perhaps in some hope of expiation for his unintentional fratricide. So, with both brothers gone, the blind sister came into the full inheritance from her father, which she spent upon the convent she had already begun.

Rheinfels and St Goar

O Rheinfels! How sad the story of your young daughter of the house, who fell in love with George Brömser of Rüdesheim, but who was half-promised by her father to the wealthier, if scoundrelish, knight of Berg. With determination the girl announced her engagement to her beloved George, and the date of the wedding was already fixed for only a short time ahead when the Emperor Albrecht summoned all good men and true to help him bring to heel the Swiss confederates, who had just broken away into a neutrality, which in fact they were to keep forever. Brömser, being indeed both good and true, obeyed the call to the colours. Not so the nasty knight of Berg.

George dug a hole in the Rheinfels garden with his sword and planted in it a lime sapling, telling his beloved that if it flourished he was safe, but if it wilted he was dead. Then he went off to fight the Swiss peasants, who trounced their attackers at the battle of Morgarten and littered the field with the corpses of Rhineland nobility.

As the months passed and a few mutilated knights came travelling home, there was still no news of Brömser. However, the lime tree was healthy and in full leaf, so the young girl did not entirely give up hope. This was infuriating for Berg, so after searching the woods for a decayed lime tree of suitable size he one night crept into the garden, flung the original sapling over the cliff and put the wilted one in its place.

Next morning, when the girl looked out of her window she uttered a piercing shriek. Then she wept for weeks on end, and it was only at the end of that interval that Berg could approach her and ask for her hand. She replied that she would be as faithful in death as in life, but certainly not to him; whereupon he impetuously drew his sword and rushed upon her.

Like most men who murder in a moment of fury he immediately wished that he had not done the deed, but there was no bringing the girl back to life. So Berg went off and hanged himself, and when at last poor George came limping back to Rheinfels he was met with a sorry tale of tragedy. He pulled out the dead lime tree and planted a bed of white lilies over the grave of his dearest love. He never married, nor did he take refuge, like most disappointed men, in a monastery. He became a minstrel and spent the rest of his life touring the castles of others, striking up the songs of his own composing which told of chivalry, and undying love, and of a great sorrow.

Castle Rheinfels was erected by the counts of Katzenelnbogen as a formidable strongpoint to protect the entirely unauthorised toll-collecting which they operated in the river below. It was one of the worst of these levies, and so the League of Rhine Towns decided that it must be reduced. In 1255 the 26 members contributed a total force of 8,000 foot soldiers, and under the protection of 1,000 horsemen and 50 armed barges the battle was begun. For 66 weeks they invested the place and on no less than 40 separate occasions attempted to take it by storm, but Rheinfels held out until at last the forces of the League had to withdraw 'amid the derision of the defenders'. The toll still survived, and I presume the dues for the ships of the League cities were suitably increased.

As for the line of Cat's Elbow, it came to an end in the fifteenth century with the death of Count Philip at the age of 77. His life seemed dogged by misfortune, for his son and heir was stabbed in an affray at Bruges when only 27, and as the father had already separated himself from his insufferable wife he could not beget another lawful heir during her lifetime. She lived to a good age, but shortly after her death Philip, who was already 71, married again – 'to please the people', as he so nicely put it. However, his relations saw in the possible fertility of his new wife a real threat to their inheritance, so they paid the old count's chaplain 1,000 gulden in cash to get rid of him by giving him poison in the chalice when he next went to mass. Unfortunately the wary old man noticed the smell or taste and declined the sacrament. Instead he had his chaplain burned alive – but after all these excitements either he or his new spouse Anna of Nassau-Dillenburg was sterile, and no heir was born.

Having withstood the League, Rheinfels again held out against a massive onslaught by the French forces of Louis XIV, who lost 4,000 men in two weeks whilst trying to force the surrender. In the end it was captured in the most ignominious fashion, for the successors to the Cat's Elbow had become careless in keeping up the fortifications and mounting a proper guard. One night in 1758 the commandant gave a splendid ball for all the neighbourhood, and this gave the Marquis de Castries his opportunity to overpower the guard and lead a small force of French soldiers into the ballroom, where all the officers were quickly relived of their swords. The gallant Marquis requested the orchestra not to be dismayed but to continue with their repertoire, and the French – full of courtesy, as was their wont on such occasions – invited the ladies to dance with them. In this pleasant way Rheinfels was taken, and during the Revolution it was blown up.

The town of St Goar is a pleasant little place of no great distinction, but it is at least unusual in that if almost every other army tried to sack it, the Swedes left it undamaged. Or very nearly so, for when Gustavus Adolphus entered the Protestant church and saw the damage done to it by the Spaniards he brought his mailed fist down with such a thump upon the corner of the altar that he broke it right off and it had to be repaired with iron cramps. As for St Goar himself, some historians have doubted his existence and have suggested that he is just a corruption of *Sand Gewer*, meaning the dangerous swirl by the sandbank at the upper edge of the town, but how they would then account for the early medieval biography of the man himself I am not certain. Personally, I like to think he existed.

Lorch

Lorch was the point at which ships were unloaded to small craft or wagons, to pass the rapids of the Binger Loch before the passage was improved. It was also the seat of Hilchen of Lorch, who followed a call to arms and went off to the Holy Land to cut the Saracens down to size. He left behind him his fiancée. But he had hardly reached the Middle East before his neighbour von Nollig decided that he would have her for himself. He fired the castle at Lorch, stormed it, killed the staff and even murdered the girl's father before taking her off. Curiously, this treatment did not endear him to her, so he locked her up in Castle Nollig until she should be willing to marry him.

News of this deed reached Hilchen by a vision – or by ESP as we might nowadays say. With a final cut or two at the Saracens he raced back to the Rhine and, drawing rein before Castle Nollig, demanded that his bride should be returned to him. Nollig's lord laughed loudly and taunted him that if he could jump his horse up the cliff into the walls, then certainly he could take the girl away. Hilchen realised that he could no more do this than capture the place by storming it, and he was just about to give up the girl and ride sorrowfully home when a face peered out of the bushes beside him.

'Psst! You want a horse to jump into the castle? OK. It's yours. Just sign this contract note.'

The speaker was of course the Devil, who was often to be found going his rounds of the Rhineland castles. Hilchen was at once aware of his identity, but thinking of his terrified girlfriend, he nobly decided to sacrifice his own soul for her freedom. He signed on the dotted line, and at once a splendid black horse was provided for him. At a single bound he was up the crag and over the walls to cut down the guards and sever the ropes of the drawbridge for his waiting men to pour in. Roused from his sleep, the abductor of Nollig perished in the fighting, lamented by none.

Hilchen's young lady was as delighted as she was astonished at such a rescue, and had just begun kissing him when the Devil hopped in through the window and thumped the contract on the table. It was time to be going to Hell, he said peremptorily.

But Hilchen's bride had great presence of mind. Snatching the crucifix that hung on a light golden chain around her neck, she tossed it on the contract, which of course immediately burst into flames. The Devil flew out again with a horrible oath and a smell of sulphur dioxide. Hilchen congratulated her upon her promptitude, and shortly afterwards they were married.

If Hilchen's romance ended happily, the same could hardly be said of the marriage of Lambert and Wiltrud, lord and lady of the mighty Fürstenberg, the next castle upstream on the starboard hand. Not that Lambert was anything but loving by nature; indeed he seems to have been a model husband, kindly if perhaps a shade susceptible. Indeed, it was his generous nature which led him to agree to the suggestion of his delicate wife Wiltrud that they should share their good fortune with those less happy, and take into their home a girl called Luckharde, orphaned daughter of a neighbouring noble family. She was only 18, but as Dr Ruland in his *Rheinsagen* states that she 'possessed a lascivious beauty very dangerous to men', we can rightly suspect that she is going to wheedle her way easily enough into Lambert of Fürstenberg's susceptible heart and bed.

Poor Wiltrud. The fact that she actually produced a son for Lambert seems to have been too much for the jealous Luckharde, who crept into her bedroom one night and smothered her with the goose-down pillows, and as Wiltrud had long been of a weak constitution there was no reason at all for the servants to believe that she had died of anything other than natural causes, particularly if one extended the term to include a broken heart.

Luckharde was now mistress of the Fürstenberg, and at least she did not murder the infant child of her predecessor. Perhaps it would have been wiser to do so, but Luckharde disposed of him simply enough by handing him over to an old woman who lived in one of the more remote parts of the servants' quarters. This same aged woman awoke one night and beheld with very understandable terror a white woman bending over the cot and kissing the boy. When she sat up in bed the apparition vanished, but in the morning the woman asked to be admitted to the new mistress of Fürstenberg to tell her what she had seen. Luckharde was distressed indeed, because the explanation that occurred to her was that maybe she had not completely asphyxiated Wiltrud, who had been hidden away in safety and had now recovered. She therefore decided to try to murder her rival a second time, and having sent the old woman to sleep elsewhere she herself took up her station in the nursery, a dagger concealed in her nightgown.

Sure enough, at midnight a woman appeared, silent and swathed in white, but instead of bending over the cot she came

105

straight towards Luckharde herself and leaned over her bed. It was enough to terrify even the boldest adventuress, but Luckharde steeled herself and suddenly leaped up to stab. The dagger went right through the apparition, and so did her arm. When Lambert awoke next morning he dressed and went down to breakfast as usual, but his beautiful young wife was not there. Instead there was a note addressed to him in which she confessed to Wiltrud's murder, told him of what had occurred during the past night, and added that the sense of her guilt was so tremendous that she had left the Fürstenberg to enter a convent. And because at least in his heart Lambert had been an accessory, she thought he should do likewise.

So Lambert handed over Fürstenberg and his own infant to the care of an upright and virtuous brother. He did not go into a monastery, but lived as a hermit in a cave on a crag overlooking the Rhine. And there, among his memories, he eventually died.

Trechtingshausen

No stretch of water in the world is so rich in legends of true loves and brigands as the Rhine Gorge from Bingen to Koblenz. And among all the tales, one of the greatest – which certainly borrows a little from the *Odyssey* – concerns the two neighbouring castles of Fürsteneck and Sooneck, which look down upon Trechtingshausen below.

Like other castles on the Rhine, the Sooneck was in its day a notorious nest of brigand gentry, and its terrible lord was in a state of perpetual enmity and feud with his neighbour in the castle of Fürsteneck. Indeed, he succeeded at last in setting a trap for him, and so took him prisoner without running the risk of falling to a bolt from Fürsteneck's crossbow – for the lord of Fürsteneck had the reputation of being the best shot along the entire length of the Rhine, and one who could invariably bring down a bird in flight.

Sooneck had his captive enemy dragged to the castle. There Fürsteneck was blinded and thrown into the dungeon, where he lay for 13 years, forgotten until the evening when Sooneck and his companions were feasting after another successful day of raiding. On that night a travelling minstrel knocked at the gate of the stronghold. He was led into the hall, and commanded to sing before the company.

But the song which the minstrel struck up was not that of

106

Roland, or of Tristan and Isolde, or of Reynaud and his brothers, or indeed any one of the favourite epics or romances which a Minnesinger would usually draw from his repertoire. It was a song, popular at that moment in the hamlets up and down the Rhine, but sung by the common people rather than by the minstrels who visited the nobility. It was not one with which Sooneck was familiar, but he certainly listened attentively when he heard the name of his vanquished enemy. For the ballad told of how Fürsteneck, the best marksman of the river, now lay in chains beneath the keep of Sooneck.

Perhaps the lord of Sooneck was flattered that his deed should be so famous. Or he may have been drunk. But his reaction was to have his blinded rival brought up from the vault of the dungeon, that he might be mocked and jeered at. And a terrible sight the bent, emaciated and sightless man must have presented as he was led stumbling into the hall.

Sooneck then ordered the blind marksman's crossbow to be brought and placed in his hand. The blind man swiftly ran his fingers over the mechanism.

'If you're so famous a marksman, shoot the goblet out of my hand,' Sooneck goaded him from the end of the hall. 'If you succeed, you shall go free and join our company. But if you fail... ' And he ended with a roar of hearty laughter in which all his companions joined.

An attendant handed Fürsteneck a bolt. 'Here,' Sooneck cried. 'My goblet. Can you not *see* it?' And once again he led the laughter, a great gust of cruel merriment which stopped as suddenly as it had begun. For Fürsteneck had not lost his skill through the long years in chains. Though blind, he had the sound of Sooneck's laughter to guide his aim, and with light-ning swiftness he set the bolt, drew the string, and fired along the hall. The bolt struck his enemy in the throat, and with the medieval equivalent of a sickening thud (which was probably a delicious, gurgling, blood-spitting crump) Sooneck fell dead across the table.

His companions leapt to their arms, but they might have guessed that the story was not yet ended. The aged minstrel threw off his cloak, tossed away his false beard, and with a whoop loud enough to summon his own trusty men-at-arms lurking outside the gate he swung his sword and sliced the heads and arms and torsos of all who approached him. He was, of course, the young Fürsteneck, who as a boy had heard of the wrong done to his father. The doors of the hall burst open, his companions streamed in, and the Sooneckers put up their weapons. Leading his blinded father by the arm, young Fürsteneck returned to his family fortress.

And there, no doubt, they all lived happily ever after, sitting along the heavy oak table in their own great hall, listening to the lays of the Minnesingers, talking of crossbows and hawking, dreaming of abducting the daughters of suitably wealthy neighbours, conversing of chivalry, of ridding the Holy Land of the Infidel, and of what a splendid idea it might be to swell the family fortune by the addition of just one more customs post down along the river, with a chain and bells to warn the guards if any wealthy merchant of Strasbourg, Mainz or Frankfurt should try to sneak a cargo through under the cloak of the new moon darkness.

The Mouse Tower

Downstream of Bingen on the Rhine, the Mouse Tower is situated on a shoal opposite the castle of Ehrenfels, of which it was originally the toll station. The name is a corruption of *Maut* (or toll). For many years the tower was the chief signal station controlling the Rhine traffic through the gorge, which begins at the tower and continues as far as Koblenz.

The Mouse Tower was built as an outlier of the Ehrenfels castle, the ruins of which peer haughtily down from the vineyards on the sharp bend immediately below Rüdesheim. It was designed entirely as a customs post, bleak and bare and practical. Its narrow tower rises most romantically from a reef at the head of a patch of shingle and a small copse of rough and scrubby trees, and sitting aloft in its upper storey a genial official of the Rhine traffic control will give to the skipper a friendly nod, leaning out of the same narrow window from which, centuries ago, a flight of arrows would have been a more likely discharge. Yet in story, and even in its name, the tower is associated with the tale of Archbishop Hatto of Mainz. The tale was retold by Robert Southey, but it is one which probably goes back to ages long before the Mouse Tower itself was built, to times when humans were sacrificed in an effort to appease the particular deity responsible for a famine. However that may be, the story which has somehow become attached to the worthy Hatto shows him in a most unfavourable light – and in an unjust one too, for he probably died before the Mouse Tower was even built. In any event he is known to have been a gentle and charitable man quite incapable of the cruelty alleged of him.

In the tenth century, it is said, there was a terrible famine in the land, and a throng of poor people made their way to Mainz to beg the Archbishop to help them with supplies from the archiepiscopal stores. Hatto had, of course, considerable stocks of grain stored in the diocesan granaries, and he invited all the poor people into one of his large barns as though he would make an issue of supplies to them. When the barn was full he had the doors secured from outside, and the building fired.

'Listen to the corn mice squeaking,' he exclaimed genially as the shrieks and screaming of the peasants rose from the burning building. And he let them squeak, on the principle that in hard times the poor were better out of the way. Were they not useless and comparatively unproductive fellows, with wives and families which merely ate up the good food which others might well need? Rather than let the rich go hungry, the poor should be burned.

But whether in real life, or in legend, or even in popular television serials, one cannot defy the moral structure of the universe and get away with it. The man on the white horse wins, the tyrant is doomed. Retribution followed as reliably in the medieval ages as in our own, and in his palace the Archbishop was soon assailed by mice which snatched the food from his fingers, fell into his cup of wine, devoured the stocks of provisions, and swarmed through the apartments, taking particular care to nibble away his name wherever it might be found carved or painted, graven or embroidered. Unable to keep the rodents at bay, the Archbishop fled in terror to Bingen and had himself rowed out to his watch-tower on the reef, where at last he would be safe. But even before his servants had pushed out the boat from the shore it was crawling with mice, and they swarmed ashore behind Hatto as he scrambled on to the islet. Other legions of rodents intrepidly swam across from the river bank, and though Hatto fled up the winding stairs and shut himself in his chamber, he was doomed. Creeping up the tower, inside and out, the mice pressed in upon him on every hand and, scrambling over the wicked prelate, they ate him. Southey added a delightfully macabre refinement to the tale when he described how the rats (which he no doubt thought more repulsive than mice, or perhaps better swimmers) 'whetted their teeth against the stones'.

The Pfalzgrafenstein

Sitting on its own rocky islet in the middle of the river, the Pfalzgrafenstein of Kaub is nowadays a signal station for the shipping. Originally built as a toll station to prey on the ships, it was also something of a medieval maternity home, and it became so as a result of a particular Rhineland romance.

Agnes, daughter and only child of the Count Palatine, fell in love with Prince Henry of Brunswick, but unfortunately the romance enraged the Emperor Henry VI, who saw that thereby the Palatinate would become Brunswick territory instead of being a dependency of his own. Agnes's father so feared the wrath of the Emperor that he decided to stop the match by confining his own daughter in the midstream castle. He locked up her mother in the same place and therein lay his error. When Henry of Brunswick arrived disguised as a pilgrim and rowed out to the Pfalzgrafenstein to beg a night's lodging, Agnes had the full support of her mother in the romantic events which followed. A priest was obtained, the wedding was conducted in private, and after a proper time Henry departed.

After some months the Count Palatine was astonished to receive the news that, out in her midstream prison, Agnes was soon going to give birth to a child. I am happy to report that instead of beheading her or throwing her out of the window, he was delighted that she had found her true love. So, too, was the

Emperor. Romance had turned away his wrath also, and the young couple received the imperial blessing on their future happiness. In due time Agnes's child was born, and ever afterwards it was the custom for the wives of the Electors to be rowed out before the onset of labour that they also might have their babies delivered in the room which had such romantic associations. Another and more practical explanation of this curious custom is that the princesses of the Palatinate had to be delivered in the midstream strongpoint to prevent the substitution of spurious offspring of ignoble blood, who thus might take over the sovereignty of the Palatinate itself.

Lorelei

The Lorelei – or Lore's Cliff – is situated on the right bank of the Rhine, below Oberwesel. It is the setting for one of the best-known Rhineland legends. At its foot there is a harbour of refuge from ice, from which the ascent can be made to the top of the 420ft cliff.

Lore, like every other maiden of Rhineland tales, was of unsurpassable beauty. She lived at Bacharach, and everyone fell in love with her. But her heart was pledged to the young man of her own choice, a noble knight from one of the score of nearby castles, and when he went away to the wars she could only console herself by retiring with her thoughts to where she could be alone. She would wander down the valley at dusk to climb the great cliff which overshadowed the Rhine, and there she would sit at its edge looking out over the moonlit gorge while she sang her strange, sad melody. Below her the river traced a silvery, serpentine course, and as her song floated away over the Wirbelei reach, borne on the still air of a clear night, the skipper of some trading ship would rashly take his eyes from the course ahead and glance up, seeking to make out her shape against the dimness of the hill-top skyline.

Er schaut nicht die Felsenriffe: er schaut nur hinauf in die Höhe; and every German child knows how the beautiful Lore lured him to the rocks and destruction. It seems, however, that this was just by the way. Lore was not a bad girl, and if night navigation was not forbidden, what had that to do with her?

The fame of Lore Lay quickly spread, and she came to be regarded as an enchantress – and a most beautiful one, too. Many fisherman and bargemasters sought to catch a glimpse of her, and most of them were drowned in the attempt. Sooner or

111

later it was bound to happen that the handsome young son of the Count Palatine should hear of her mysterious charm and decide to see her for himself. His somewhat square father forbade the enterprise, but the young man was not to be put off. Under pretence of going out hunting he went to Oberwesel and hired a boat, ordering the boatman to let the craft be wafted down towards the cliff.

And sure enough, far up on the cliff edge there sat a beautiful maiden, combing her golden tresses by the light of the moon and singing her famous, powerfully emotive melody as she did so. The adventurous hero stood up in the rowboat, and with a mighty spring he leapt for the shore, only to experience exactly what others have found when leaping from a rowboat – that the boat moves away but the leaper stays more or less where he is. Then, as now, it was all a matter of relative motion, mass and inertia, and if the son of the Count Palatine had known more about these things he might not have allowed himself to be impelled by love to an action which accorded so ill with Newton's Laws. But as it was, he leapt, fell short and sank.

The Count was not at all pleased when he heard the fate which had befallen his impetuous heir, and rather unchivalrously he decided to be revenged upon the unfortunate Lore who had lured so many to their death. He at once sent out a troop of his own horsemen, who surrounded the riverside cliff to prevent the escape of the wicked wench. The captain of the band then chose two or three lusty and intrepid comrades, with whom he climbed to the summit.

Lore was peacefully sitting there, thinking of her own absent loved one and perhaps adjusting her hair. She also happened to be holding a pearl necklace. No doubt she was surprised when the captain advanced uninvited and somewhat baldly announced that she was to be flung down into the river below, but she did not lose her composure.

'The Rhine will fetch me,' she declared, and flinging the necklace far out so that it fell into the 30-foot deep off the point of her rock, she struck up a new and urgent melody, crying to the river in a strange, mysterious cadence.

> *Vater, Vater, geschwind*
> *Die weissen Rosse schick deinem Kind,*
> *Es will reiten mit Wogen und Wind!*

Send, father quick, the white horses to save,
And your daughter shall ride on the wind and the wave.

112

And who could doubt the legend, which goes on to tell that the dutiful *Vater Rhein* obeyed? The great stream foamed and frothed and threw itself into swift confusion until two huge white curling crests (which must have had a height of at least 420 feet) swept up to the top of the rock and carried Lore away into the depths. As she vanished from their sight the men of the count's punitive expedition just had a chance to see the flukes of her tail. For she was, of course, no ordinary mortal but a fresh-water mermaid, a Rhine-maiden.

Although the rough count may have thought her a cruel and heartless girl, Lore was really a kindly soul. Already she had persuaded her father Rhine to send another wave to wash up the body of the impetuous young man, not dead but alive; and even if she did not restore the love-struck bargemen who had fallen under her spell and run upon the rocks, she never again let herself be seen. And yet they say that she is still there, hidden among the bushes, or in the clefts of the rock – for how else could one explain the soft answering voice which floats back in mimicry of that of the skipper, or the experienced certainty with which it declares that the Burgomaster of Oberwesel is really rather an ass (*Esel*).

Assmannshausen

Across the river from this wine village on the right bank of the Rhine, Castle Rheinstein stands magnificent, even if only a shadow of what it was in the years of highway robbery of the shipping. Below it and right against the shore stands a chapel, the Clemenskapelle. Standing on its own, it is a memorial to yet another deed of medieval violence. The lord of Rheinstein had put into a state of imminent maternity a virtuous girl who lived in a valley on the further side of the river, and for some reason which I have never fully understood, this caused him to be ridiculed by his neighbours who, one would have thought, might have been expected to regard this as the most common-place situation. The Rheinsteiner was stung by their taunts and decided to show that he was capable of going further than a mere clandestine meeting by night. He would seize the girl and carry her off to Rheinstein.

With an adequate force of toughs he crossed the Rhine and abducted her, but on the return voyage the poor girl stood up in the boat and called upon St Clement, promising him a new chapel if he would rescue her. And lo, in a moment the saint appeared on the water, scaring the robbers out of their wits with his unearthly shining light. Clement took the girl by the hand, and she stepped out of the boat to walk over the water with him to the bank. As for her captors, the boat was overset and every one of them was drowned. Which I think probably served them right.

However, another tale of its building is less romantic. When the unauthorised tolls levied by the gangsters in their Rhine castles had become too oppressive to be borne any longer, the Emperor Rudolph of Hapsburg decided to have done with these aristocratic brigands for ever. After his warnings had been disregarded with contempt, he appeared in the Rhineland with a mighty force of men, swelled by the burghers of the towns which suffered at the hands of the robbers. His system was not to storm the castles but to fire incendiary materials into them until they were well ablaze. From Reichenstein, from Sooneck and the Heimburg the clouds of smoke drifted down into the valley, and as the robber lords issued from their burning nests they were seized and taken for trial, then led through the streets of Assmannshausen amid the cheers of the merchants and vintners (and particularly the women, I imagine) to a place of execution on the bank of the Rhine.

It seems that the relatives of these men were very naturally concerned about the fate of their souls, and a priest advised them to cut down the trees on which their fathers and husbands had been hanged, and to use the timber together with stones from the burned castles to build a chapel of expiation for their misdeeds. When it was finished, the bodies were all exhumed and brought up the river in a macabre procession of barges, to be buried a second time in the Clemenskapelle, under the special grace of an absolution pronounced over them by the Archbishop of Mainz.

But this little chapel on the river bank is also connected with another of the most dramatic tales of the Rhine gorge, for it became the burial place of Gerda of Rheinstein and Helmbrecht of Sterrenberg. Gerda's father Diethelm was a highly successful robber baron, and he did not confine himself to plundering Rhine barges. On one of his forays he abducted a beautiful girl named Jutta, a girl of such winning ways and golden character that, according to Dr Ruland, 'as the delicate ivy twines itself round the rough oak and clothes its knotty stem with shimmering velvet, so in time the gentle conduct of this maiden changed

114

the coarse baron to a noble knight who eschewed pillaging and carousing' – and actually married her. But alas, she died when her baby was born; and that baby was Gerda. Needless to say, she was wondrous fair, so that those familiar with the Rhineland will already suspect that she was destined to have the most alarming experiences, which are almost certain to end in either defenestration or suicide.

Old Diethelm wanted to marry his daughter to anyone who had enough money (the ivy which had twined itself round the rough oak now being dead), and he was not at all averse to the suit of Helmbrecht of Sterrenberg, who had fallen in love with Gerda when she appeared as Beauty Queen at a tournament at Rheinstein. Gerda was in love with Helmbrecht, so everything seemed set fair for a wedding approved by all. But in those days it was the curious custom to urge one's suit through a relative who was a contemporary of the bride's father, and so Helmbrecht of Sterrenberg put his uncle to work on his behalf. Needless to say, the man was a wicked uncle, and as he was also very rich he easily persuaded the rough oak Diethelm that it would be much better if he married Gerda himself. The girl had no great wish to be espoused to this crafty old schemer instead of to the man of her own choice, but in those days young ladies were rarely consulted as to their desires. She was bluntly informed that she was to be married to Helmbrecht's uncle.

Looking up from the river towards the ruin of the great castle, one can even now imagine the events of the fateful day and see the wedding procession winding its way down the steep track from the Rheinstein towards the Clemenskapelle on the shore, the chapel in which so many noble brigands lie interred. None can now intervene to save the lovely girl from the wicked uncle of her lover. No mere human, that is, can stop the train of events. But insects are a different matter, and suddenly a squadron of horseflies buzzes out of the bushes and collectively they bite Gerda's horse on the rump. The steed rears and breaks away, racing down the dangerous path ahead. Gerda screams, the wicked uncle puts spurs to his charger to save his precious bride. So does old Diethelm.

There is a clatter of hoofs, then the uncle's horse trips on a stone and goes over the edge of the cliff with its rider still in the saddle. There is a crashing from below as rider and steed bounce from rock to rock, but the wedding party is more worried about Gerda's fate. Her father has now nearly reached the bridle of the fleeing animal but before he can seize the reins the steed rears, raises a hoof, and lodges a well-aimed blow upon his leg. Moaning, the knight is carried back to the castle, and the doctor is called.

Gerda's horse is now out of sight, the wedding guests and horseflies all left behind. Nor has the animal any inclination to stop its wild galloping. And then, as it careers round a bend, a man bursts from the wayside bushes and grabs the reins. It is – as the reader will have guessed – the faithful Helmbrecht, who was lying in wait to have a farewell glance at the bride who was not to be his. Gerda has already swooned away with fright, and when she awakes it is in the strong arms of her own dear, dear Helmbrecht.

I am glad to say that, after a few days in bed nursing his bruised leg, old Diethelm came to his senses enough to decide that Helmbrecht was not such a bad young fellow after all. Besides, one must assume that he had inherited his uncle's wealth. The old man gave the youngsters his blessing and rode in their wedding procession to the Clemenskapelle, accompanied by his sister Notburga from the Nonnenwerth convent – who must surely have been there to see that he behaved himself.

Rüdesheim

Rüdesheim, on the right bank of the Rhine, immediately above the defile of the Binger Loch, with a good harbour, is not everybody's choice. Not everybody's but very nearly so, to judge from the scores of thousands of visitors from Britain and the Netherlands who are brought there on package tours. A representative of the place told me how many visitors spent the night in the village during the year, and though I rarely remember such statistics, I know it was a very large number indeed. More than 3,000,000, if I recollect rightly, and when one considers that nearly all of them arrive during the brief summer months, one can see that Rüdesheim is hardly the place in which to seek solitude. Its few streets are thronged with the English indulging their favourite interest of looking in the shop windows, laboriously calculating the prices into sterling, and then deciding that a packet of cigarettes, or a bottle of beer, a jar of mustard or a pair of socks is either a tremendous bargain because it is a few pence cheaper or outrageously expensive because it is slightly dearer than its counterpart in Britain.

116

The village is famous for its Drosselgasse (Thrush Alley), a passage lined from end to end with pubs and wine bars, some of which are very much better than one would expect. There is music and dancing, mostly of a rather old-fashioned kind, because on the whole it is the tired middle-aged English and the solid retired Dutch or Scandinavians who come there to drink the wine. Over all the din, the little carillon on the Schloss inn just makes itself heard, as several times each day it sends the melody pleasantly over the grey slated roofs. And up at the back of the town there is a cable-lift to the top of the Niederwald, where stands the truly astounding figure of Germania.

'The visitor will hardly waste his time in going up the cogwheel railway to see the Denkmal of Germania above Rüdesheim', wrote Baring Gould. 'From a distance it looks like a shattered windmill. The absurdity of putting a huge elaborate piece of sculpture halfway up a mountain could hardly be surpassed.' But the fact remains that the Kaisers often did just that, and in the case of the Niederwald memorial there were no half measures.

Hurra, du stolzes schönes Weib, Hurra, Germania! Wie kühn mit vorgebeugtem Leib am Rheine stehst du da!

Proud she certainly is, but I am not so sure that Ferdinand Freiligrath was correct when he described her as beautiful, though it is perhaps difficult to judge the charm of a lady of such unusual size. For the figure of Germania is huge. She weighs 30 tons; and I hope it is not immodest to say that she measures just over 23 feet round the hips. She is not quite so spiky and masculine as the Germania on the old pre-1914 German stamps, who was modelled on Anna von Strantz-Führing, an actress of some renown and not the all-in wrestler one might have thought from her portrait. The postal Germania shared with the Marianne of France a curious embattled sexlessness, but the Germania of the Niederwald monument is definitely feminine, although in a rather militant, suffragette way. It is surprising to discover that she was in fact modelled from a Bad Ems bath attendant who was renowned for her beauty; but maybe even one of Rüdesheim's graceful wine queens might appear rather overpowering if blown up to such dimensions.

Kaiser William I unveiled the mighty Watch-on-the-Rhine memorial, and in so doing he had a surprisingly near escape, though probably the 30-ton Germania was in fact too heavy to have been toppled by the bottle of nitro-glycerine carefully buried beside it by two Anarchists. Leading to the flask was a buried fuse-cord with only the tip protruding from the ground, and the plotters had merely to set this alight and the fuse would burn swiftly to its destination. And that would be the end of the Hohenzollerns.

Or so they thought, but unfortunately for the Anarchist cause the night before the opening was one of incessant rain. Their Excellencies and the other important personages took their seats, and still the police had not so much as noticed any interference with the ground where the fuse had been laid. One of the men lit a cigar and touched the end of the cord. Nothing happened. He puffed to a red heat and tried again, but in vain. The fuse was too wet to light. Still the police were unaware of any plot, and they remained so until 15 months later, when the two men were foolish enough to try and claim their travelling expenses at a workers' meeting in Elberfeld. A police agent noted what they said, and one of the men was executed for treason; the other, being then only 20 years of age, received a life sentence – and in Germany, a lifer meant a lifer.

The waterfront of Rüdesheim is pleasantly stately, and the hotels beloved of the English grand tour travellers still have an air of superiority, hardly deigning to notice the railway which so unfortunately thunders past them on the other side of the riverside road. A little further back stands the amorphous and rather ugly ruin of the Brömserburg, now a museum with a fine collection of ancient wine presses, pruning knives and drinking glasses from Roman times onwards. Certainly the Romans had plenty of vineyards in the Rheingau, even if they may not necessarily have developed the slopes at the back of Rüdesheim itself.

Locally it is asserted that it was Charlemagne who was responsible for Rüdesheim's rise to fame as a wine village. He often resided at Ingelheim, a little further upstream on the other shore, and as he froze in the winter wind which drove the snow around his quarters he noticed that the hill across the river faced south and was free of snow, basking instead in the winter sunshine. As this happened regularly, it occurred to the great Emperor that the slope would be an excellent one for viticulture, and he despatched riders to Orleans to fetch some stocks. Sure enough, the vines flourished and three years later the first grapes were pressed. The vintage proved an excellent one, as have hundreds of others in the succeeding eleven centuries. Rüdesheimers used also to claim that whenever a year was to be a good one for its wine the Emperor would rise from his tomb in Aachen and transport himself to Rüdesheim, where he

The Graslei, Ghent.

Zieriksee.

Huy.

The Mouse Tower.

Pfalzgrafenstein.

Bad Ems.

Diez.

Karlstadt.

Heidelberg.

would stride up and down the river bank, blessing the vines which had originally been established there at his command.

The solid and rather featureless remains of the Brömserburg recall the very human story of Engelhard Brömser, a stubborn but upright man whose lot it was to live at the time when Bernard of Clairvaux was stumping Western Europe to raise a force for a determined attempt to wrest Jerusalem from the dreadful Saracens. Every man of honour or money or property was obliged to swell the ranks of the Crusaders, and no doubt most of them did so very willingly. Yet in the case of Brömser, the anticipation of slaughtering the Infidel was slightly dulled by his having to leave behind him his only child, the fair Mechthild, whose mother had recently died. After much deliberation he decided to place her in the care of his friend and neighbour at Castle Falkenstein, and then he rode away to Regensburg on the Danube to join the 70,000 other mounted knights who were massing for the campaign.

After much savage fighting beneath the hot sun of the Middle East, Brömser of Rüdesheim was captured alive, and as a prisoner of war he became a slave. In his despair he made the usual vows to encourage the Almighty to arrange his deliverance, promising that he would build at Rüdesheim a church to the Virgin and the Apostle James the Elder, and also a chapel to recall the agony on the Mount of Olives. He repeated these vows over and over again, then as a final bait he added that he would place his only daughter Mechthild in a convent.

Shortly afterwards, a new invading wave of European knights bore down upon the Holy Land. Quickly the Saracens drove their prisoner slaves far into the interior, but in the confusion Brömser escaped and hid in a disused sepulchre until the fresh force of Crusaders had overrun his place of hiding. Free at last, he did not hasten home to the Rhineland until he had again fought the Saracens in bloody contests, and it was some years before he came riding across the low hills of the Rheingau to his castle at the entrance to the river gorge, and to his own daughter Mechthild. At once he gave a banquet to all his friends and neighbours, and in his after-dinner speech he told them of his stirring adventures at the hands of the Infidel, of his vows, and how he now had no thought but to put them into practice at once. There was to be a church for Rüdesheim, a chapel also, and he had promised his daughter to a convent.

The shriek with which Mechthild greeted this last item caused a chill to fall over the company. At once the young Falkenstein

119

stepped forward, said that he and Mechthild had been in love for years, were engaged, and intended to marry at the earliest possible moment. He was sorry, but that last bit of his host's vows would not, could not be fulfilled.

Brömser was silent for a moment. In his anxiety to be free he had never even considered that his daughter was growing up and might have developed a will of her own. But he was an obstinate man, and soon he was declaring to the company that no Brömser had ever broken his vows, least of all to the Almighty, and as last of the line he certainly was not going to do so. To which his daughter replied that precisely the same went for her. She had promised to marry the young Falkenstein, and she did not wish to be the first Brömser girl to break her word. As for the convent, her father could keep it. And she swept out of the room, followed by the Falkensteins and their friends.

For two days the obstinate man argued with his equally obdurate daughter. Neither would move from their intentions. In the third night an ingenious idea came to Brömser. He would agree to the engagement in principle and then travel to Rome to ask the Pope to annul the part of his vow which related to putting his dear Mechthild into a convent. It might cost a little – such favours were rarely obtained free –but the Pope would surely agree to the request of a stalwart and faithful Crusader. Then the wedding could take place, and everyone would be happy. Even he himself.

Brömser jumped out of bed and sent a servant to fetch Mechthild. But the maid came back and reported that the daughter of the house was not in her room. Her bed had not been slept in.

Those confounded Falkensteins, Brömser thought. Unable to get Mechthild by fair means, they had obviously contrived to take her by stealth. Girding on his sword, he galloped off to Castle Falkenstein and hammered furiously on the door. But the Falkensteins were so genuinely surprised that they quickly convinced him that they knew nothing of Mechthild's disappearance, and they roused their own men to join in the search. No trace of Mechthild was found. It was two days later that her body was washed up on the shore below Assmannshausen.

How Mechthild had come to be drowned was never known. It might have been an accident, but I doubt it – just as in his heart Brömser doubted it, too. The girl was just one more victim of the perennial problem that nearly every family has to face.

Nowadays we would talk of the generation gap, an unbridge-able gap in understanding that the young may have their own ideas.

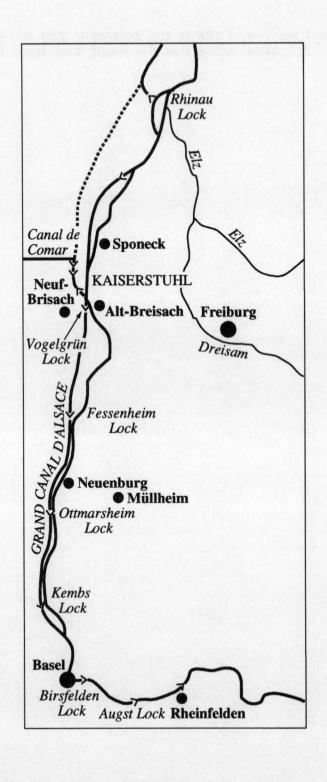

8

The Upper Rhine: Worms, Mannheim-Ludwigshafen, Strasbourg, Breisach, Colmar, Saverne and Basel

The Upper Rhine is here considered as the stretch upstream of the Gorge to the limit of navigation. That is, at the moment, at Rheinfelden, upstream (by two Swiss locks) of Basel. Opinions differ as to whether to make the remainder navigable past the Rhine Falls at Schaffhausen and into the Lake of Konstanz, which would give Austria an outlet to the sea at Rotterdam. Though there is much to be said for the idea, conservationists pointing to pollution by heavy craft have up to now succeeded in preventing any extension.

The area upstream of Strasbourg is one of vineyards, including the excellent Kaiserstuhl wines from the volcanic hills near Freiburg and Colmar. The whole river upstream of Karlsruhe has now been made properly navigable as far as Rheinfelden, the length abutting on Alsace being known as the Grand Canal d'Alsace. This was established for hydro-electric purposes under the Treaty of Versailles.

Worms

The joke about the Diet of Worms is as old as the teaching of history in English private schools. Yet the fact remains that Worms is an odd name, particularly for such an august and episcopal city as that which bears it. However, the name seems to have puzzled local chroniclers long before Martin Luther, and from them we have the assurance that the city was in fact named after a giant worm or dragon which had fled to the Rhine from some middle-eastern desert, a creature with a wormy tail, two feet, sharp teeth, a flame-thrower in its gullet, and an altogether rather unnerving appearance and manner. It ate humans as readily as cattle, and all efforts to appease the creature's wrath failed. Once a year the dragon had to be bought off with the sacrifice of a human. This was, of course, quite usual, and I have never yet sailed across the trail of a dragon of which this was not true. The Tarasque of the Rhone, the creature of the Drachenfels in the seven Hills near Bonn, the fearful Roggenbuk of the Trave estuary below Lübeck, each of these had to be propitiated in just the same manner. An annual meal of hominid was, it seems, the regular requirement of dragon metabolism.

At Worms (though the place as yet did not bear that name) the persons to be devoured were chosen by lot, but after a while the council refused to conduct the lottery any more, and the people feared that the delay would lead the animal to attack them wholesale. However, they had a worthy and self-sacrificing young queen who promptly decided to set a good example by putting herself and all her court officials down for the draw.

When the queen's number came up, a young man stepped forward and said he would try to save her on condition that he might marry her if he succeeded. To this she quickly agreed, and the young man went off to prepare for the encounter. In fact he was no fearless St George but one of three brothers who were cutlers, experts in fashioning and sharpening blades. The three men had together built a special suit of armour of a new design, entirely set with sharp projecting knife blades, hedgehog fashion. In this ingenious casing the young man was thrown by his brothers to the dragon, which foolishly swallowed him whole and died in the greatest agony. When it had ceased to squirm and twitch he climbed out unharmed to marry the queen, and everyone lived happily ever after. As for the 'worm', it was commemorated for ever in the new name of the city.

The famous Diet was held very much later, and it was on an April day in the watershed year 1521 that Martin Luther reached the gates of Worms under Imperial escort. Swiftly the news spread through the streets, and many of the citizens rushed out to meet him and to escort him enthusiastically to the Johanniterhof, where he was to reside. There was no doubt at all which side the people were upon in the great debate which was breaking over the city. They had seen too much of the materialism of the church dignitaries and the political scheming of rich clerics.

The Emperor and his brother, 6 Electors, 24 dukes, 8 margraves, 30 prelates and a host of earls and counts and diplomatic representatives made up the magnificent establishment audience before whom Luther was called upon to recant and to withdraw his writings. But no, he could not. After explaining that everything he had written came from his conscience and through a profound study of the Bible, he could not and would not withdraw one word, because it was neither safe nor right to do anything against one's conscience. 'Here I stand,' he concluded. 'I can do naught else. God help me! Amen'.

One further day was spent in fruitless attempts to reason with the obstinate reformer. He was then given 21 days in which to recant, without punishment. Slowly the time of grace passed, but Luther had nothing more to say. On the day after his span for reflection was up, he was conveyed to the Wartburg. The Reichstag having declared against him, a ban of excommunication was pronounced and the public executioner burned his writings in the open air at the market place. Inevitably, the great split begun further up the Rhine by Geyler of Kaysersberg and enlarged by Luther was not breached by these actions but widened still further, and it was to be more than four centuries before the first faint stirrings of a spirit of reconciliation made themselves felt.

As for the city which had been chosen as the venue for that momentous meeting, it was from then onwards to be continually rent by a split in its loyalty. Backed by the mass of the townspeople, the city council declared uncompromisingly for Luther and reform. Yet the city itself actually belonged to the Emperor and to the powerful Holy Roman Empire which had consigned Luther to damnation. Worms had to pay nominal homage to the Catholic bishop who ruled over its church, but in its heart and conscience the city had declared irrevocably for Luther, and to this day Worms is predominantly Protestant.

Once a place of ecclesiastical glory, Worms was almost annihilated by the bombardments of the Second World War. Much was lost for ever, but the cathedral has been restored from a ruin, and the Reformation memorial still stands under the trees near a piece of town wall which may well go back to Roman times. The monument is huge – it was put up in the period when Germany was sprouting giant memorials without hesitation – and whether or not one likes the scatter of earnest and more than life-sized reforming theologians surrounding the central figure on his pedestal, it would be impossible to conceive of Worms without it. Probably no event in history was, in the long run, more far-reaching in its results than the meeting of the Diet at Worms.

There is also the famous church with the baroque altar and the statue of Our Lady to which pilgrims had once come in their thousands. Our Lady – *Unsere Liebe Frau* – and the vineyards stretching up from the harbour to the edge of the old town itself were of course those from which Liebfraumilch (Milk of Our Lady) was once produced. But that was long ago, when no grape was worthy of that designation unless it grew within the area of shadow cast by the church of *Unsere Liebe Frau* during the course of the year – a patch which would be much larger than one might at first imagine, for at sunrise and sunset the shadow stretches as far towards the horizon as intervening buildings will allow. Leibfraumilch has now changed, the name having been extended to cover any wine in the whole of Rhein-Hessen sour enough to have been sugared before bottling. This is not a very attractive description, but it comes from the German wine trade itself, and no German vintner would ever attempt to fool the German public about the appellation. Not that some brands of Liebfraumilch may not actually be quite pleasant; but in Britain the old romantic association still lingers on, and many a grocer genuinely thinks (particularly if he only drinks beer) that he is doing his customers a real favour by securing for them a wine in which, if he only knew it, many Germans would not so much as wash their dogs.

Beyond the outer harbour wall and just below the bridge with its tall-arched gateway a figure stands in the bow of a boat which in turn is placed solidly on a stone pedestal, which in fact was that of a former medieval crane for unloading Rhine cargoes. The man wears a tunic and has a mighty sword hung from his belt, and in his upraised arms he holds a shield, using it as a tray to carry a pile of objects which he appears to be ready to cast into the river. This mighty fellow is the tough but evil-natured Hagen, and the objects on the shield the famous treasure hoard of the Nibelungen, whose land had once been conquered by the mighty Siegfried of Xanten.

Siegfried gave the treasure as a wedding gift to the fair Kriemhilde when he married her, but our hero was slain by the crafty Hagen, who waited until Siegfried was stooping to drink at a spring and swiftly ran him through with a spear which he deftly thrust into him at the one spot on his back where a falling leaf had caused a defect in his outer garment of invulnerability. Kriemhilde was inconsolable, and it was after she had refused for three years to speak at all that her brother Günther sent for the Nibelungen hoard to cheer her up. Twelve truck-

Worms bridge. Hagen with the Nibelungs treasure

loads of riches were loaded on a barge which set off up river and eventually docked at Worms.

Kriemhilde was indeed somewhat cheered, but being a worthy girl of responsible outlook she began to distribute the riches to the poor and needy. This very naturally made her extremely popular, and her husband's murderer went down even further in the estimation of the common people. Hagen soon realised that her charity must be stopped, and with the connivance of one of her brothers the key was stolen, the whole remaining hoard quickly laden on a ship and, at some point unknown to the Wormsers, flung overboard.

If none of it has ever been recovered by dredgers, that is merely because the Rhine Maidens who were told to guard it are so good at their job.

Actually, the *Rheingold* is not just a legend and a Wagnerian opera, nor even a crack Bundesbahn express. The Rhine gravel is in fact to some extent auriferous, and the Celts used to extract gold from the shoals anywhere between Basel and Mainz. It was in that period that the stories of the Nibelungen first began to take shape; and that Rhine gold was a real enough article is shown by the fact that Bishop Remi of Strasbourg in the year 777 assigned to a convent in Alsace the right to extract the gold

127

in one particular reach of the river. This monopoly was of real value; certainly it was in the upper reaches of river, the gravel stretches of Baden and Alsace, that most of the gold was found, and the metal itself was of high quality being of 22.4 carats, not far short of the 24 carats of complete purity.

Mannheim-Ludwigshafen

These twin industrial cities face each other across the Rhine; the Neckar flows in through the Mannheim docks. Ludwigshafen is on the left bank, with the long range of wharves of BASF, the Badische Anilin und Soda Fabrik. At first it is puzzling that this factory, with its marshalled yards of dye-stained tanker-wagons and its nostalgic laboratory odours, is there, for it is not in Baden at all, though Mannheim on the right bank is. However, it seems that the Badische works were once genuinely Badische, but, outgrowing their site on the right bank, they had no choice but to jump over the river and extend into the land of another state. A clue to what that state must have been is contained in the name of Ludwigshafen itself. The Ludwig was Ludwig I of Bavaria, and the territory was Bavarian-Hessian.

Charlemagne once decreed that the workshops for women on his estates should be equipped with supplies of certain textiles for weaving, teasels for teasing, and woad and madder for dyeing the cloth. The madder plant was still a mainstay of the dye industry as late as the nineteenth century, and the revolutionary government in France sponsored plantation of it in Alsace, on the left bank of the Rhine. The dye came mainly from the skin of the roots, which contained a substance (now known to be ruberythric acid) which could be hydrolysed to form sugar, and the actual dye itself, alizarin. So much in demand was this colour that 70,000 tons of it were used in Europe alone in the year 1868, when something happened. The something was that a pair of German chemists, lured by the rich prize of stealing this old-fashioned trade for the laboratory, succeeded in elaborating a series of reactions to produce alizarin synthetically. The only drawback was that the process involved using bromine, the cost of which was prohibitive.

It was just then that the BASF happened to have a large quantity of anthraquinone, an apparently useless by-product of one of their factory processes. One of their employees, a calico-printer named Heinrich Caro, wondered what would happen if he mixed it with oxalic and sulphuric acids. It was just one of those strange musings to which men of scientific bent seem unusually prone, but Caro decided to try the reaction. He mixed the three materials together and heated them.

No, the roof is not going to be blown off the BASF factory (though this occurred in 1921, when more than 500 were killed). Very much to Caro's disappointment, nothing occurred at all, except that the oxalic acid decomposed. He was still frowning over the undramatic nature of the results when a messenger brought him an urgent note to go to another part of the works. He left his room so quickly that he forgot to turn out the flame under his chemical cookery, and when he later returned he found a charred mass in the bottom of the dish. But there was also a bright pinkish crust. Accidentally, Caro had produced the dye of madder by a simple process which involved little more than strong heat.

Caro raced ahead to take out a patent for he knew that in England, Perkin was also hot on the scent. The race was such a close one that Perkin had his patent granted on 26 June, but Caro just beat him to the post by 24 hours. Caro's patent was taken over by BASF but they generously rewarded Perkin by granting him a monopoly licence to make the dye in England. As for the men who farmed the thousands of acres of the madder plant *Rubia tinctorum*, they were ruined overnight. The factory dye was far cheaper, and the growers had to turn over to maize or tobacco.

BASF's other great achievement also came about as the result of chance. The firm had spent a million pounds in trying to synthesise indigotin, the dye found in the woad and indigo plants, when one day the mercury thermometer used to control an experiment broke. To the astonishment of the chemists, the mercury acted as a catalyst and indigotin was produced. The way to make cheap blue dyes and large profits lay wide open. In India alone, one-fifth of a million acres of land which had been entirely given over to indigo-growing were put out of commission, but Ludwigshafen flourished more than ever.

Strasbourg (Strassburg)

This city lies on the Canal de la Marne au Rhin, the River Ill, and the Grand Canal d'Alsace, or Canalised Rhine. There is excellent mooring at the Quai des Pecheurs, near the centre of the city.

If there is one thing in particular which at the first glimpse distinguishes Strasbourg from other great cities, it is the row upon row of dormer windows which crowd every slope of mottled tiles, as though the Alsatians are unwilling to leave an inch of roof space or gable unused. From the top of the cathedral tower the visitor can have an astonishing view over these myriad little openings, and if he has keen eyes he can also scan the rooftops for the patches of white which mark the whereabouts of a family of storks. And if the storks live in the modern bustle without obvious concern, the rows of little houses dating back to the sixteenth, fifteenth or fourteenth centuries seem to stand with just as little fear of the greater speed of the modern world around them.

Strasbourg contains enough of history and of beauty to occupy the visitor for many days. There is the courtyard of the Corbeau Inn, the magnificent palace of the Rohans, the Maison Kammerzell, the Cathedral with its famous clock which attracts thousands to its daily performances. But besides these, every street and alley has treasures of little houses and courtyards, and if the town did not altogether escape bombardment in the last war, it has at least been spared too much replanning and 'improvement'. It was the siege of 1870 which wrought the most destruction, when Strasbourg alone resisted for six weeks the Prussian occupation of Alsace, and as punishment had to suffer bombardment of the interior of the city by 50 pieces of artillery. The copper roofing melted in the heat of the flames which surged in the Cathedral, and much of the exquisite stained glass was destroyed. Perhaps worst of all, the 300,000 volumes of the library went up in flames, among them the *Hortus Deliciarum* of the Abbess Herrade of St Odile, probably the most celebrated book of the twelfth century, and a collection of everything that a pious lady might be expected to know – passages from the Bible, hymns and prayers, history and geography and simple science. Its particular importance lay partly in the drawings which the abbess herself had made, showing contemporary scenes of every kind, from peasants at work and children at play to knights jousting and kings at their banquets.

In the fourteenth century, an earthquake which killed 16,000 in Strasbourg alone was interpeted as a punishment of God for general impiety and mercenary inclinations. Then came such a pestilence that the churches could not contain the dead. Offerings were made to various saints, but when naught availed the favourite European scapegoat was brought out, with the allegation that the plague was caused by poison thrown into the wells by Jewish merchants. Rioting citizens and craftsmen demanded the death of the Jews (to whom, by a curious coincidence, they happened to owe very considerable sums of money), and only three men of the council stood out firmly and refused to sanction such a barbarous act. Yet each of these was soon forced by the mob to withdraw from office, and their leader – the brave *Ammeister* Peter Schwarber – was made to hand over the keys of the city before being deprived of his rights and property as a penalty for striving to maintain a standard of humanity.

The burning of the Jews – 1884 adults and 900 children were herded naked into one great bonfire – was one of the blackest stains on the history of Europe in the fourteenth century, and well might the chronicler record that *'es war ein jämmerlicher spectakel: Gott verzeihe ihnen allen!'* The hearts of some of the burghers themselves were softened at the sight, and several citizens plunged into the flames to rescue children from their mothers' breasts. Altogether some 500 children were saved from the flames, and the recorder of the period also noted that women who were beautiful were not burned.

With the slaughter of the rich Jews, the loans which they had issued were conveniently considered to have lapsed, and the city councillors divided their property among themselves – although several refused their portion. The ashes were hardly cold when a great procession of wailing flagellants descended upon Strasbourg, calling upon all to whip themselves morning and evening for 33½ years in penitence. 'From the waist up they were naked. They lay down in a great ring, and each one showed wherein his sin lay. He who was a murderer beat the ground with his fists; he who was a thief opened and closed his hands continually. The adulterer lay on his belly, those that ate and drank with delight barred their mouths.' Then they went home and whipped themselves till they bled.

Before the year closed, a letter was reported to have been brought from heaven, delivered by the angels. It recounted how God was so incensed with the wickedness of the world that he had determined to destroy it, and only through the imploring of Maria and the angels had he till now been withheld from doing so. At this news the people wept, the rich opened their doors and invited the penitents to sup, the flagellants were joined by a flock of women, and even young children took to flagellation.

131

Then, as quickly as it had come, the hysteria vanished and Strasbourg settled down to a more orderly existence, with nothing but an occasional drowning of some poor criminal in the Ill to add excitement to the daily round.

A curiosity is the connection with the Guilds of Zürich. On the wall of the Protestant church a tablet records the gratitude of the parishioners to the Guilds of Zürich, who had sent them the sum of 1,000 pounds in the great distress which followed the bombardment of 1870 in the Franco-Prussian war – a callous attack which incidentally destroyed almost the whole of the incomparable collection of medieval illuminated books in the library of the Cathedral.

It happened this way. In 1576 there was considerable unrest in the city, and to prevent disturbances the magistrate boldly decided to distract the people with a great contest of shooting with the arquebus. It might seem highly dangerous to invite shooting societies into a city seething with discontent, but he had judged rightly and the scheme was a great success. Strasbourg went *en fête*, and from far and near the teams of marksmen responded to the challenge. Among them were 54 from the Guilds of Zürich, trade guilds of which many exist in that city to this day and are very similar to the Livery Companies of the City of London.

In those days the journey from Zürich on the River Limmat to Strasbourg on the River Ill was most easily accomplished by water, but the distance was considerable. Although the voyage was entirely downstream, one had to reckon four days, but the Zürichers decided to make the run in a single day of strenuous non-stop rowing. As a demonstration that it could really be done, they placed in the centre of their boat a large iron porringer, which was filled with hot gruel at Zürich. The 'original' pot is still to be seen in the museum by the Ill in Strasbourg, carefully preserved for nearly four centuries, even if it suffered a chipping in the bombardment of 1870.

The oarsmen of Zürich performed their extraordinary feat, which even today must be a challenge to any boat club, and they were received in Strasbourg with wild enthusiasm. Their leader then made a speech of thanks, in which he declared that if ever Strasbourg were in need, the Guildsmen of Zürich would come to their assistance in less time than it took for a pot of porridge to cool – for the cauldron in their boat was still hot enough for the contents to be served to the astonished Strasbourgers.

Breisach

So boldly does the magnificent Romanesque Cathedral of Breisach stand on its rock overlooking the Rhine that it is hard to realise that this tight-clustered town was more totally destroyed during the Second World War than was Hamburg or Cologne, or indeed any place other than the shippers' town of Emmerich where the Rhine crosses into Holland. Breisach stood immediately in front of the muzzles of the big French guns across the water, and its elevation also made it an excellent spotting platform. Not all its Martin Schongauers or the fame of its glorious carved altarpiece could save it.

This astonishing piece of work is renowned for three reasons – its vast size, its brilliant carving, and the curious fact that its creator is unknown, beyond the fact that he created the work in 1526 and his initials were HL. In German art books he has the simple and straightforward title of 'Meister HL', but tradition in Breisach identifies him as a certain Hans Liefrink, a young man who fell in love with the beautiful daughter of a wealthy town councillor. Naturally, this important person was not inclined to part with his daughter to a mere travelling apprentice, and a woodworker at that. Sadly Liefrink took himself off to Nürnberg, but not before he had sworn eternal devotion to his girl and planted in the corner of her garden a rose tree so that the flowers might remind her of their love.

Time passed, and the day came when the prosperous Breisachers wished to adorn their Cathedral with a work of art which should have no equal in all the world. The advice of Albrecht Dürer was sought, and as he recommended a young woodcarver of Nürnberg named Liefrink, the worthy Hans was invited to his own town of Breisach and commissioned to carve an altar finer than any in existence. He called once more at the house of his true love's father, who was now somewhat better disposed towards him; but unable entirely to swallow his pride, the councillor jestingly brushed the young artist off with a remark to the effect that he might certainly have the daughter if he could carve an altarpiece higher than the ceiling of the Cathedral nave. This, if taken seriously, meant that to win the girl Liefrink would have to carve a work more than 45 feet in height, a formidable task indeed. Besides, it was not easy to imagine the Cathedral containing something higher than its own roof.

But that same evening Hans met his beloved in her garden, and together they went to look at the rose tree he had planted. It had grown strong and healthy and the weight of bloom caused its tip to bend right over and point downwards. In a flash Hans saw the answer to the mechanical part of his problem.

And that, they say, is how Breisach's amazing triptych, brilliantly carved in limewood, came to be made higher than the ceiling, so that only when the craftsman had steamed its central pinnacle and bent it over permanently could it be brought into the Cathedral at all. It was a pleasant way to win a beautiful bride, and I have always thought that the Meister HL must have made an excellent husband.

If the year 1945 saw Breisach second only to Emmerich in the extent of its destruction, that town of the Lower Rhine had a certain inherent internationalism on account of its trade, and so the lot of being chosen for a referendum fell upon Breisach. In 1950 the natives voted in secret ballot on the question, 'Do you wish political and economic national boundaries within Europe to be removed, and all its peoples to be merged into a single European Union?'

That 19 out of every 20 Breisachers answered 'Yes' astonished everyone; traditional animosities were evidently not so strongly inbuilt as might have been expected.

Colmar

The city of Colmar, reached by the Embranchement de Colmar of the Canal du Rhone au Rhin or, if this is no longer navigable, by bus from Breisach, is beautiful beyond imagination. Bustling and humming with the industry of vintners and coopers, crowded with country people bringing their wares to the market, its centre contains an astonishing number of splendid domestic buildings from earlier centuries. Narrow lanes wind between timber-framed buildings with their skeletons painted in ochre or black, red or blue, and at almost every street corner there is a slender oriel capped with tiles in a cross-stitch design of brilliant colours, or the upper storeys of the houses lean across the roadway to gossip with their neighbours opposite. The Pfisterhaus, with its wooden galleries meeting under the tall night-cap of a corner turret, is as fine a patrician house as one could find in Alsace, and the Maison des Têtes with its curious grimacing faces is another, but these are only two out of dozens. The town has street upon street of unpretentious charm lifted from the pages of fairytale. The fifteenth-century Ancienne

Douane, with its arches and gallery gay with geraniums and its two elegant high-pitched roofs chequered in glazed tiles of green, orange and red, is one of the finest municipal buildings in a country where beautiful town halls and towers are to be found on every hand.

Down by the Krutenau, the district of the market gardeners, the stream of the Lauch flows into the town crystal clear and rippling over the gravel, swaying the long feathery weed from side to side as it sweeps into its own Petite Venise or Kleinvenedig, where low roofs of tiles project out across the water to shelter the washing stages and landings. In the background the tower of the church of St Martin peeps over a medley of ear-flapped chimney pots and mellow tiled dormer windows of the riverside houses, and it is in this church that the most famous of the paintings is to be found which came from the hand of the young Martin Schongauer, whose house – the Schwanenhaus – can still be seen close by.

Schongauer was himself a Colmarer, and he was probably born about 1450, son of a local goldsmith. That he must have wandered far and wide when young is shown beyond any doubt by the detail of the exotic plants and animals in such

135

engravings as his *Flight into Egypt*, for these things could not have been extracted so correctly from any works of his contemporaries. This young man was so well-known during his life that people called him 'Martin Hipsch' – or *hübsch*, the beautiful – 'Martin Schön', and in other lands 'Bel Martino' and 'Le Beau Martin'. Albrecht Dürer himself wrote upon one of Schongauer's sketches, '*Dz hat der hübsch Martin gerissen im 1470 jor do er ein jung gsell was. Dz hab ich A.D. erfarn und im zu ern doher geschriben im 1517 jor.*' He was also so technically competent that the *Madonna in the Rose-bower* was one of his first paintings and was almost certainly completed by the time he was 20.

How much else he may have created is unknown, but many of his works must have been destroyed when army after army laid waste the towns and villages of Alsace. Both the Reformation and the French Revolution caused further heavy losses to the artistic treasures of the churches, and had Cromwell's lieutenants or the Dutch sectaries visited Alsace it would no doubt have been made as sterile of beautiful things as a public convenience. But the *Madonna* of the St Martin's Church was lucky enough to escape – probably being hidden on several occasions. Against the gold background the red roses of the trellis bloom freely, and among their stems the little local birds stand to chirp to each other, goldfinch and robin, chaffinch and blue tit. In front of them the Madonna sits on a bank with the infant Jesus, a simple but beautiful country girl with an expression of haunting sadness and melancholy, heightened by the gaiety of the flowers behind her and the perky attitudes of the little songsters on either side.

Colmar also boasts several other paintings of Schongauer, and in the Unterlinden Museum there are two side-wings of an altarpiece from the monastery of the Antonites of Isenheim. In the cathedral of Alt Breisach, not far away, patches of fresco had for long showed through the colour wash, and when in 1932 a professor of fine art began to scrape away the overlying layers he revealed, little by little, a *Last Judgment* which beyond any doubt is the work of Schongauer, whose sketches for this same fresco are extant. As a fresco this work could not be removed during the Second World War, and it was damaged by bombardment in 1945, but Schongauer's Colmar paintings all escaped. And just how many there really are is something of a problem, for in the Unterlinden the altar of the Church of the Dominicans is to be seen, with its 24 panels, of which one or two are obviously the work of the master, whereas others were more probably

136

executed to his stock designs by apprentices, or added independently.

The Unterlinden Museum, which houses the works which Schongauer executed for the monastery of the Antonites at Isenheim, was until the Revolution a community of Dominicans. And however alluring the Schongauer panels may be, and however horrific the head of the tyrant Hagenbach, who was executed at Colmar in Schongauer's lifetime, these things will hardly be noticed by any who step through the doorway of the chapel to be confronted with the ten astonishing panels of another altarpiece from the monastery of the Isenheim Antonites that of the Master Mathis Gothardt, who was later and for some quite unknown reason to become known as 'Mathias Grünewald'.

The Master Mathis was born half a century later than Schongauer, and he came from Franconia, from the valley of the Main. He settled himself in Seligenstadt on the Main, where he set up his workshop and studio as court painter to the Lord Bishop of Mainz, whose arms appear in some of his scattered works. At the same time he seems to have served as official architect to the bishops, and in his capacity as hydraulic engineer he was responsible for constructing the fountains at Bingen, Aschaffenburg and elsewhere. It seems very likely, to judge by the writings that were among his possessions at the time of his death, and from the fact that in 1526 he was discharged by the Cardinal from episcopal service, that he had been involved in the Peasants' Revolt of the previous year. And this would be entirely in keeping with his pictures, which in themselves were violently revolutionary in that they cried to earth and heaven against the soft, sumptuous, traditional and rich presentation of the Incarnation which adorned the churches and cathedrals of his day, and glorified the Christ as a man of the people, more hideously pain-racked than he had ever before been seen – and yet more starkly real, perhaps, than any other painter has ever made him, before or since.

Though Master Mathis was separated from Martin Schongauer by only a few decades, their work belongs to different ages. Grünewald himself was a sign of the new and turbulent time, a part of the great movement which was to strip religion of sickly sentiment and revolt against abuse. In Alsace the stirrings in the minds of men first broke out in powerful form in the strong voice of Geiler de Kaysersberg as he preached to vast crowds in the Cathedral of Strasbourg, castigating the hierarchy for its

137

abuse of Christian doctrine and practice, and demanding a return to a truer and purer form of worship and churchmanship. A man of extreme piety and charity, Geiler inveighed against a corrupt priesthood throughout 32 years of his ministry, and it was about the time of his death that Master Mathis was at work on his magnificent altar for the monastery of the Antonites outside Colmar.

Saverne (Zabern)

At the foot of the descent from the Arzviller tunnel on the Canal de la Marne au Rhin, Saverne was the Roman Tres Tavernae. Odd bits of Roman columns are built into the wall of the towpath. The canal was deliberately cut across the magnificent vista of the famous Cardinal Rohan. The town is not notable, but it gives easy access to the castle of Haut Barr, either by bus or on foot, a trip which every visitor should make – not least for the wide view up the Zorn valley and over the divide into Lorraine, and eastward across the plain to the cathedral of Strasbourg and the misty outline of the Black Forest hills beyond.

Most astonishing of all is the fortress itself, for what appears from the valley to be the high wall of a keep is found to be three gigantic lumps of red sandstone mysteriously perched on the summit and separated by ravines. Sheer-faced and even overhanging, these pillars, 60 or 70 feet in height, provided such an impregnable site for any castle which could laboriously be erected on their tops that it is not difficult to understand how a single farming lad could keep at bay a detachment of crack troops. Considerable ruins are still there, but in its days when it guarded the pass into Alsace from the west the Haut-Barr must have been a formidable sight, with its towers and turrets ranged on the rocky columns and connected to each other with drawbridges which could be lowered across the gaps.

The Haut-Barr was not the only castle which once looked out over the Zorn valley, and as one drops lock by lock towards Saverne, one can see that almost every prominent cliff and hill bears a crumbling tower or the heaped remnants of a keep. Immediately opposite the Haut-Barr is the Greifenstein, the ruin where, towards the end of the eighteenth century, Hans Klein had a very remarkable adventure. Hans Klein was a stonemason of Saverne, and he played the flute. Having neither wife nor family, he spent his Sunday afternoons walking through the woods until, in some pleasant clearing, he would seat himself upon the soft moss and blow an air on his favourite instrument. The Greifenstein was one of his particular haunts, and on a certain Sunday afternoon in the springtime he was surprised to hear a voice singing the same medieval air which he happened to be piping. So lovely was the voice that tears came into the eyes of the worthy mason, and when he stopped playing and looked up, then the singing stopped abruptly also.

Above him, perched on the edge of the tower, sat a lady dressed entirely in white, and as he hesitated she waved to him, so he doffed his hat. Being a sensible and practical man, he begged leave to draw her attention to the fact that she was sitting on stonework which might very easily crumble. He was a mason, he said. And she could be assured that he knew what he was talking about. The ruin was in a sorry state, and if she was not extremely careful she would be killed, he said. The lady thereupon pointed out that this could hardly happen, as she had been dead for three centuries already.

Hans was somewhat taken aback at this statement, but the lady now came down to him. She was extremely beautiful, and she told him that she had once been mistress of Greifenstein. For living so richly at the expense of the poor and the outcast of her domain, she had been sentenced to wander eternally amid the ruins of the castle to which the lords and knights had once flocked to flatter her, and from this fate she could only be freed if, on a Friday, some man would kiss her – because on Fridays she was metamorphosed into a particularly unpleasant toad. If Monsieur Klein would return on the following Friday and liberate her she would sleep peacefully for evermore, but before doing so she would lead him to the hidden vault in which the treasure of gold and jewels from her earthly days still lay buried. She was only asking him, she said, because she had noticed that her singing had moved him to tears, and she was sure that in that case he must have a very kind heart.

Hans looked at her and, moved with pity, promised to return on the following Friday. And so he did, and there among the ruins he saw a toad as huge as three porkers, a fat and slimy beast, its skin warty and greasy, and the body covered with horrid secretions. As the creature advanced towards him he told himself that this was really a fair lady, and that it would be a kindness to free her. Besides, there was the matter of the treasure. All this he told himself as he stood still, moistening his lips for the kiss.

And then, just at the very last moment, he turned and fled through the wood. A cry of inexpressible sadness followed him as he stumbled between the trees, but he did not stop. And he never visited the Greifenstein again. Nor, all his life long, did he ever blow another note upon his flute.

Almost from end to end the chain of the Vosges falls away on its eastern side to hills and spurs capped with the same extraordinary sandstone bluffs, standing erect like square cairns built by a race of giants. There is not one of them which is not crowned with the ruins of a castle built of the same rosy stone, and between Saverne at the northern and Thann at the southern end of the range there are more than 60. From any one of them, others are always in view, and from the Haut-Barr one may look across a few miles of forest to the round hill of Dabo, where the capping rock once provided the foundation for the castle of the lords of Dabo-Egisheim. It was there that the Bruno de Dabo who became Leo IX was probably born, and though the castle itself was destroyed by French artillery in the late seventeenth century, the wind-scored rock now bears a more modern chapel in honour of Dabo's own Pope.

Basel (Basel)

The great commercial port of Switzerland, Basel stands at the head of the Grand Canal d'Alsace. Its harbour has a fascinating museum of the history of Rhine shipping. Three countries meet in midstream off the Dreiländereck.

Basel is the pharmaceuticals centre of the world, and it became so in a peculiar way. Centuries ago, when the Edict of Nantes was revoked and freedom of worship vanished overnight from France, the Catholics began to attack their Protestant fellowmen, sometimes murdering them but at the least driving them to flee for their lives. Many escaped as refugees to Britain or Germany or the Netherlands, but those who lived closer to Switzerland fled across the frontier to Basel. Many of these refugees were weavers, and they set up little workshops for making silk ribbons. Ribbon-making soon became a great business in Basel.

As time went on, ladies' fashions changed and new colours were needed for the ribbons, so a dye-making industry followed hard on the heels of the ribbon-makers, but its tremendous expansion was stimulated mainly by the discoveries of Perkin,

140

the young London student who set up a simple laboratory in his parents' house and in the Easter Vacation of 1856 actually succeeded, when he was still only 18 years old, in elaborating the synthetic dye mauveine. With his brother he set about the manufacture of the first artificial colouring materials derived from coal tar, and in so doing he laid the foundations of organic chemistry. The colour-makers became organic chemists.

Now it so happens that dyes are very complex chemicals, and once a firm has all the know-how to make them it is well placed to step out into other products. The industry expanded into the drug field, and many drugs in everyday use were first perfected in the laboratories of Basel. All across the world tablets and pills from Basel are in daily use, and the Swiss are very conscious of their prowess in this field. 'Every disease has a cure already growing in Basel,' they proudly declare, and this is hardly an exaggeration.

Basel was well placed to develop its trade beyond mere colour-making, for it also had a chemical industry of longstanding. The famous firm of Geigy had been there since the 1750s and was joined by others, particularly by chemists emigrating from France – not on this occasion for religious reasons but because of the very restrictive patent laws. The forerunners of CIBA were soon established in Basel, and also those of Sandoz. These firms were originally concerned with dyes alone, and sometimes they came up against unexpected difficulties – as when a chemist in the Müller aniline works (later united with Geigy) elaborated an excellent new dye in a strong shade of blue. So pleased was Müller that he at once gave the man a reward of 1,000 Francs and sent him off to Paris to enjoy himself. This the worthy researchman did, but he was so swept off his feet by the entertainments of Paris that he somehow lost his notes of the process and Müller was unable to manufacture the dye. At least that is what is related, but I have always found it difficult to believe that a man could really make such a discovery and within a few days entirely forget how he had done it.

CIBA extended into plastics, waterproofing, paint pigments and almost every possible branch of chemical synthesis, but perhaps it is most famous for its pioneer production of hormones. These complex substances are normally manufactured in endocrine glands such as the pituitary, thyroid or adrenal glands, and the simplest way to obtain them is by extraction from the tissues concerned. Yet a simple method is not always a

141

sensible one. To produce a mere tenth of a gram of adrenalin it would be necessary to obtain two tons of adrenal glands from a slaughterhouse and render them down. Much better, thought the CIBA chemists, to find a way of building up the right molecules from less complex ones. Besides, the medical consumption of hormones is now so great that the slaughterhouses could hardly produce enough bits and pieces of cattle to keep up the supply.

Geigy became interested in mothproofing, then moved from the clothes moth to insects in general and became specialists in pest control. One of the Geigy products must have saved many millions of lives around the world – though cynics might add that this has merely made the population explosion detonate earlier than it might have done. The substance was of course the famous dichlorodiphenyltrichloroethane, which may be just a greenhouse aid in Britain, but elsewhere has almost exterminated the insect carriers of some of the greatest killer diseases – malaria, yellow fever and plague. Dr Paul Müller of Geigy certainly earned the Nobel Prize which was awarded to him for producing that first of the great insecticides, known for short as DDT.

There is no end to the chemical conjuring of Basel. The Sandoz company specialised in plant drugs, and long ago isolated the active principles in the purple and yellow *digitalis* (foxglove), and the deadly poison in the arrow-tips of South American Indians. Once a chemical has been analysed in its molecular structure there is a chance to make it artificially, yet drugs are not such an easy way to wealth as one might think. Out of every thousand complex substances built up in the laboratory, only one will have properties which are medically useful.

The last of the great drug names of the Swiss city by the Rhine is Roche. Hofmann-La Roche specialised in vitamins, and it was Roche who developed the manufacture of vitamin C – something that might have been most useful to the crew of a ship if they had voyaged centuries earlier and found their teeth dropping out from scurvy. Vitamin A later appeared in the Roche line, and B_1, B_2 and E have all been run to earth in the Basel research laboratories. Altogether the chemists of Basel spend some 10,000,000 pounds annually on research, and every now and again a real winner is found which will bring in money from all over the world. It may be a new anti-depressant for the suicidal, or perhaps a systemic poison which can be spread on the ground so that plants take it in by the roots and are made poisonous to insects. One bite at a leaf, and a bug falls down dead – unfortunate if one is the bug, but very good if you are a gardener or a shareholder in the chemical enterprise of the city and involved in the export of drugs and biologicals and pesticides, which together flow out of the factories to the pleasant melody of more than 700,000,00 Swiss francs a year.

PART III

THE MIDDLE RHINE TRIBUTARIES

The Middle Rhine has two navigable tributaries, the Moselle and the Lahn. The first of these was fully developed as the International Moselle Waterway in 1965. It is a major shipping route connecting the industrial areas of the Saar and Lorraine with the Rhine. It joins the Rhine a few kilometres below the Lahn, which flows in from the East and is nowadays not a commercial waterway of any importance, although it was once a major route for the export of marble. Schemes to make an extension through to the Fulda at Kassel have been abandoned.

9

The Moselle, Metz, Ehnen, Igel, Trier, Pfalzel, Neumagen,
Veldenz, Alf, Stuben, Bernkastel, Kues, Zeltingen, Alken,
Kobern and Dieblich

The Moselle

The Moselle has been navigable, with difficulty, since Roman
times, when it was a major highway for bank-hauled cargoes to
and from the Mediterranean via the Rhone. The poet Ausonius
wrote a poem in its honour, and throughout its course it passes
Roman antiquities.

Rising on the western side of the Vosges, it becomes properly
navigable from some short way above Toul, and thence flows
past Pont-à-Mousson to reach Metz, and the industrial basin
around Thionville (Diedenhofen). It then becomes the International Moselle Waterway, opened in 1965, flowing with the left
bank in Luxembourg, the right in Germany, to Wasserbillig,
where it becomes German from side to side all the way to its

confluence with the Rhine at Koblenz.

Famous for its wines, its twisting course leads past one pretty wine village after another, many of them with their legends. Its locks take the giant consignments of coal from the Ruhr to the foundries below Metz and to the Saar basin, but it is an extremely beautiful river, and every care has been taken to ensure that the navigation works, power stations and locks do not intrude upon its justly famous landscape.

Metz

The capital of Lorraine, Metz is where Venantius Honorius Clementianus Fortunatus, Bishop of Poitiers, took ship in the sixth century and descended the river in the company of the young Merovingian King Childebert and his mother Brunehaut (Brunhilde) of the lovely bronze skin, widow of the King Sigbert who had been murdered when Childebert was only five years of age.

On an earlier visit to Metz Fortunatus had his boat stolen by one of the palace cooks, as he related in his poem *De coco qui ipsi navem tulit*. Vilicus, Bishop of Metz, came to his aid with a skiff, but this boat was too light for him and his companions, and soon the water was over his ankles. Fortunatus did not omit to make a proper comment. *'Obesquium,' dixit 'remove, modo nolo lavari.'* 'Thank you, but depart. I do not want a bath.'

When he told Sigbert of his sad adventures the king laughed, but told his knights to find the bishop a new craft, and eventually he was waterborne again.

On the occasion of his later voyage down to the Rhine Fortunatus arrived at Metz on horseback, as he tells in *De navigio suo*, and there he at once took to his rowboat. Now and again his craft was caught in the rapids, and he was in danger of taking in water, but soon he was in calmer waters, enjoying every moment of his journey. Even then the river was one of vineyards, and downstream of Trier the bishop gazed in admiration at the rocky heights on either hand, their shaly slopes green with the dressed vines in full leaf, and the vintners hanging from the rocks to gather the bunches. Somewhere downriver he managed to buy some, for he held the grapes in his hand as he sped down the stream in the wake of the royal watermen.

And what a happy voyage it was. All along the Moselle Childebert and the dowager queen were served with dishes of the fresh fish in which the river abounded. The musicians played until the rock-faces echoed with the sound of their brass, and the mellower tones of the flutes seemed to be repeated by other instruments hidden in the woods. It was merely to delight the people that the king had ordered music and singing to accompany him down the river, and as the royal craft sped along the stream the songs of those in the boats were taken up and swelled by those ashore. The Dark Ages! There is something Pepysian about the scene, and one can only regret that none of the Merovingian music has survived.

Ehnen

At Ehnen, a village of vintners, the Moselle (Musel in the local language) is a river of great beauty. It flows through a country-side particularly rich in local legends, such as that of the Iceman.

It is only when the river is frozen that the Iceman appears, a little fellow with a white beard who resides all through the day in a fissure of the ice. After dark he will often leave his crevasse and wander ashore, not to do harm but instead to slink furtively through the alleys of Ehnen, seeking out widows and waifs and others who are in need. Sometimes he gives advice, for he is wise and experienced, but wherever he can help in a practical way he will do so. A widower with starving children may find a kid in his garden, and another poor person will perhaps discover some food or money pushed inside their door. Such things can only be the work of the Iceman, so a hard winter in the valley is not altogether without its blessings.

The Iceman, however, is not the only spirit to have inhabited the Ehnen reaches. Between there and Wormeldange people used to see a headless ghost, and no doubt some of them still do so, particularly at the time of year when the pouring of the new vintage is celebrated. This apparition is unusual, for it is not a white lady or a fiery coach, nor anything merely Freudian. It is nothing less than the ghost of a *Moselhalfe*, one of those rough and hardy men who bank-hauled the ships upriver.

The Iceman is a kindly little fellow, the headless *Halfe* certainly does nobody any harm. He rises from the water on the towpath side and eventually he sinks again, and that is all. But the third spirit of the Ehnen waters is malignant, even if he is not such a murderer as the 'Hakenmann' of the Neckar, who pulls people in with his crook to drown them. Ehnen's 'Steip-

149

männchen' is ill-disposed, but he is not a killer. The object of his malevolence is invariably the skipper of a boat, so I thought a short study of his habits was desirable before I ran the reaches between Stadtbredimus and Grevenmacher locks. Yet there was no cause for alarm. The canalisation of the river had done away with the rapids where he lived, and driven the poor spirit to find a home elsewhere.

The Ehnen rapids were a dangerous feature of the river before canalisation. As at many other places on rivers, a statue of St Nicholas was placed there, to which the skippers of passing craft paid due deference (he being the patron of bargees). The St Nicholas of Ehnen is still there, standing on the German shore opposite the village.

The statue dates from 1764, when two vintners, Kohl and Kieffer, were coming upstream with a boatload of grapes for the wine-press. At the Ehnen rapids the boat broached and tipped over, throwing the steersman Kieffer into the river. Kohl was on the towpath with the hauling line, and he could not reach his companion to save him.

Kieffer himself was unable to swim, but as he struggled in the swirling water he had sufficient presence of mind to recall that St Nicholas was the patron of shipmen and a reputedly reliable rescuer from just such a danger as that in which he found himself. He called upon the saint and promised to build him a chapel on the shore if his own life was spared.

The vintner fought on in the waves, and sure enough he came safely to land. He did not fail to do what he had promised, and from the shrine that he built against the rock-face a statue of St Nicholas was soon looking out upon all passing craft.

The statue had not long been there when it was carried away by the floods. It was a wooden effigy and so it floated, but it had nearly reached Trier before a bargeman saw the body bobbing awash on the waves and rescued it. He at once recognised it, and took the saint back up to Ehnen in his boat.

The St Nicholas of Ehnen seemed to be unusual in that he paid very great attention to the manners and behaviour of those who sailed by, for several tales are told by the Luxembourgers of the remarkable powers exercised by this particular effigy. It is said that a French merchant was travelling up the Moselle one day with a convoy of three heavily laden ships filled with goods that he was importing to his own country. As was the custom, the steersmen of his barges took off their caps and bowed their heads to the statue of St Nicholas, an action which greatly amused such an agnostic child of the Revolution. Instead of bowing, he laughed and shouted various improprieties at the figure.

The boatmen were almost speechless with horror, but not quite. They reproved the businessman and assured him that the saint would not forget. The Frenchman was not impressed by such bumpkin superstitions, and no doubt he had little difficulty in falling soundly asleep in the inn at Ehnen when the convoy halted there for the night. But about midnight the mooring line of the last of the three craft mysteriously parted, and the vessel began to drift unmanned down the river. Hastily roused from his bed, the merchant ran to the river bank, but was not quite in time to see the vessel strike on the St Nicholas reef and founder, taking all the most valuable part of his goods to the bottom. Cursing and swearing he raged along the towpath, but all the comfort he had from the shippers was a reminder that he had behaved badly. With fortitude he accepted the loss and swore once more – this time to the effect that he would never again be so imprudent as to abuse St Nicholas.

Then there was the case of the bargemaster whose ship got into difficulties in the fleet passage of shoal water which used to exist at Ehnen, and who prudently called upon St Nicholas for help. If his ship should come through unscathed he would present the saint with a candle as big as the mast of his vessel, he said. St Nicholas must have been fond of candles, for at once the current seemed to slacken and the ship began to make headway. The barge captain, a somewhat parsimonious fellow, thereupon reduced the size of the candle he would present. Finally, as the ship moved out of the upper end of the difficult passage he shook his head.

'So, that's that, and now you'll get nothing at all, Nikläschen,' he cried with a laugh as he steered the boat upriver.

Probably he thought no more of the matter, but St Nicholas did not forget. The very next time the bargee came down with his ship, he had no chance to mock the statue, for as the vessel came to the rapids it immediately struck on the reef and the captain was drowned.

The International Moselle Company has put the barrage of Grevenmacher a few miles further down river and so raised the level of the river that it glides slow and smooth and deep over the point where Kieffer was nearly drowned. The saint still stands among the nettles on the railway embankment to watch the French pusher-craft, the smart passenger vessels and the heavy ships lumbering up from Rotterdam and Antwerp and

151

Duisburg towards the smoky factories of Lorraine. I doubt if many of the skippers from other lands pay much attention to him, but at least when I was following a small Luxembourgish barge down the river below Palzem-Stadtbredimus I had the pleasure of seeing the skipper take off his cap and bow as he passed the little shrine on the starboard bank. I did not then know what it was, and at first I imagined that he had probably seen a friend over on the German shore. But no, he was saluting St Nicholas, who now has to be content with such rare courtesies as he may receive from a few skippers of old-established bargee families of the Moselle, and with the flickering candles left at his feet by children who have rowed over the river in early winter to make known their requests to Santa Claus while there is still time.

Igel

Igel is a pleasant name for a village, for it means 'hedgehog'. The village is only a small one, cramped on the shore and bounded by a railway embankment on the river side, and without even a footpath along the bank, for the old towpath with its nostalgic memories of the days of the *Moselhalfen* sitting the plodding horses which slowly hauled the cargoes from the Rhine to Wasserbillig, or Thionville, or the free state of Metz, is on the opposite shore. The pretty church stands tightly cramped on a rock as though expecting another hideous persecution under the Romans, and as it is thus raised above the level of the dwelling of ordinary mortals, it is not overtopped by the memorial to the drapers. For that remarkable stone column is large enough to tower above the signals on the railway embankment and to look down upon its village neighbours with undisguised disdain. It is more than 70 feet in height.

I suspect that the Secunduni may have been the Selfridges of third-century Trier. The family had their residence at Igel on the Roman highway from Reims to Trier, and the imposing memorial of grey and red sandstone which two of the sons raised to their parents must have been the envy of many less wealthy merchants. Its particular interest for ourselves, seventeen centuries further down the line, is the great detail in the scenes of everyday life which are shown in relief. Some have weathered away, but there are plenty left to tell us how the drapers traded, and how they conducted their business. One main relief shows us the father, chairman and managing

152

director of the firm and a former volunteer in the imperial forces, taking leave of his two sons as he sets out upon his journey into the land of the dead. If the monument was not broken down in the early Christian centuries, this seems to have been because this relief was so magnificent that it was mistakenly thought to have shown Constantine, the first Christian emperor, and his mother St Helena.

There are gods and goddesses, of course, both Roman and Greek, but more interesting is the kitchen scene, with the chef receiving from servants and tenants the mutton and poultry, game, Moselle fish and fruits. Another picture shows us the family at dinner, doing justice to the *haute cuisine* which they could afford to keep. Then there are the warehouse scenes, with assistants examining and grading cloth, and baling it for storage. A four-wheeled cart brings another load of bales to the merchant's house, and other wains carry away the consignments despatched to meet special orders.

But there still remains one relief, at the base of the huge memorial and on its upstream side, which no boatman should miss, for here we see a Roman barge of the third century, a direct if distant ancestor of the Europa-ships which now send the waves of their wash to slop on the stones of the Igel shore.

Trier

'I see the imperial buildings rising to such a height that they almost reach the stars in heaven,' Eumenius wrote of Trier in the year 310. Eumenius was an eulogist, a public relations man, and thus given to slight exaggeration, but Trier must certainly have been a magnificent place, and even if it did not contain skyscrapers it had some luxurious institutions. One of these is still to be found as an area of ruin at the upstream edge of town. When St Matthias is on the starboard beam the first of the bridges is already in sight, but before it is reached one is gliding past the *Barbara-thermen*, tantalisingly hidden behind the trees.

These Roman baths merely came to be known by the name of the medieval suburb in which they lay, and nowadays there is little left above ground to hint at the richness and splendour of an amusement place which survived into the era of the Franks before people began to strip it and use it as a stone-quarry. In the heyday of Roman Trier these baths, even more luxurious than the Imperial Baths in the same city, must have been a bustling scene of gaiety, and physical culture, of dining-out and gossip, laughter and plotting and amorous intrigue. Merchants, vintners and shipmasters, aristocrats with their attendants carrying the bathing-wraps and changes of clothing, all came and went at their leisure in the marbled passages and ante-rooms. There were masseurs and manicure attendants, and no doubt it was a good place for a lady to have her hair made up in the newest mode. One could have a warm swim there, too, and then retire to a quiet corner to pick at bunches of sweet grapes while listening to poets and musicians; or, if one was thoroughly tired of culture, there was a skittle alley very much as one might find it today in a riverside pleasure garden.

The bridge which crosses the river just below the site of the Barbara baths is one of the most astonishing sights on all the Moselle. It has eight arches, two of which are occupied by the navigation channel, but the curves and the roadway they support sit somewhat curiously on the massive buttresses, as though they were a job-lot bought second hand. On the balustrade over the buttress some way to the right of the centre there stands a crucifix, and below it, with his feet just above the bulk of the bullnose itself, is St Nicholas.

With seven buttresses standing in the water, one would expect both the statues to be on the fourth or centre one, but they are not. They are where the centre of the bridge used to be, two arches on the right bank having long ago been buried under the embankment. The earliest picture of the bridge in its original form is on a fourth-century coin of Constantine, for the bridge is in fact a Roman one. Or, more correctly, the buttresses are Roman, the flat wooden roadway of Roman times having even-tually been replaced by medieval stone arches, which in turn came to be changed for more modern ones.

It is only a short walk to the market, which suddenly opens out as a bustling and colourful centre to the city. At one side is the site of the old 'Steipe' where kings and emperors would stay. Sadly it was blown to pieces by a bomb and now there is a pleasant space where one can sit and drink wine or eat cream cakes and wonder at the inscription boldly carved on the rose-pink wall in letters of gold – *ante romam treviris stetit annis mille trecentis*. It is a splendid boast and one which can hardly be true, but as it is such a large lie it is confidently believed by many a patriotic native of the city.

Trier was founded – in popular imagination, if not in fact – by a certain Prince Trebeta, of whom Sebastian Münster related in the fifteenth century that he was driven out of his Asiatic homeland by Semiramis, who had been busy founding Nineveh. His expulsion must have been violent, for he never stopped in his headlong flight until he reached the beautiful and happy valley of the Moselle, where he decided to settle. Wise, strong and no doubt handsome, he built himself a great palace on the tall sandstone cliff, and across the water at its foot he established the town which he called after his name, Treberis. 'This happened in Abraham's time,' wrote Münster. 'Founded more than 2,000 years before Christ, the city is 1,300 years older than Rome.'

Merian, the famous engraver of prospects of German towns and cities, is even more precise. 'It is the oldest city in all the world,' he wrote. 'It stood for 1250 years before Rome, and was founded in the sixteenth year of the Patriarch Abraham – that is, in the year 1966 after the creation of the world, 310 years after the flood and 39 years after the death of Noah; although perhaps we cannot be entirely certain of this.' Much truth lies hidden in that last remark. Trier was certainly a Roman foundation in the land of the Treviri – a people of whom Tacitus wrote that 'They make out that they are Germanic in origin. Indeed they do so with particular pride, hoping that by claiming such distinguished blood relationship they can dispose of any similarity to the flabby Gauls.'

At the end of the main street of Trier there stands one of the most famous of Roman buildings, the immense and powerful Porta Nigra, time-blackened and sturdy, its massive stones still held together with iron cramps. It is 16 centuries old, a fortified gateway built as a bastion against the menacing Germanic tribes of the untamed country outside, and so designed that invaders could be shot down from the sides or trapped and slaughtered from above. Though never completed, it rises three storeys high above its own archway, a formidable memorial to the power of Rome, but the Romans had long vanished when it came to have a stranger tenant than any guard of the watch.

In the year 1026 Archbishop Poppo went on a two-year tour to the Holy Land, accompanied by a scholarly monk who had come from the famous monastery on Mount Sinai and so knew his way around. This man was named Simeon.

Upon their safe return to Trier, Poppo asked Simeon what he would wish to have as a reward for his services. No doubt he expected his companion to ask for a canon's stall or some other appointment in the Cathedral, but to his surprise Simeon asked

155

to be allowed to withdraw completely into a life of prayer, removed altogether from the world. He wished to be walled up in a cell in the Porta Nigra, with neither door nor window but only a hole in the roof through which some food might occasionally be dropped to him.

His wish granted, Simeon lived for seven years, immured in the ground-floor chamber of the eastern tower. When he died, Archbishop Poppo decided to convert the Porta Nigra itself into a great church in his honour – a two-decker church, the upper of which was for the inmates of the *Simeonstift* (or St Simeon's Foundation) next door. It must have presented a most extraordinary appearance, for one Roman tower was later capped with a steeple and the other with a choir and gallery walk. The entire ground floor and the Roman archway were buried in a great ramp of earth, on which was set a broad flight of steps which would have done justice to St Peter's in Rome. When Trier came under Napoleon's sway, the emperor ordered the demolition of everything non-Roman in the construction of the Porta Nigra, and he had the arches dug out again, but eventually the gallery and the choir were allowed to remain as curious embellishments of the original Roman design.

Just as the Roman gate became a hermit's cell, then a church and finally an ancient monument, many others among Trier's famous buildings have changed their use across the centuries. The Archbishop's palace, built in a riot of Rococo in the eighteenth century, testifies to the splendour to which the clergy of Trier had risen, yet it only held the Elector for a brief eight years before he moved his residence to a new palace in Koblenz. When the troops of the French Revolution streamed over Trier they converted the Palace to a hospital, and later it became a Prussian barracks, with stiff-booted troopers stamping up and down the marble stairs and strutting along the elegant garden walks. Then came the Second World War, which reduced it to a ruin and provided the opportunity for the palace to be restored again in all its splendour of pink and cream, with little putti amusing themselves in the nooks and bowers of one of Germany's most delightful public gardens, or impudently blocking their ears with sandstone fingers while the brass band of the fire brigade plays beneath the trees on a Sunday afternoon.

The palace is strangely – and I think mistakenly – built on to one of Trier's other great buildings, the Basilica, in such a way as to obscure about half of one end of it. One can hardly imagine an architect of the Baroque having done anything quite so extraordinary, but there it is – even if each building would be better on its own. As for the Basilica, that too has changed its use across the centuries. Once this huge building was actually the judgement hall of the Emperor Constantine. Then it became the residence of the Frankish rulers, and later of the Electors. It was eventually converted into a church, and sharing the fate of the Rococo Palace in the destruction of 1944 it was finally rebuilt as a great evangelical church in the heart of the oldest cathedral city of Germany.

Pfalzel

Pfalzel (Palatiolum) was the residence of the Elector-Archbishops of Trier. Little remains except for the convent church, the scene of the strange tale of a nun who played a particularly ingenious trick on the Archbishop. With the assistance of the Devil, she made a most unusual cope or cloak, which she then presented to him. Upon wearing it he was immediately flooded with terrible carnal desires and felt as though he was being dragged off to hell, but being a strong-minded man he promptly took off the garment and handed it to one of his attendants, then to another. Each in turn was seized with the same lecherous longings.

This would never do, the Archbishop thought, and so he had the nun ejected from the convent. But it then appeared that each nun was as bad as her sister, and having begun the clearance in the interest of institutional purity, the Archbishop had to carry through his purging until the whole institution had been emptied. And that, says the tale, was how the convent of Pfalzel came to an end; but the English traveller Octavius Rooke, who descended the Moselle by coach more than a century ago, remarked darkly that 'the garment, however, still exists and is worn by many.'

But Pfalzel is also the scene of the legend of the fair Genoveva, the pure and beautiful wife of the Count Siegfried, who was coveted and hungered after by the wicked bailiff Golo. Continually repulsed, he managed like Iago to poison the mind of the husband, but at least Siegfried did not strangle his guilt-less wife. Instead, he merely drove her out of the castle to die of hunger or as the prey of wild beasts – which one must assume to have been boars, or conceivably wolves.

So generous by nature was Genoveva that she did not wish

157

her husband to be guilty of her death, so as she left home she took off her ring and flung it into the Moselle, not from anger but merely to release him from his vows – for in those days marriages could be dissolved without further ceremony than that. Then she disappeared into the night, and no doubt Siegfried thought he was well rid of her.

The months passed, and then it happened that Count Siegfried was out hunting. At the end of the day he pitched camp with his retinue somewhere beside the river. In deference to the presence of their lord, two fishermen came to the camp and presented him with a splendid fish which they had just taken in their net. When the creature was cleaned for the pot, the cook found in its gut a ring, which proved to be that of Genoveva.

Certain that she had been drowned, the Count was overcome by a mixture of satisfaction and remorse, and when at last he fell asleep he dreamed of Genoveva in all her loveliness and beauty – but, alas she was being pursued by a horrible dragon. Yet only a few nights later the count had an even more distinct dream, one in which he saw a hind of purest white fleeing through the forest before a relentless huntsman whose only thought was to hound the creature to its death. Waking suddenly with a sense of horror, Siegfried was certain that the albino deer must be Genoveva, and himself the cruel man hunting the defenceless creature to kill it. Calling his men, he ordered everything to be made ready for a hunting party. There was no time to be lost.

The retainers must have been surprised at this irrational demand, but they did as they were told, and at first light the party set off with Count Siegfried in the lead. Sure enough, they had not ridden far from Pfalzel when a white doe was started from cover. The Count spurred his horse in pursuit, and racing after the creature he at last came within range and let fly an arrow. The hind faltered, then seemed to summon a final burst of energy, for it bounded ahead into a thicket and there fell, exhausted. It collapsed at the feet of Genoveva herself, who was huddled in the entrance of a rough cave, crouched on a bed of branches and moss, her little child clutched to her bosom.

Siegfried flung himself on the ground and begged her forgiveness, which she gave freely. The doe which had kept her alive with its milk lay dying, but now Genoveva was taken back in triumph to her castle. As for the baby boy, the inheritance of the Count's own features dismissed any doubts about his parentage, and he was later to become the Count Palatine of the next generation. Golo very rightly came to a well-merited end, and his head was exhibited on the castle battlements, as a warning to any who might feel inclined to bear false witness against another.

Neumagen

Neumagen – Noviomagus to the Romans – is an old-established wine village on the right bank of the Moselle, below Pfalzel. Near the shore is the famous Roman wine-ship, a sculpture which once adorned the sarcophagus of a local wine-exporter of Roman times.

Until quite recent times the wine of Neumagen was sold ex-cellar, barrel included. To move a cask of anything up to one ton weight was not easy, and until pumps came on the scene it was the task of a special guild of *Schröter*, or barrel-pushers, to convey the barrels along the roadway and down to the waiting ships. A close look at the arrangement on board the Neumagen wine-ship of Roman days suggests that the same system was then already in use, for the sculptor has provided enough detail to show that even then the casks were designed for shoving, just like those still used by some of the Moselle vintners – that is to say, the thin hoops of iron which held the staves in place are covered over with withies, the ends of which are carefully shaped and bound with willow. The object of this was to prevent the thin iron bands being damaged when the barrels were moved, for there was always the risk that such a metal hoop could be scored and might give way, so that the barrel would burst and the wine be spilled.

Before the system was changed to selling the wine in bottles, the *Schröter* received one thaler and a gallon of wine for each barrel they moved, in return for which they stood the entire loss if any damage occurred between the cellar and the barge or railway wagon to which they conveyed the cask. It is no wonder that they invariably started work by reciting the Lord's Prayer with bowed heads.

To lift a barrel, an inclined barrel-ladder would be placed between the cellar and the pavement, much like those still used by brewer's lorries when supplying inns. Two men hauled on ropes hooked to the rear edge of the cask, and a third walked backwards up the ladder, shoving with his back. In this way the barrel was brought up to a wagon, and when loading it on a barge the cask was slid down the same ladder into the vessel.

Old prints show that from medieval times onwards the barrels were loaded lengthwise in the ships, just as they are in railway wagons. This prevented rolling when the boat or train accelerated or slowed. But the Neumagen wine-ship shows them laden crosswise, and no doubt a larger cargo could be carried in a comparatively small craft if they were placed in this way, a lower layer of barrels on special stands or cradles, and an upper layer resting between them.

Veldenz

At Veldenz, a small wine-village a short way upstream of Bernkastel, the heroine is the lovely Irmina who had sadly to be parted from her beloved when he went off to the Middle East to cleave the Saracens to the navel. As he spurred his horse down the valley Irmina wept and wept, but as soon as her mother judged that the time was opportune she bade Irmina to stop crying, take stock of her own undoubted beauty, and realise that there were plenty more fish in the sea. There would be no lack of suitors, she would see to that.

But Irmina still wept and wept. She would ever belong only to her true love, the one who had pledged himself to her with the ring she always wore night and day and which somehow seemed to whisper to her of his devotion.

Irmina began to waste away, as such girls will, and her mother decided that to cure her the attachment must be broken. She reasoned and reasoned that Irmina's fiancé must surely by now be dead – cleft to the navel, no doubt, by a Saracen scimitar. Better forget him, dry the eyes, and start again. If she would be a sensible girl Irmina would throw away her ring, and by so doing she would be simply absolved from any further bond to the dead warrior.

Curiously enough, Irmina let herself be talked round, and at her mother's suggestion she dropped the ring down the well. It disappeared into the depths, but it seems that neither mother nor daughter had noticed that the bucket was at the bottom. So the ring was eventually brought up in a pail of water, and returned by the serving-maid.

The mother decided next time to bury it in the garden, but once again she had not reckoned with all the probabilities of nature. When the ring was buried a bean was inadvertently interred beneath it, and the shoot passed through the lover's token and brought it back to the light of day and right up the side of the house to shine outside Irmina's own window.

Irmina, it is said, was much frightened at the sight, or perhaps merely at the size of the bean plant. Yet to have her ring back delighted her, and once again she lost herself in thinking only of her departed lover. This infuriated her scheming mother, who already had the succession arranged. She now demanded that Irmina rid herself for ever of the silly token. Together they would put it in the fire, and there it would melt.

Her daughter reacted firmly. It would be a sin to destroy a pledge given in love, she said. Whether her young knight were still alive or long since dead, she felt herself wedded to him in her heart, and she could never marry another.

The mother's patience broke. She snatched at Irmina's hand and there was a struggle. Irmina was no match for her mother in strength, and she felt her ring being pulled off. Yet the old woman had not yet managed to fling it into the fire when the door burst open and her hero was there just in time, safe and sound, ready to clasp his faithful Irmina to his breast and make her his bride. And that he did, immediately with the original ring, thereby acquiring at one and the same time a most happy and adoring wife and a decidedly unpleasant mother-in-law.

Alf

Just below the harbour at Alf the Alfbach flows into the Moselle. In the angle the village lies huddled, with hotels which have known generations of visitors. And from just past the confluence one can see right up the valley to where Burg Arras stands proudly on the top of its private hill, a castle at first sight very like Burg Landshut above Bernkastel.

Arras is in fact still one of the most handsome castles of a modest and defensive type, for in the early 1900s the ruin was tidied up and restored to form a private residence. Below the square keep there is a pleasant house with towers and turrets, with half-timbered gables and delicate slated roofs. Seen from the Moselle it shimmers elusively in the distance, but it is no great way by the path that leads up through the orchards and pinewoods from Alf and breaks out into the open beside the vines which cascade down the slopes below its walls.

The name Arras was that of a charcoal-burner and smith who

lived in the valley of the Alfbach. He was a man of mighty physical strength, and he had 12 strong and hearty sons who worked with him in the smithy or on his simple small-holding. Thus they were engaged when, in the year 938, the Huns came sweeping over the Eifel towards the valley of the Moselle.

The only bastion which might have obstructed the passage of these terrible marauders was Castle Bertrich, further up the Alfbach valley, but the Count of Bertrich seems to have been a cowardly man who preferred to look after himself rather than to accede to the request of the Archbishop of Trier that he should block the way of the horrible Huns and cut off their road to Trier, or at least hold them at bay until the Archbishop himself should arrive at the head of his own forces. It may be that the Count assessed the situation coolly and decided that if the Huns had forced the Rhine they would certainly not be held up by the Moselle. Rather than bring their fury upon his own house and home, he would sit tight in his keep and let the invaders stream past his domains and attack the Archbishop.

News of this betrayal reached Arras the smith, and according to the chronicle he summoned his 12 sons. They in turn roused the peasants, and with what simple weapons they could muster these country people made their way in the darkness to the crags overlooking the defile of the Alfbach. There the sons of the smith arranged them in companies, and when in the early morning the vanguard of the invading column appeared in the narrow pass it was met by an avalanche of rocks prised loose and rolled from above. After a certain amount of confusion the Huns retired, then returned again and again to renew their attempt to break through towards the valley, but each time the stones and rocks took their toll. By night and by day the battle went on, until at the end of a week the force from Trier arrived and finally put the marauders to flight.

Stuben

Very beautiful is Stuben, alone on its low tongue of land at the edge of the vines. In floodtime the river will creep up the bank and wash the ruins of those same walls where once the sisters chanted. Outside its walls the nightingales would long ago take up their own evening refrain, singing a throaty chorus of wild delight. That they did so was the result of a very curious incident.

One of the foundations which owned much property along

the Moselle was Himmerode, where in course of time the monks lapsed into bad habits and led lives which were far from blameless. Bernard of Clairvaux was sent to reform the place and restore it to order, and betaking himself thither he embarked upon a campaign of sermons and lectures and reprovings. Yet the monks were not moved by his exhortations, and to all his carefully reasoned discourses they turned deaf ears.

Bernard was depressed. He retired to his room and shut himself in so that he might think up yet further arguments and reasoning which might move the monks to better behaviour and a less dissolute life. When the air became somewhat heavy and stale he threw open the window, and at once he heard the chorus of nightingales singing in the bushes of the monastery garden. The sound sent a wave of sweet relief over him, a curious sense of bliss. And then, gradually, he found to his horror that awful carnal desires were creeping into his mind.

Leaping up, Bernard slammed the window to shut out the destructive sound. Pondering the matter, he eventually came to the conclusion that if nightingales by their song could raise unspeakable thoughts in such a well-disciplined man as himself, they must play havoc with the minds of mere ordinary monks. He saw the birds as the workers of iniquity responsible for the vice which afflicted Himmerode, and he decided to act. Striding out into the moonlit garden, he ordered the nightingales to depart from there for ever. And because Bernard was a man whom even the birds had to obey, the nightingales took wing and flew off.

It so happened that the good abbess of Stuben heard that Bernard had driven out the nightingales, and that the poor birds were still flying forlorn from one place to another, longing for a home where their song would be appreciated. A gentler soul than the forthright Bernard, she called to them and offered them the freedom of the trees and meadows around the abbey she ruled. So the nightingales came to Stuben, and they stayed there until the coming of the French Revolutionary forces, who stripped the abbey roof, tore down the Baroque doorway with its angels and smashed everything of beauty.

By boat one turns so closely round the flat point of shingle, on which only the bare walls remain, that one can see the remnants from almost every angle.

There is something inexpressibly sad about the crumbled and weathered building, standing as deserted as an abbey of the Yorkshire dales. And it has a sorrowful tale attached to it, as

163

seems only appropriate.

The first Abbess of Stuben was Gisela, who in earlier years was a girl of such incomparable fairness and beauty that one might well guess that some terrible tragedy would certainly be lying in wait for her. She had given her heart to a noble and upright young knight – another sign in the life of the Moselle valley that doom was surely impending. He happened to be away, though whether on a campaign against the Saracens or merely on a visit upriver I do not know. One version of the tale says that it was Gisela's wedding day, and she was awaiting his arrival for their marriage. Whether or not that was so, she was sitting at her window, looking up towards the bend of the stream, watching and sighing and longing for her own true love.

At last, just after sunset, she saw his boat come sweeping round the cliffs below where St Aldegund lock now stands. She could make out his figure in the dim light and, leaning from the window of the tower, she waved to him. No, she did not fall out, but her lover was imprudent. Aglow with ardour, his heart beating with the longing to hold her in his arms, he stood on the prow and leaped for the shore. Unfortunately he had not reckoned with the weight of his armour, and his spring fell short. Gisela no doubt saw the splash as he fell in the water and sank.

She did not weep, the story says, 'but her bosom became cold as the waters that closed over his head'. Her father endowed a convent to be built on the flat meadow beside the river, and she was the first to enter it, the first of a long line of Abbesses of Stuben.

Bernkastel

Bernkastel's river frontage is disappointing. It is Victorian from the age of wealthy visitors who came by coach or carriage, and only the one-time Electoral Cellars and the Michaelsturm break the mediocrity. This tower is splendid, a thousand-year-old bastion of the vanished walls, square and solid and built of rough slate, with eight little turrets around its conical top. It is in fact this tower which makes the appearance of the town when seen from the river, for it tactfully draws the eye away from the hotels and bus parks and the car-laden foreshore. Yet the real beauty of Bernkastel lies behind, around its exquisite market-place with the half-timbered houses gay in all their brightness of newly painted corbels, and the little Spitzhäuschen which seems to have been added as a bold afterthought to fill a

Bernkastel, the Michaelsturm

small remaining gap and yet leave room for the wains to pass beside its tight-waisted lower storey. It is a Grimm, even a Disney creation, and surely either a witch or some superior kind of gnome must inhabit it.

Bernkastel owes its fame to its wine, which is very rightly celebrated. The best is certainly not shipped abroad, but is to be found in the little parlours of the vintners themselves, tucked away in the alleys. Most famous – but perhaps no better than others – is the one which leapt to fame in 1360.

> *Eile die Weile! Die Sage gibt kund,*
> *Der Kurfürst wird von dem Weine gesund.*

Thus the boys and girls of the valley still hear in rhyme about the Elector Archbishop Boemund II of Trier, who lay sick in his summer residence above the town.

> *Hurry and hear what is rumoured abroad,*
> *The Elector by wine of his sickness is cured!*

165

The illness is said to have been gout, a not uncommon afflic-
tion of medieval archbishops, and yet the mode of cure makes
this seem a little unlikely, for it is said that when his chaplain
mentioned the matter to a local knight, in whose charge the
defence of Bernkastel lay, the man declared that he was personally acquainted with a doctor who would fix the Archbishop
quickly enough.

Quaffing another bottle of his favourite vintage to give him
extra strength, the knight set off for the Bishop's quarters with a
whole barrel of the wine on his shoulders. He persuaded the
prelate to admit this specialist doctor he had brought with him,
and when the sick man had taken a gulp of the wine he felt
new life tingling in his body.

'That wine is the best doctor of all,' the Archbishop declared.

Kues

The son of a bargemaster, Nicholas von Kues (or Cusanus) was
never active in the world of his father's shipping, and his
younger years were very similar to those of Trithemius half a
century later. His liking for learning being despised by his
father, who is even alleged on the basis of legend rather than of
record to have pushed his bookish son overboard when on a
voyage downriver with a barge, he left home (or swam ashore,
if one believes the unlikely embellishment) and set out to study
where he might. Count von Manderscheid aided him, and soon
he was at Deventer in Holland, next in Heidelberg and Padua.
Trained as a lawyer, he returned at the age of 23 to his
homeland, and accepted a brief in a case at Mainz. He lost the
case, threw up the law in disgust, and turned to theology. Not
many years passed before he was addressing the delegates to
the Council of Basel, undertaking diplomatic missions for the
Pope, advocating ecclesiastical reforms, and taking up his post
as Lord Bishop of Brixen in the Tirol. He was the intermediary
in peace talks between England and France, a continual comer
and goer in the courts of Europe to which urgent diplomatic
missions had to be sent. Trithemius referred to Cusanus as 'an
angel of light and peace in the midst of darkness and confusion.'

Modestly riding on horseback, he travelled through the Netherlands, to Vienna and Salzburg, to Trier and Magdeburg,
Cologne and Aachen, indeed throughout all of western Europe
east of France, preaching reform and striving to raise the stan-

dards of ecclesiastical administration and justice. But Nicholas of Kues was more than a reformer and a church diplomat. He was absorbed in studies about the nature of the universe, which he saw as a reflection of the wisdom of God, and more than a century before Copernicus he decided by reason rather than by any observation that the Ptolemaic cosmology could not be true. In his *De docta ignorantia* he wrote that it was inconceivable that the earth itself could be the centre of the universe. 'There are no fixed and immovable poles of the heavens, but every part of the heavens themselves must be in motion; from which it is clear that the earth itself is in motion.' He also considered the earth to be 'a star among many stars, of just such materials as the heavenly bodies, moving as they do in similar and imprecisely circular orbits. Its form is roughly that of a sphere.'

Cusanus bought some mathematical and astronomical instruments in Nürnberg, and engaged in many speculations in the mathematical field. He tried to calculate the precise value of π, and came very close to the right answer. He was also intrigued by the problem of weight, and developed a hygrometer to measure atmospheric humidity by the increase or decrease in weight of a ball of wool. As a result he put forward the opinion that one should be able to forecast probable changes in the weather by observing alterations in the water content of the air. His studies also led him to try to produce a scheme for improving the accuracy of the calendar, and he suggested at the Council of Basel the reform which in fact was introduced one-and-a-half centuries later by Pope Gregory XIII.

Yet Nicholas of Kues is known best of all for the gift he bestowed upon his village. When he came home to rest before returning again to his unruly diocese of Brixen, he drew up the plans for the Hospital of St Nicholas, which is still one of the glories of the Moselle valley. The foundation was to provide a home for 33 poor men, aged 50 or over, free men of honourable employment and solvent, bachelors of the diocese of Trier and if possible out of the immediately adjacent villages. Six were to be priests, six nobility, the rest common people.

Zeltingen

Like so many of the Moselle villages, Zeltingen has a uniform charm rather than any outstanding feature. It is just 'a nice place', as one might write on a picture postcard. But it has its tales, one of which concerns the excellent wine produced in the monastic vineyard of the Martinshof, a wine so renowned that the Elector Philip of Cologne wished to experience it for himself. He frequently let it be known that he would appreciate a barrel of the vintage, but the monks seemed not to understand even the broadest of hints. The truth was that they did not like the Elector with his high-handed ways.

Philip at last decided that the only sure way to sample the wine was to carry out an inspection, and in due state he set out from Cologne on an official visit to Zeltingen. The Abbot easily guessed why his lord spiritual seemed at last to be taking an interest in the life of the brethren, and he quickly laid in a stock of other wines from the Rhine, Nahe and Moselle. These he set before the Archbishop and his entourage, without revealing their identity.

On leaving, the Elector thanked the Abbot for his generous hospitality, praising in particular the excellent wine which had been provided. He insisted that the Abbot should visit him at Cologne, but regretted that he could not offer in return such fine vintages as that of the Martinshof.

'Thank you, my Lord,' the Abbot calmly replied. 'And if one day you should come here with the intent to interest yourself in our institution rather than our cellar, then the Martinshof wine may indeed be set before you. Until then we shall prefer to reserve it for those who are our true friends.' And he bowed the Elector out.

Alken

Alken lies at the foot of Burg Thurandt (or Thuron), a stronghold famous as the site of a remarkable wet seige. The fortress was named in memory of the stronghold of Tyre by one of the sons of Henry the Lion, who accompanied the Emperor Barbarossa on the Crusade and returned to the Moselle in about the year 1200. It had not long been built when it became the scene of strange events.

Although it was the residence of the Emperor Otto IV himself, who ruled his Holy Roman Empire from within it, the castle eventually came to be administered by a certain Zorno, a rapacious count whose activities provided an excellent excuse for the forces of law and order to attack it. However, the idea of capturing Thuron seems to have occurred to two energetic Electors simultaneously, and so it was that in 1246 Archbishop Arnold II of Trier and Archbishop Konrad of Cologne joined forces to put down Zorno, the enemy of peace and security. Each hoped to seize Thuron for himself.

The seige developed into a two-year campaign, which must have been one of the pleasantest in which a soldier can ever have been involved. It happened that the two years were ones of good vintage, and after prolonged attempts to breach the walls with rocks catapulted from a nearby height, the besieging troops resorted to attack by winemanship. Thuron had great stocks of food, and a well which reached the water-table far below, but its defenders soon ran out of wine. Shrewdly judging the psychology of Zorno's men-at-arms, the commanders had a *Fuder* of fine wine brought up, which was broached and given to the investing forces in full view of the wineless defenders. Next day some more tuns were dragged up by wagon, and the soldiers again relished the fine wine of the sunny slopes. The defenders watched, with a thirst slaked only by water, a thirst which each day grew greater.

Every house and vineyard within reach of Alken was searched by the ecclesiastical forces, and if we can believe the thirteenth-century chronicle which tells the story of the seige, no fewer than 3,000 barrels were drunk, or about three-quarters of a million gallons of wine, before the defenders gave in. Ringed about with a mountain range of empty casks and having nothing to see or hear but the wine-happy, singing soldiery, the garrison at last could stand it no longer, and forced Zorno to surrender. Naturally, the soldiers of the Archbishops were far from pleased. To spend two years drinking wine was a pleasant enough form of military service, and they were angry that the besieged had not held out for another year or two. The Alkeners, however, were delighted. They were long tired of having their own wine commandeered without any payment.

The Archbishops having won, there now remained the question of which of them was to have the prize. Over this a deadlock was quickly reached, and it may be that one of the pair of Holy Terrors remembered the judgement of Solomon in the case of the disputed ownership of a child. They agreed to have the premises cut in half with a wall, so that each Elector could reside when he wished in his own half. It was a Berlin Wall in miniature, although I doubt if either of the Electors were quite as neurotic and sensitive as the modern wall-builders. And the strange division is still there, dividing Thurandt into isolated halves.

A condition of the surrender was that Zorno and his garrison should go free, but the victorious ecclesiastical forces excepted a village official in Alken who had acted as a spy for the men of Thuron. What became of him is not very clear, for one version states that a rope was stretched across the valley of the Alkenerbach to the tower of the Bleidenberg, the emplacement where the besieging catapults (or *Bliden*) had been installed. The official was told to walk this quarter-mile of tightrope at a height of several hundreds of feet above the ground; and he did so, afterwards building in thankfulness a chapel at the end of the traverse. The remains of this chapel can still be seen, although in fact it seems to have been built by Archbishop Arnold in thankfulness – either that the seige had ended without his men becoming alcoholics or perhaps that he at least secured half the castle for himself.

Another version states the official to have spied for the episcopal side, and to have been suspended by the garrison midway between the Bleidenberg and Thuron towers so that he might contemplate the errors of his ways. An even more attractive story says that after the surrender the spying official was carried up to Thuron, placed in the sling of the great catapult with which the defenders had shot at the military works on the Bleidenberg, and flung high through the air to meet a death which he prudently averted in mid-flight by calling upon the name of the Virgin and promising to build her a chapel if she should bring him to earth unharmed.

Kobern

Up by the ruins of Kobern's castle is the hexagonal chapel of St Matthias, splendidly crowning the vineyard hill. It is said to have been built as a one-fifth-scale copy of the Church of the Holy Sepulchre in Jerusalem when Heinrich of Kobern returned from a Crusade early in the thirteenth century. Once it held the head of St Matthias himself, brought back by the same knight from the Holy Land, and so it became the goal of an immense annual pilgrimage from Koblenz and Trier.

Kobern itself is the scene of one of those appealing and tragic romances, the memory of which has come down from the Middle Ages and yet still has a wistful freshness about it. Else, the fair and noble daughter of the Lord of Kobern, had given her heart to a worthy young noble named Johannes, and every-

170

thing was set fair for an unclouded romance when Johannes somehow came into conflict with the Archbishop of Trier, who declared him an outlaw and excommunicated him.

Forced to flee from the land of his beloved, Johannes hid himself in the forests of which Germany then as now had an abundance. There he might have pined away with thinking of Else, but being a very practical young man he purchased a harp, and in the woods he would spend his evenings teaching himself to play it. When he had become proficient enough he set out for Kobern, where a feast was planned at the castle. As a minstrel he was made welcome, and at dinner he struck up his harp and played an air that in modern sentimental days would be known as 'our tune, darling'.

Else listened, and as she heard the melody and the voice of her outlawed beloved the emotions surged so swiftly to her head that she fainted. When those at the table had lifted her to a couch and restored her to consciousness, the minstrel had gone.

However, the faithful Johannes was not far distant. The mere sight of Else made him unable to bear the thought of never seeing her again, and though his passion was hopeless, he decided that at least he might hope to behold his beloved at a distance. So, discarding his harp, he set up as a hermit in a rude shelter beside the road down which she would sometimes ride.

One night he was lying awake under the bushes, looking up at the stars and thinking of Else – and perhaps less charitably of the Archbishop of Trier – when he heard footsteps in the roadway. Soon some men drew level with where he lay. There were several of them, and they were talking earnestly.

'So be it,' said the one who seemed to be the leader. 'At midnight then, at the postern gate. It will be handed over to us, and the entry will be simple. The famous fair Else will be ours tonight – ha ha!'

Johannes lay still until the men had dispersed, then he hurried to the home of his beloved to give the alarm. The retainers were roused and stationed in ambush in the passages to wait for the robbers. Sure enough, the postern gate was found to have been treacherously left unlocked, but instead of securing it the Lord of Kobern decided to let the robbers enter and take them by surprise.

At midnight the attack came, and the intruders were beaten back or slain. Johannes the Hermit was constantly in the thick of the fighting, and there he was mortally wounded. As he lay dying he at last revealed his identity, begging that he might be buried in the chapel below the castle. Then, his eyes upon those of the girl who had always loved him as he had faithfully loved her, he stretched out his hand toward her, and died.

Dieblich

The Moselle sweeps round past Dieblich at the foot of the hill to which so many poor women were dragged to be put to the sword as witches before their bodies were burned in fires that could be seen far across the country. Often the belief that the women had brought hail upon the grapes or disease to the cattle was no doubt sincerely held, but one case of alleged witchcraft at Dieblich was quite deliberately planned.

There happened to be a particularly beautiful girl in the village, in whose honour many a bottle of wine had been emptied – so many, indeed, that her mother became too convinced of the girl's market value. When a local squire himself came to demand her daughter's hand in marriage, the mother bluntly refused him. At that moment the belle of Dieblich herself came in, and the squire, already smarting at his rebuff, decided to address himself somewhat peremptorily to her. But beauty had gone to her head. She laughed at the squire and mockingly asked him if he would not prefer to marry her mother instead, if matrimony were so urgent.

Thus insulted, the man took himself off and promptly denounced the elder woman as a witch, and although many testified for her, she was sentenced and killed. The daughter knew very well that the same fate would overtake her, so she flung herself into the Moselle and drowned. Yet the reader will be relieved to know that justice occasionally strikes, and in this case it did so in the form of a flash of lightning, which so startled the horse that was carrying the squire home from the scene of the execution that it reared, galloped wildly away, and flung him with such force that he was killed instantly.

Dieblich once had a small convent, a place which was little more than a retreat for eight female recluses. They were girls of noble birth, and as they were also young the gallant knights of the neighbourhood had a curious tendency to gather outside their windows to sing songs of romance and whisper words of love. It may even be that some did not always remain outside the walls for a very upright knight of the neighbourhood became so shocked at the goings-on that he eventually

172

appointed himself the guardian of the ladies, and every evening he took his stand at the convent gate in full armour and with sword in hand.

Yet the male heart cannot always persist in such rigid and righteous determination. Little by little the guardian himself began to feel the remarkable impact of one particular pair of sparkling eyes which smiled down upon him every morning when, at sunrise, he prepared to march home from his night of dutiful vigil. At last he could resist no longer. One night the office of sentry was abandoned, the gate left unguarded as the knightly watchman himself stole inside. Alas, his unselfish chivalry and virtue were so transmuted by love that the visits of this noble knight who had sought to preserve the chaste peace of the devout ladies eventually led to the convent of Dieblich being closed and moved elsewhere.

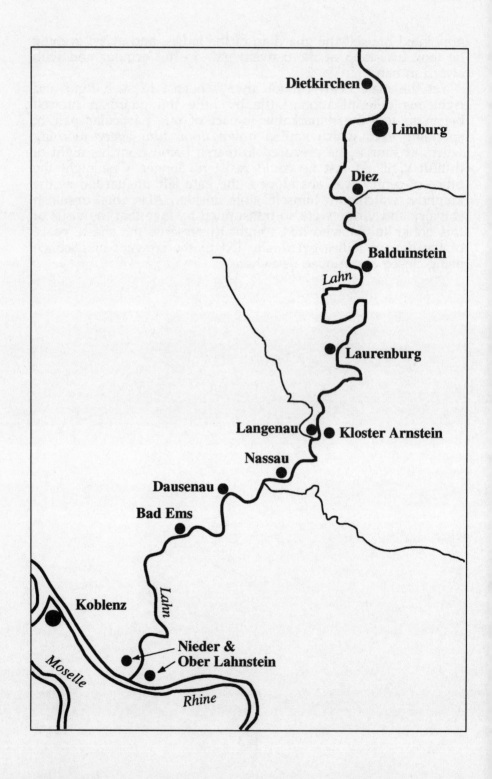

10

The Lahn, Bad Ems, Langenau, Diez, Limburg and Dietkirchen

The Lahn

The river Lahn flows into the Rhine just upstream of Koblenz. It is navigable for comparatively small Lahn-ships, but is a popular cruising ground on account of the scenery through which it flows. Originally the navigable reaches extended further, but nowadays the limit is at Dehrn, just beyond Dietkirchen. The main transport was of marble from the quarries above Diez, the loads then being transhipped at Niederlahnstein into larger Rhine vessels.

The river is one of great beauty, and many of the small towns upon it are notable, such as Nassau, with its connections with the House of Orange, and Limburg. Reasonably safe, free of 2,000-tonners racing for the next cargo in Rotterdam, the Lahn is a right little, tight little stream flowing past one village after another until it finally does a double twist to the last lock at Niederlahnstein and opens up to the junction with its mighty relative, the Rhine. Yet it rarely sees a foreign cruiser, and only the more enterprising and less flashy German craft deign to notice its existence at all.

Even the mouth of the Lahn is intriguing. Close on the point to port stands the ancient church of St John – but of where? Presumably of Niederlahnstein, which is the nearest settlement, but I suspect that it once belonged to an abbey perched on the Rhine bank and long since vanished. Ahead, the square keep of Lahneck stands a little bit tired, half-asleep after its centuries of guarding the entrance to the valley, and perhaps a little horrified at the bright yellow renovations of Stolzenfels across the Rhine. The main course of the Lahn curves a little to the left along the pretty and rather tumbledown waterfront of Niederlahnstein, and to starboard the cranes in Oberlahnstein's harbour are busily loading cargoes from the small Lahnships into their

175

greater cousins of the Rhine trade. Beyond them a tower or two and some fragments of medieval town wall remind the boatman that Oberlahnstein was once a proud town and not just the rather scattered and nondescript place of small factories which it has now become.

In fact, Oberlahnstein has the unusual distinction of being the place at which an Emperor of the Holy Roman Empire was actually relieved of his office. The man was Wenceslas of Bohemia, an individual who paid little attention to the responsibilities of his office. That was the reason why the four Electors of the Rhineland met together in June 1400 and sent him a stern letter to the effect that he was to come to Oberlahnstein on a certain day in August and tell them what he proposed to do to stop the rot which was spreading in both church and state, or else.

Wenceslas did not even reply. He preferred to remain in Prague, where things were easy enough. He had no intention of visiting Oberlahnstein to explain his conduct. However, on the appointed day the four Electors were there right enough, together with a great assembly of lords and knights and representatives from cities throughout the empire, and as the Emperor evidently did not consider them worthy of his attention Archbishop Johann of Mainz stepped out in front of the people and read a remarkable proclamation.

'For many weighty reasons, and because of his insupportable failure, we hereby remove and depose Herr Wenceslas from the Roman Empire, declaring him useless, idle, and thoroughly inept as head of the Roman Empire, and we release all lords, nobles, knights and gentry, cities, countries and peoples subject to the Roman Empire from all fealty due to Wenceslas in the name of the Roman Empire, and from all and every such oath, and we further instruct them in their oath to the Empire, never more to obey Wenceslas nor to render him any service such as would be due to a Roman Emperor, but rather to reserve such obedience and service for him who, by the will of God, shall be elected as Emperor. The foregoing verdict and sentence is read and delivered by us, Johann, Archbishop of Mainz, upon a throne constituted as a throne of justice.'

Cheers rose above the town, and no doubt the good wine flowed in many a tavern as the four Electors returned into Oberlahnstein's Castle and completed the formalities for the installation of Ruprecht of the Palatinate, who was duly elected on the following day, across the Rhine at Rhens.

Goethe was enough of an inland waterways man to take an occasional trip by water, and it was as he rowed with his friends down this last reach of the Lahn and looked up at the mighty towering keep of Burg Lahneck that he began to form the lines which I presume are diligently taught to every school-boy and schoolgirl of both the Lahnsteins.

Hoch auf dem alten Turme steht
Des Helden edler Geist.
Der, wie das Schiff vorübergeht,
Es wohl zu fahren heisst:
'Sieh, diese Sehne war so stark,
Dies Herz so fest und wild,
Die Knochen voll von Rittermark,
Der Becher angefüllt...
Mein halbes Leben stürmt ich fort,
Verdehnt die Hälft in Ruh,
Und Du, Du Menschenschifflein dort,
Fahr immer, immer zu.'

High on the ancient bastion stands
The hero's noble shade,
And bids the shipman sailing by
A safe untroubled voyage.
'See, once these sinews too were strong,
This heart so sure and bold,
Sturdy the marrow in my bones,
The Rhenish in my glass...
Through half my life I fought and thrust,
To spend the rest in peace,
And you, you little human barque,
Sail ever, ever on.'

Probably the tendon so strong, the heart so firm and wild, the bones full of knightly marrow – to say nothing of the beaker filled to the brim – belonged to the last of the Templars of the Rhineland, whose tale is woven in to the fabric of Lahneck. For however peaceful the keep may look as it stands high in the night sky above the lock, bathed in the glow of summer flood-lighting, it has certainly had its great moments, and none more dramatic than that which is said to have occurred in the year 1315. The Knights Templars had begun as a noble and chival-rous institution, but as time went on and there was little hope for their original purposes they became corrupt, a sort of semi-

177

brigand society of toughs. That was why, in 1313, Pope Clement V excommunicated the Templars one and all, and Philip the Fair expelled them from France. Outlawed, these fierce and tried men of undoubted bravery had either to give up their order or to find some place where they could maintain themselves by force of arms against the rest of the world. Thus it was that 12 of these knights forced an entry into Lahneck Castle and appropriated it for their own fortress.

Lahneck belonged to the Archbishop of Mainz, who had built it to protect his territories from marauders, so the Pope immediately sent an order to the Archbishop instructing him to have the Templars ejected. An archiepiscopal army was sent to surround the Castle in force and demand their surrender. The knights, however, did not trust the offer that they might keep their lives and liberty if they laid down their arms. They knew the Pope too well. Defiantly they withstood the onslaught of the enemies and killed many of them. Again the Archbishop demanded surrender, with the promise of a pardon, and again the knights refused. Pardon belonged only to God, they said, and God would be able to know well enough who it was who needed to be forgiven. As for trusting the men of the Roman Church, unfortunately this was something which they were unable to do. The 12 men must certainly have by now known that death faced them whichever way they turned, and they had resolved to sell their lives as dearly as they might.

So, at dead of night, the troops of Mainz were made ready for a final assault. But the scaling ladders had not yet been thrown up when the massive gate swung open, the drawbridge fell, and the 12 knights in armour poured out of Lahneck, slashing and thrusting as they came.

How many of their enemies they cut down in this last desperate sadly is not known, but at last 11 of the 12 were among the heap of dead at Lahneck's gate. Only one remained, an old man in shining armour.

At this moment a messenger from the Archbishop broke through to the front, calling that the fighting was to stop. The Emperor himself had guaranteed freedom to the Templars, he proclaimed.

The old man stood still for a moment. Then, leaping over the prostrate bodies of his companions, he cut and thrust his way through the men at arms to where the commander of the besieging army stood. Grappling with him, he dragged him to the edge of Lahneck's cliff, and flung himself and his enemy, locked

178

together, over the precipice.

From Lahneck's terrace, where once the last of the Templars grappled with the last of his enemies, the view of the confluence of the rivers is a fine one indeed. And a little to the right a Lahnship is slowly being raised by the water flowing into the lock, beyond which a not very beautiful dye-works occupies the site of an old watermill, the Weissmühle. Millers have a way of being the fathers of beautiful daughters, and the miller who ran the Weissmühle in the 1450s was no exception. Wondrous fair was his Elisabeth, the loveliest maiden in all the country round about. Many a young man had tried to win her affection; but no, Elisabeth was not interested. Secretly she was deeply in love with the choice of her own, a mere fisherman from the Lahn. She cared nothing for competitors.

At least, that was how matters stood when one day a remarkably smooth and handsome young knight appeared at Lahneck. In fact, he was the son of that noble house, who had spent his youth in the service of the Bishop of Mainz, and now emerging fully fledged from the archiepiscopal court he was just ready to fall head over heels in love with the miller's daughter. This he did, and he haunted the vicinity of the mill whenever he could, to catch a glimpse of her, and to lure her into his arms.

Now it is one thing to be loved by a Lahn fisherman, and quite another to have the heir of Lahneck as boyfriend, so it is hardly surprising that Elisabeth found it easy enough to respond to the thrill of laying her head on a metal breastplate in preference to the homely and perhaps somewhat smelly jacket of her first true love. All the same, she did not tell the young fisherman of her new romance, but met him every evening as before and lay beside him in the soft grass of the river bank, beneath the willows.

One evening, however, the fisherman waited in vain. Elisabeth did not come. Worried that something might have happened to her, or perhaps stung by the first prickings of a well-justified suspicion, he made his way to the mill and peeped in at the window. What he saw there one can guess, for at once he went down to the river bank and sat there as though dazed.

He had been there some time before he heard steps, and maybe a slight clanking sound. The young knight of Lahneck saw the fisherman on the bank and commanded to be rowed back down the river toward the foot of the castle hill. Without a word, the story says – though it is difficult to see how anyone can tell – the young man pushed out his punt and conveyed his rival downstream.

But he did not stop at Lahneck. He let the boat be swept on, out past the Lahnsteins, and into the turbulent Rhine. Perhaps he did not even need to rock the boat to ensure that it was swiftly overset in midstream. Both men were drowned, as probably the broken-hearted young fisherman had intended.

As for Elisabeth, she waited in vain the next day for the arrival of her romantic lover. When she heard that the fisherman had disappeared, and the boat also, she must have guessed what had happened. She flung herself into the mill race, and that was the end of her. The affair was also the end of the Lahneck line, for the gay knight had been the only son, and with his death the family became extinct.

Bad Ems

This is a rather faded spa of great elegance. Nowadays its customers come mainly from the German health service. The springs are extremely hot. One of the first to try the waters was Agrippina, the wife of the Emperor Germanicus. From earliest times, one particular spring at Ems was reputed to have the property of determining the sex of future children, in that pregnant women bathing in the Bubenquelle (Boys' Spring) would even-

180

tually produce a boy. Its working upon Agrippina was disastrous, for she shortly afterwards gave birth to the boy who afterwards became the notorious Caligula, probably the most revolting creature ever to have been born in the Lahn valley. Yet this spring certainly achieved a great reputation for male progeny. If a boy was born, then it was the water which had done it; but if the child was a girl, then of course the woman must have made her visit too late. No doubt this would account for the case of the English lady who, the Emsers assert, already had eleven daughters when she came to Bad Ems, bathed in the Bubenquelle, and promptly had a twelfth. Many people still believe in the special property of this gusher, whatever the rest of the world may prefer to think about sex being determined by the XX or XY mechanism of chromosome assortment. And, even though I used to be a geneticist, I would not wish for one moment to interfere with such a charming belief.

Bad Ems is perhaps more famous among historians for its telegram than for being responsible for the birth of Caligula. It was in July 1870 that the Kaiser was taking the waters when he was visited by the French Ambassador Benedetti, who had been sent to Ems by Napoleon III with instructions to request the Kaiser not to permit Prince Leopold of Hohenzollern-Sigmaringen to put himself forward as candidate for the throne of Spain. Not surprisingly, the mission failed. One day the men met on the promenade beside the river and Benedetti raised the matter again. But the Kaiser had 'nothing more to say'. The exchange was short and perhaps not very diplomatic. The famous telegram drafted by Bismarck swept along the wires from the local post office, heading for Berlin. The Franco-Prussian war was launched, Strasbourg was bombarded, Alsace and Lorraine attached to Germany for nearly 50 years. On the promenade a discreet stone recalls this event so typical of Franco-German relations of a past age, but nobody is particularly proud of the recollection.

Langenau

In the meadows on the right bank of the Lahn stands the long, low building of the Castle of Langenau. And here, as in the case of Heisterbach, there is a tale involving travel through time.

It so happened that the fair mistress of Langenau was walking beside the river, along the bank where nowadays the campers from the Ruhr and Rhineland pitch their tents. She held her small son by the hand until they came to a place where he could play in the grass, and there she sat down. As the day was pleasantly warm, she dozed off. She did not sleep for long, but the moment she awoke she realised with terror that her child had vanished. Scrambling to her feet she searched the meadow, the river bank. Not a sign of the child was to be seen. The mother ran to the Castle, and at once a search party was sent out. All day and throughout the night the men combed the woodland, and at dawn the fishermen dragged the river. But never a trace of little Heinrich was found. He had simply vanished.

In the course of time the sorrow of his disappearance faded, and as the years flowed by like the River Lahn, he was forgotten. Eventually his parents died also. It was 70 years after the event that a knocking on the gate of Langenau Castle one evening caused the porter to open. Before him stood a small boy who told him some hare-brained tale of how he had been playing at the water's edge when a hand (that of the Lahngeist, I presume) rose from the water, clutched his arm and pulled him in. A kind beautiful lady had taken him into a hall, where he had played with a host of boys and girls until at the end of the afternoon he had said he must be going home. And here he was – though he did not recognise any of the servants as those he had left only a few hours before.

The young Lord of Langenau was summoned, together with his bride – for he was only recently married. He looked the child up and down, shrugged and said he had never seen him in his life. Yet his wife recognised a family likeness in the features, a fact which aroused her suspicions in what happened to be an entirely wrong direction. But while she was speculating on possible previous amorous adventures of her husband, the chaplain remembered that sometime, somewhere, he had read something in the family archives. Hurrying to the library, he began to blatter through the papers until he found what he was seeking. Yes, there it was, written in the hand of two or three generations earlier.

'My son Heinrich was lost. The silver cross on his rosary bears the date 1506.'

The chaplain raced back to the group which still surrounded the stranger boy. The rosary? Yes. The lad felt inside his shirt and drew it out. The silver cross, with the date 1506 – yes, it was there right enough, but were we not now already in the 1580s?

'It is he! Heinrich!' The lord of the manor steps forward, hesitant.

The company do not know what to do, to say. Here is the lost child, 70 years old but still a small boy in appearance, in speech and in fact.

'Heinrich, dear. Come in...' The young mistress of Langenau takes him by the hand and leads him into the court he knows so well. And yet, as she does so the transformation begins. Within only a few moments he runs through 70 years of physiology and ends up in the realms of gerontology. He is a lad, a young man, middle-aged, elderly, then an old and rheumaticky fellow all in succession, growing and wilting like a plant seen in a speeded-up film of its development. At the door into the great hall he is already decrepit, and there on the threshold he collapses, his frail body no longer able to support him in his old age. Heinrich of Langenau dies, in the home where he was born.

Somewhere there must be a moral in this tale. Maybe it is concerned with the Lahngeist and its curious ongoings, but personally I prefer to find in it a reminder that time – as the monk of Heisterbach also discovered – is relative, that the railway time-table of school-leaving at 16 or 18 and retirement at 65 is an invention of man rather than a facet of real truth. And perhaps it also holds a hint that we are much closer to another time-scale than many of us would care to admit, except in those dreams when we experience a new dimension as vividly as did Heinrich of Langenau when the Lahngeist stretched her arm above the waves and drew him down into a new level of being.

Diez

Just outside Diez is the Manor of Dirstein, once a convent which drew its novices from the aristocratic families of the neighbourhood, and because so many of the novices were related to the nobles in the area they were allowed passes into the outside world to an extent that was probably unusual. The young knights of Diez and Nassau and other seats were not at all averse to the decorous visits which the young ladies from Dirstein were permitted to make.

There happened to be in the convent a nun named Jutta, who was in fact the Countess of Diez, and being a high-spirited woman she decided just before Lent that it would be a pleasant idea to help her particular friend Clementia to go to the Shrovetide Carnival at Limburg, of which they had heard so much from the relatives they visited outside. Undoubtedly such an

Diez on the Lahn

escapade would have been against the rules, but perhaps she bribed the portress. However that may be, Clementia slipped out of the convent and into the Diez family carriage, which Jutta's brother had brought there in readiness. By the time they reached Limburg, Clementia was made up as a most ravishing mermaid.

Now, girls in convents are not necessarily more immune than others to feelings of romance, and amid all the fun of the fair the mermaid Clementia succeeded in falling head over tail in love with a neighbouring young gallant, Gerlach of Limburg. Back in the convent she could not sleep for thinking of him, and whenever she was allowed out to the Diezers or the Limburgers, sure enough her adoring Gerlach was there. One day he persuaded her to elope.

Clementia may or may not have been torn in her emotions, but returning to the convent she stole into the chapel and hung upon the statue of the Virgin the veil which she had taken upon her admission. Then she slipped out through the gate again and accompanied her lover for a time of decidedly human enjoyment.

And yet, as the days of blissful adventure passed, Clementia began to feel disappointed and to regret her rash action. She slipped away from her lover (who by this time may also have been having second thoughts, for he made no effort to pursue her) and after some little while she stood forlorn and weary before the door of the convent she had left. Her mind made up, she knocked at the wicket gate and the portress opened to her.

It was then that the errant girl had a surprise. The woman who opened the door to admit her was not the familiar gate-keeper but none other than the Virgin Mary. Naturally, the prodigal girl dropped to her knees, but the Virgin told her to stand up.

'You have sinned much,' she said. 'But because you have loved so greatly, it will all be forgiven to you. While you were away I took your place and did your work. Nobody knows that you have been absent. So off you go, take up your service where you left off, and sin no more!'

Limburg

At the very foot of the tall rock on which the Cathedral of Limburg stands, towering up beside the splendid former Episcopal Palace and Castle of the Electors of Trier, the Lahn pours over a rough weir of stone, burbling as it passes the water mill and then hopping over the stones to divide and flow past the two sides of an island. This peaceful haunt of warblers and ducks and moorhens was the *Pestinsel* of earlier times, the Plague Island to which were banished all those who might infect their fellows. The chronicler of Limburg mentions one of these unfortunates, a 'barefoot' Franciscan, a mendicant brother from the Main valley, who was a leper. This man 'made the best songs and ditties in all the world, both in rhyme and in melody, so that none along the Rhine or in all the land was his equal. And the people sang with delight the songs that he made, and master musicians and pipers and the other minstrels carried copies of his melodies and verses with them.'

The name of this poor leper friar is not known, but the chronicler gives the words of some of the plaintive songs which he sang as he sat in one of the willows over the Lahn cheering his fellow men with his music as he waited, blind and wasting away, for his release in death.

In fact, those were terrible times for the people of the town. First came the terror of the Black Death, and then the eerie procession of the flagellants, a long column of wandering men and women carrying crosses and flags, torches and candles, and the sinister whips with which to flay themselves for their sins. In an effort to keep the dread disease at bay, they would fling themselves on the ground, each by his particular posture indicating what was the nature of his evil deeds. Those who had broken their marriage vows lay on their sides, murderers were face upwards, oathbreakers raised a thumb and two fingers, and to each in turn came the two chosen master-whippers, who gave every penitent a lash, followed by an unauthorised absolution. All would then sing one of their strange dirges, and after beating their breasts they scourged themselves until the blood ran. In the evening the people of the town would invite them into their homes, and early on the following morning the flagellants departed on the next stage of their 30-day penance.

The penitents even went to Rome – from where, relates the chronicler, who had no sympathy with such unauthorised movements, they came back even worse than before. Nor was the epidemic halted by these attempts at preventive confession, and a more horrible explanation was found for the spread of the dread disease. The Jews were said to have poisoned the water supply, and they were quickly rounded up to be butchered or burned alive. The good chronicler did not approve of this, but he remarked that the curse had certainly been fulfilled 'which they made on Good Friday: *Sanguis ejus super nos et super filios nostros.*'

Dietkirchen

When Lubentius died at Karden on the Moselle, he was buried with suitable ceremony at Koblenz, and as this happened well within the era of wonders, we must not be surprised to know that the grave could not contain the bones of such a holy man. A flood invaded the town, the water swirled over the grave, opened it, and carried the body away to the Rhine. At Deutsches Eck the corpse of Lubentius turned to starboard and forged upstream against the full force of the flood to Niederlahnstein, where the saint entered the valley which had been the scene of his labours and floated up the stream for more than 40 miles (there were as yet no locks) before running aground on the river bank at Dietkirchen, where the delighted inhabitants rushed to the bank to load the body of their old friend on an ox-cart to take it to the burial ground. But behold, the worthy and obstinate beasts refused to haul anywhere but to the top of the hill, and there Lubentius was duly buried.

The name Dietkirchen suggests that the great Romanesque Basilica which so splendidly crowns the solitary cliff was actually built by a man named Dietrich. And so it was. In a Saracen prison the crusading knight Dietrich of Dehrn – the village a mile or more upstream of the rock – who had had the misfortune to be wounded and taken prisoner by the Infidels, languished in a hot cell, longing for his wife and child, and eventually made a vow to build a church if ever he should see once more the lovely Lahn. With this pious resolve in mind he went to sleep upon the hard floor of his cell, and one can imagine how surprised he must have been to awake next morning in full sunshine under a great oak tree. Before him stood his familiar castle, and he was so delighted to be home again that he leapt to his feet, rushed into the family home and flung himself into the arms of his dear wife, who was as astonished as he, and I hope had the sense to realise her good fortune to be born in the Middle Ages, when such curious things could happen.

Dietrich of Dehrn was very, very human, and the thrill of being miraculously transported to the banks of the Lahn made him forget all about building the church he had promised. However, one day when he was out hunting he narrowly escaped being electrocuted when an oak tree beside his path was struck by lightning, and the very next day he had the work put in hand. A site was chosen on his own land, close by his castle, and the masons set to work.

Yet every piece of material would vanish overnight and be found next morning piled up on top of the rock where Lubentius had founded his chapel in the fourth century. And this was of course a much better site, except from the point of view of the people of Dehrn, who had a much longer walk to church. Dietrich lived to see the work completed, and when he died he was buried in one of the transepts.

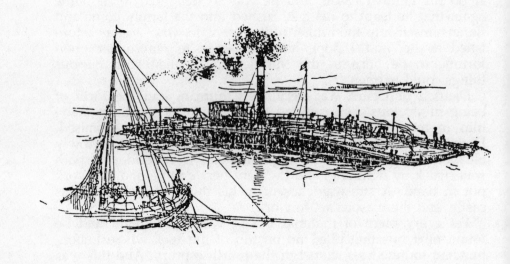

PART IV

THE UPPER RHINE TRIBUTARIES

The Upper Rhine has two navigable tributaries, the Main – now extended through to the Danube by the Rhine-Main-Danube Canal, a modern replacement of the Ludwig's Canal. But the idea of forming a link with the Danube is as old as Charlemagne, the remains of whose Fossa Carolina are still to be seen. However, lack of any means of ascertaining the levels led the monarch to abandon the attempt.

Upstream of the Main, the Neckar joins the Rhine at Mannheim. It is navigable to a short way above Stuttgart, but plans to extend it further have now been abandoned. It is fairly well used by large inland ships as far as Neckarsulm and Stuttgart.

Both these rivers are excellent cruising grounds, and flow through forested country and past villages of great beauty. Both are well supplied with vineyards which produce excellent wines.

11

The Main, Karlstadt and Rothenfels

The river Main is the most important tributary of the Rhine, into which it flows at Mainz. It is a large shipping route and flows through Frankfurt, where it noticeably changes colour. Its upper reaches, in Bavaria, pass through vineyard country (the Main wines are excellent) to reach Bamberg. At this point it was formerly joined to the Ludwig's Canal, named in honour of King Ludwig of Bavaria, and although this route to the Danube was open (with difficulty) until after the Second World War, it has now been replaced by a big-ship route, the Rhine-Main-Donau Canal. Many of the places along the river course have splendid examples of Rococo architecture, especially Würzburg.

Bamberg

Karlstadt

At the end of a narrow street stands the Gothic Town Hall, with a high gable mounting in eight steps to a belfry, below which there stands in a niche above the clock the figure of a young man with flowing locks, dressed in a gay coloured jerkin and baggy hose down to his knees, and with a smart military hat decorated with a cockade. In his right hand he holds a straight trumpet. His uniform is not that of any bygone Karlstadt militia, for in fact he was a trumpeter of the forces of Gustavus Adolphus of Sweden.

However much the Swedes may have been disliked – and not without reason – the *Schwedenmännlein* of the walled town of Karlstadt is the town hero, and it is only right that he has been given the honour of standing high above the market place, where he may continue to raise his trumpet to his lips when the hand of the clock points to the hour, for his trumpeting once saved the town, even if it cost him his life.

The story of the Little Swedish Man is probably founded on fact, and it tells how the mighty Gustavus came storming up the valley ahead of the cloud of smoke which rose from the villages his troops had sacked, and the citizens of Karlstadt were very naturally filled with alarm. They had their town walls, but they had very little inclination to suffer bombardment and siege, so very prudently they opened the gates and let the Swedish monarch enter without a shot being fired. They even invited him into the Town Hall for a beaker of wine, and the sea-green enamelled glass from which he drank is still to be seen in the council chamber.

Whilst these courtesies were taking place, elsewhere in the town love at first sight was impelling the royal trumpeter to court a beautiful girl of Karlstadt. Her name is not recorded, but whoever she may have been she was not one to resist the advances of the gallant young Swede – at least, only so far as to make a very proper bargain with him. She would be his, this heroine of Karlstadt declared, and he might come to her that very same night if he would just do one simple little thing to prove to her that he really loved her, to show her that he was not a mere unfeeling unit of licentious soldiery.

Driven by gallantry or desire, or perhaps by love, the young man said that he would do anything that she wished – as young men so frequently and foolishly do. Whatever she should ask of him, the request would be a command which he would

192

Michelstadt

not hesitate for one moment to obey. History does not relate whether he was surprised when she whispered to him that all she asked was not that he should bring her some victuals from the quarter-master's stores but just that he should take up his trumpet in the small hours of the morning and blow a signal to indicate that a force was approaching the town to relieve it.

The bargain was kept. The girl took her new-found lover to her arms, and in the middle of the night he left her to break the slumbers of the Swedes by sounding the Retreat, or the Advance, or whatever it was that conveyed the appropriate message. The tired troopers stumbled sleepily from their beds, the cavalrymen flung the saddles over their horses, the officers shouted their commands, and soon the entire Swedish contingent was issuing from the town to attack the relief column, which they believed to be approaching in the darkness. When the last of them had passed through the gateway, the burghers emerged to swing the stout gates shut and to bar and bolt them against a return. But the Swedes did not come back – at least not then, for it was not until some time later that Gustavus

193

Adolphus returned in person to supervise the improvement of the walls so that Karlstadt might become a Swedish fortress town. For the gay-hearted young trumpeter the story did not end so happily. Gustavus was not the man to treat such a matter lightly, and the unfortunate youth was hanged, but even today he is thought of with affection and gratitude by the people of Karlstadt as he raises his wooden arm to blow a mute call upon his trumpet.

Yet the town's particular pride is of a very different kind, and a modern fountain of red sandstone in the form of a pestle and mortar, set in the market place, reminds visitors that Johann Rudolph Glauber was a man of Karlstadt. Although his name is usually associated with his 'miraculous salt' (sodium sulphate), this young man who set out to tour Europe as a mirror-silverer and apothecary was in fact one of those who laid the foundations of the chemical industry. It was not theory with which Glauber was concerned, but practical experimentation, and most of his discoveries are given – if somewhat incompletely – in his *Furni Novi Philosphici*, which was actually an instruction handbook on building laboratory furnaces but also gave the rough outlines of the experiments which a chemist might carry out with them. From this book, which had a great influence on Robert Boyle, it is clear that Glauber had discovered much about the preparation of metallic salts, and that he had prepared benzol and phenol, acetone, strychnine and morphine, nearly 200 years before these organic substances were again to be isolated. He also showed the effect upon crops of an artificial fertilizer (potassium nitrate), and the manufacture of nitric and hydrochloric acids is even today carried out by the process he developed.

A kindly man, tolerant in matters of religion and even when his first wife was unfaithful to him, Glauber's life was one of misfortune. After hard years in the Netherlands he removed to Bremen, but he was soon obliged to flee from the city on account of his debts, and he set off by ship up the Weser to reach Kassel on the Fulda and from thence cross by wagon to the Main at Hanau, bringing his wife and children, his furniture, books and laboratory apparatus with him. Continuing again by ship, he landed at Wertheim to establish his laboratory, but very soon he was to be evicted by his landlord. He moved on up the river to Kitzingen, where he again founded his laboratory. Soon he was engaged in quarrels with another chemist, to whom he had sold certain of his recipes, and he became even more secretive than he had been before.

It may have been such experiences which led Glauber to announce as his maxim the principle, 'Do not all that thou canst; say not all that thou knowest; believe not all that thou hearest.' Certainly he lived up to the second part of it, for he tended to keep to himself some vital detail of any chemical process and only release it under licence and against payment. This may sound a very mercenary procedure, but it must be remembered that Glauber was not an alchemist working in the pay (or perhaps in the prison) of a wealthy patron, and he could only support his research laboratory and his assistants out of the takings. Nevertheless, the secrecy was strongly disapproved of by Boyle, who very much criticised the way he described the preparation of sodium sulphate from salt by 'pouring in A', without saying what 'A' might be. (Boyle repeated the experiment and rightly concluded that 'A' was sulphuric acid). But if Robert Boyle found Glauber's experiments 'described so darkly and ambiguously that it is not easy to know with any certainty what he means,' he himself had no need to sell his discoveries, for he lived in great affluence upon a private income of several thousand pounds a year. And even if he disapproved, he recognised the remarkable ability of the Franconian chemist and read his works as soon as he could obtain them.

Glauber eventually returned to Holland, and it was his horror at the sufferings of the Dutch sailors on their voyages to the East Indies which led him to perform the experiments which were published in his book *Trost der Seefahrenten* (The Navigators' Comfort), a work in which he recommended various remedies for hunger, thirst, and scurvy. He prescribed a malt extract from which a beer-like drink could be made by sailors, and he prepared experimentally a kind of dried biscuit-bread which was concentrated and yet would not become mouldy. He even attempted to tackle the age-old problem of how to make fresh water from the sea.

But Glauber's health was already declining, and during the last ten years of his life he was to suffer terribly from mercuric or arsenical poisoning, contracted during his experiments. Racked with pain, and often vomiting blood, he was at last unable to leave his bed and he could only direct others to carry out experiments for him. Eventually he was obliged to dismiss his assistants and even to sell his books and apparatus in order to have the means to feed himself and his family. He died in poverty at Amsterdam, in 1670.

Rothenfels

Rothenfels (Redcliff) lies three miles upstream of the pottery village of Hafenlohr, and is one of the most dramatic sights of the middle Main. Below the barrage the actual village itself turns only its less attractive side towards the stream, and it is when one is first ashore that one finds just what a wealth of pretty houses lies along the village street. Behind it the great cliff of red sandstone from which the village takes its name stands squarely to form a backcloth for the houses, and before the canalisation of the Main a finger of the same cliffside lay submerged in midstream to form a red and rocky reef which was such a menace to shipping that it has since been dynamited to increase the breadth and depth of the fairway. The village itself is one of fishers rather than shippers, and its Guild of Fishermen was already flourishing nearly a hundred years before the twelfth-century castle was built at the very top of the rock face to protect the village at its foot. The ascent to the castle is a steep one, more than 300 steps zigzagging up the face of the cliff, and by the wayside there is a *Bildstock*, showing the figure of a young woman praying, and glancing up towards a ray of light.

Pillars, richly wrought or plain, tall or short and stumpy, sandstone crosses, even occasionally a gallows such as the double-pillared one at Wörth through which the wild ghostly army is said to rush shrieking in the dark – these curious mementos of bygone times are a familiar feature of the Franconian countryside, and one finds them at crossroads, by the side of a vineyard pathway, or standing alone in a field or deep in the forest. The crosses – not calvaries, but plain crosses of stone – are usually set at the site of a murder. The old Germanic law demanded compensation from the killer, usually in an agreed sum of money, and if this were not forthcoming a blood feud would begin which might continue for generations. The coming of Christianity substituted an emphasis on prayers for the soul of the murdered man to be offered by his killer, and after the cash value of the slain had been agreed the guilty man had also to erect a cross, or sometimes a chapel or other memorial, either at the scene of the crime or at some other more prominent point which the victim's relatives might select.

When in the sixteenth century killing became punishable by hanging, the form of the memorials changed. Until then it was the killer who had been responsible for the monument, and he rarely had any great inclination to inscribe upon it his own name and the details of what he had done. But now that the cross or other memorial was erected by the family of the victim, details of the crime and its perpetrator were usually added.

So common are these murder-marks, penitence stones and the like that a single vineyard wall in the Tauber valley has no less than 14 of them built into it, but the *Bildstock* is more often to be seen standing in its original position. It is a memorial which consists of a pillar, sometimes simple but often beautifully carved, ending in a top-piece which will probably have a cross or a group of angels on one of its faces, and on another perhaps something representative either of the dead person, or of the event which happened there. It is not necessarily a reminder that one man met his death at the hands of another, for it may commemorate any form of sudden death, such as falling from a horse. Or perhaps a village girl returning from a country dance was so terrified by the sounds of the forest that she ran, stumbled, and fell to her death. A *Bildstock* near Zwingenberg is on the spot where seven musicians were killed by lightning when sheltering under a tree, and it specifically warns the traveller not to do so.

A *Bildstock* on the path from Rothenfels to Hafenlohr begs the passer-by to say a prayer for the poor soul of the victim, that his sins may be forgiven. This memorial dates only from 1844, and it relates to the death of a tanner of Rothenfels who had gone into the forest for a pleasant evening's poaching when a gamekeeper came upon the scene. The tanner took to his heels, but without warning him in any way the gamekeeper fired and shot him dead. Where the man fell, the stone was put up as a warning to all those who might be tempted to fire on their fellows as though they were rats or other vermin. Its erection had a curious sequel, for more than 20 years later the gamekeeper concerned in the incident shot himself and was found dead beside the *Bildstock*, which no doubt had always brought back to him the memory of what he had done, the recollection so preying on his mind that he at last took his own life.

It is not always a violent death which is commemorated in this way, and the memorial beside the steps leading to the Castle of Rothenfels, which shows the young woman and a shaft of light, has a very different origin. This stone was put up by a Jewish girl who had wished to adopt the Catholic faith, but was fearful of the anger of her family. On that spot, it is said, she stopped to pray in her bewilderment as to how she should live if she were to be turned out of her family home, penniless. A ray of light struck her as she prayed, and she heard a voice assuring her that she would gain something of far greater value than all her earthly possessions. So, leaving her home, she became a Christian and was taken in and cared for by her fellows in the church community.

Occasionally the origin of a *Bildstock* is less easily made out. There is one in the Spessart which baldly declares that it was 'erected in 1705 by the salt-carriers to the honour of the crucified Lord'. One account suggests that a salt-carrier fell and was trampled upon by the pack-animals, yet survived; another that it commemorates the safe and unexpected arrival of the carriers after a journey across several customs areas where they might well have expected to be robbed officially of much of their goods and money. Another stone, set in a little shrine, reminds one (if one happens to have heard the tale, for there are no details upon the *Bildstock* itself) of how a young farmer's lad, returning home at dusk, heard screams in the forest, and hastening to the spot found two girls being savagely attacked by a wolf. He rushed to their assistance and beat the animal off with his stick, and when later he and one of the girls were married they together put up the little shrine in gratitude.

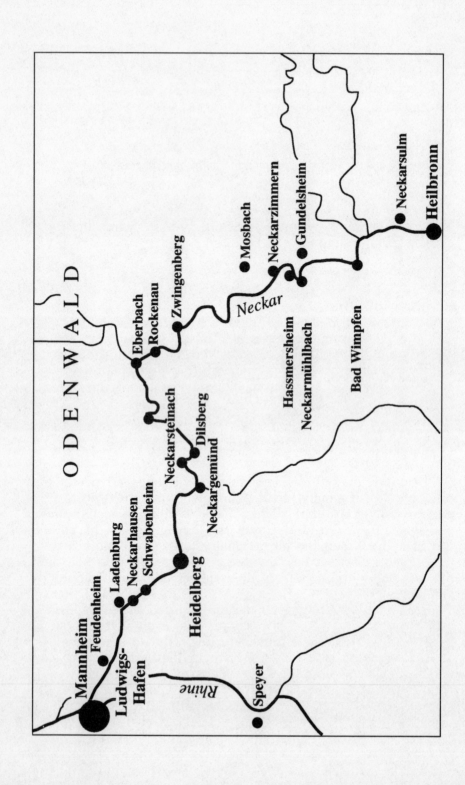

12

The Neckar, Heidelberg, Ladenburg, Gundelsheim, Hirschhorn and Neckarsulm

The river Neckar flows into the Rhine in Mannheim docks. It is known far and wide from the student song,

Ich hab' mein Herz in Heidelberg verloren,
In Heidelberg am Neckarstrand....

And certainly Heidelberg is one of the world's leading universities. But the river has patches of industry too, such as NSU at Neckarsulm. It eventually reaches Plochingen, at the edge of Stuttgart, 202km up from Mannheim. It is a popular river with canoeists, winding to and fro along the edge of the Spessart Forest.

Heidelberg

So famous is the city of Heidelberg, from song and poetry and on account of the many great figures who have held posts at its ancient University, that visitors flock to it in their thousands, and few dare to go home until they have climbed the path to the castle and seen the gigantic wine-tuns. On a more learned note, the main street has a statue of the great Dr Bunsen, with the burner without which no school laboratory would be complete.

Heidelberg must be one of the most visited places of Europe, and a most attractive city it certainly is, even if it is now no longer only a quiet little university town. But to see Heidelberg at its best one must cross the river in the early evening, and climb the narrow winding alley steps of the Schlangenweg to the height of the Philosophers' Walk and look out across the Neckar to where the ruins of the magnificent Castle stand out from the trees on the hill above the Church of the Holy Ghost.

Below, the mellow tiled roofs are fading in the evening haze of woodsmoke, but if one has chosen just the right moment and the proper meteorological conditions, the rosy sandstone of the ruined wings of the castle glows warm and radiant in the last rays of light before the sun slides behind the hill and a sombre shadow falls across the view.

Though wistfully beautiful, the Castle of Heidelberg is only a faint shadow of its former glory, and even the magnificent formal gardens are but a fragment of those that were laid out by Friedrich V for his Stuart bride, Elizabeth, the daughter of James I. Although the castle capitulated to Louis XIV and was promised immunity, the retreating French forces blew up many of its finest buildings, and on their return four years later burned down most of the remainder during a drunken orgy. The loss to the city was tragic, and yet the Protestant Kurfürsts of the Palatinate seem to have accepted the disaster with resignation, viewing it as divine judgement on their line for the deed of their forebear Ludwig III who, at the Council of Constance, had ordered John Huss to be burned.

Without a dinghy one can reach the Philosopher's Walk by crossing the Old Bridge at the foot of the lock. Foolishly destroyed by the German army in 1945, this most beautiful of all the Neckar bridges has since been rebuilt in its original eighteenth-century form, a costly undertaking on the part of the citizens but certainly a wise one, for its six high arches of the same rosy stone of the Odenwald complete the beauty of Heidelberg in a way that no other bridge could have done. The Elector, Carl Theodor, who was originally responsible for building it, still stands proudly on a buttress on the townward side, whilst Pallas Athene watches over the Neuenheim end of the crossing. Beyond her, near the foot of the Schlangenweg, stands a statue of St John the Nepomucene, or Jan of Pomuk.

The figure of this Bohemian priest is more usually to be found right over the arch of a bridge, for he happens to be the patron saint of bridges – and also of those in danger of drowning if they fall in. The Nepomuk is probably the only saint to have a halo with a specific gravity of less than 1.0, and in confirmation of this unusual property it is said that when he was flung into the river Vltava at Prague his halo with five stars not only appeared as he sank, but actually floated.

As chaplain to the Queen of Bohemia, Jan of Pomuk incurred the wrath of her husband, King Wenceslas IV, a ruler who seems to have begun his reign moderately enough but to have turned tyrant and drunkard after an unsuccessful attempt had been made to poison him. It was to Jan that the Queen turned for advice in the constant work of caring for the sick and the poor in the city, and as her confessor he was naturally enough her trusted confidant. But, as so often happens, heavy drinking led the King to imagine that his Queen was guilty of all manner of deceptions and, knowing that she would have revealed them to her confessor, he summoned Jan and demanded to know the secrets entrusted to him in the confessional. Probably there were none, but Jan did not argue that particular point. He merely declared that he could not break his trust, upon which Wenceslas threatened him without avail, and then had him beaten, imprisoned, starved, and tortured. It was only the intervention of the Queen that saved his life – for a while.

Jan of Pomuk continued to serve the Queen, but one day the King, in a fit of inebriate fury, seized and tortured almost the entire clergy of Prague. He reserved his special wrath for the Queen's confessor; yet even when burned with red-hot irons Jan courageously refused to speak, whereupon he was dragged through the streets of Prague, horribly burned and mutilated. At the bridge his head was tied to his feet and, with his hands bound and his mouth forced open with a block of wood, he was flung from the parapet, to the cheers of his royal master. It was then, the story tells, that the halo with five stars rose to the surface and floated away down the river towards the Elbe.

Ladenburg

One of the more curious structures in Ladenburg is a turreted and machicolated four-square structure which looks very much like a keep to which the local people might have driven their cattle when threatened by raiders. In fact it is the oldest garage in the world, for it was built by Carl Benz to accommodate his horseless carriages in suitably impressive style. Perhaps the most beautiful of all the buildings is the local museum, a fine Renaissance house with carved galleries open to the street. And here it is not the remains of the Celts or Romans or Jesuits which attract attention so much as a yard or more of heavy chain hanging from a nail in a beam. This is a short length of the famous *Kette*, preserved for posterity when the chain was collected from the river in 1935 and taken away to be melted down – the end of a curious chapter in the history of the Neckar valley. It was to this chain that the famous Lion of Handschuhsheim was tethered.

The village of Handschuhsheim lies at the very edge of the foothills of the Odenwald and is now continuous with the suburbs of Heidelberg. Local tradition relates that it was there, on a spring day, that was heard the growling of a ferocious beast, somewhere down in the valley beyond the woods. It was generally known that a circus was playing at Mannheim, a mere ten miles away, and the people of Handschuhsheim at once realised that a lion, or possibly several, had escaped from the cages and was roving up the valley, tearing to pieces every living thing in its path. As the roaring of the beast and the screams of its terrified victims grew continually louder, the women and children were ordered to lock themselves in their houses for safety, whilst the less timid of the men armed themselves with pitchforks, flails, scythes and such implements of battle as their houses could furnish, and set off through the woods under the leadership of a gamekeeper.

The sound of the fearful beast grew louder as the men marched towards the Neckar, ready if need be to die in the jaws of the lion rather than have their loved ones devoured by the raging animal. But when at last they emerged from the trees where the open fields led down to the river bank, they stopped short. Creeping up the valley was no carnivore but a curious ship, a long black vessel with smoke belching from its two slender funnels set side by side. Behind it a string of barges hung in the current, and the roars and screams were no more than the creaks and groans of the winches and capstans on the monster's deck as it clawed its way up the Neckar by hauling a chain out of the water below its bow, passing it round drums and pulleys to drop it into the river once more at the stern. The creature was in fact the first of the seven *Kettenschiffe* or chain-ships of the newly formed Neckar Chain-Towage Company.

The intrepid hunters dispersed and made their way back to the village, where no doubt their womenfolk were greatly relieved to know that any immediate danger of death was past. But the tale of their sortie could not be kept from others in the neighbourhood, and one of the chain-ships was promptly given the name of *Hendsemer Löb*, dialect for *Handschuhsheimer Löwe*, or the *Lion of Handschuhsheim*. Another was to be known as the *Neckaresel*, or donkey, on account of the braying sounds which it emitted, and although these intriguing vessels are no longer in existence, the traveller who is curious to know just what they were like can see an excellent picture of one of them painted on the outside wall of the ferryman's cottage at Zwingenberg, further up the river. Or, if he prefers to drink a glass of wine in the *'zum Kettenboot'* at Eberbach, he can see there a model of one of these curious beasts of the river.

The chain-system was not an invention of the Neckar valley. It

205

had already been used on many other waterways where the course was tortuous and shallow and unsuited to screw or paddle-ships, or where other special conditions made it a particularly suitable means of propulsion – as on three watershed levels of French canals, and in the Ham tunnel on the Meuse, where there was so strong a current that poling was impossible and where the lack of a tow-path in the tunnel prevented the use of horses. Besides, theoretical calculations showed that where the gradient was steeper than 1 in 3,300, chain-towage was the most economical form of haulage – even if not the most convenient, particularly when the chain parted and the ends had to be recovered with grappling irons and linked up again by the smiths aboard the chain-ship. For these various reasons, at one time or another chains were in use on the Seine, on the Rhine between Bonn and Bingen, and on the Elbe. This last was 407 miles long, and it was laid in a single piece from Hamburg to Usti in Czechoslovakia.

Gundelsheim

The Hornberg or Götzenburg is generally connected with the rough and turbulent character of Götz von Berlichingen, who spent many years of honourable confinement within the walls of the castle which still stands as a romantic ruin, looking out defiantly over the sweep of the Neckar towards its tight loop below Gundelsheim. It was here that he wrote the memoirs upon which Goethe drew when he wrote *Götz von Berlichingen*, or *The Knight with the Iron Hand*. The bluff and doughty Götz was perhaps the most famous political character the Neckar valley was ever to know, and in the hands of Goethe he was to be shaped into an even more glamorous and heroic figure than in fact he was.

As the tenth child of his parents, Gottfried von Berlichingen could have no hope of a stake in the family estate at Jagsthausen, and the inheritance due to him was paid out in cash. Leaving home, he joined the forces of the Emperor Maximilian at the early age of 17, and when he was only 24 he lost his right hand in battle. The smith in his home village of Jagsthausen forged for him his famous hand of iron, which is still to be seen there in the family castle, and which was provided with such an ingenious mechanism that its owner was still able to ride and to fight. And the young Götz was certainly of a restive, warlike

206

Gundelsheim

nature; although he himself was not actually a robber knight, he aided one of the more notorious ones, and he indulged in sufficient raiding and quarrelling of his own for the Emperor to be forced to outlaw him.

In 1512 he was deprived of all his rights, and even his marriage was dissolved by the official declaration, which stated that his consort was now a widow, and his children orphans, his inheritance and property forfeited to his children, his body and flesh to the beasts of the forest and the birds of the air. Where every other man enjoyed peace and company on the high road, he would by right have none, and he was 'directed into the four corners of the world in the name of the devil'. For Götz this was a severe blow. He lost his property, but within two years he managed to buy himself free of the proscription with a heavy sum. Yet for him to change his spots was impossible and he soon became involved in further quarrels, most of which stemmed from a curious sense of rough justice, and a hatred of the duplicity and intrigue which marked the dealings of so many of the aristocracy.

In 1517 Götz bought the castle of Hornberg on the Neckar, and he had not long been there when the Peasants' Revolt broke out. Rising against the bishops and landowners, the farmers and labourers advanced to the Neckar, burning and destroying and torturing as they went, and when they had taken Gundelsheim a short way upstream of Götz's new seat at Hornberg, the massed rebels realised that they could not hope to win the struggle unless they had an experienced and competent commander. They there and then decided that Götz should lead them and, advancing upon the Hornberg, they announced their decision. At first their chosen general declined the honour, but as the only alternative was that he should be slaughtered in his own castle he gave in, and no doubt he was not altogether averse to assisting in the destruction of some of the enemies he detested.

After four bloody weeks, during which the relations between the thick-headed peasantry and their appointed leader were often extremely strained, the revolt was crushed. The landowners had won, and the end of feudal days was deferred for centuries. Götz was put on trial, and the statement made in his defence reads curiously like that made by many before the De-Nazification courts four centuries later. He had not wanted to help, but on the other hand he had not particularly wished to be disembowelled for refusing. In such a situation, what else could he have done? What could any man have done? And although he had joined the party, he had of course tried to temper its violence with wisdom, and if there had admittedly been atrocities might things not have been infinitely worse if he had not acted as he had, and exercised his restraining influence?

Götz lay for two years in prison, but he was sentenced to 'retirement' in his castle of Hornberg. He might not go out, nor was he to mount a horse. He continued, however, to quarrel, particularly with the town of Mosbach, but throughout ten frustrating years he served his sentence honourably enough to be pardoned by the Emperor, whom later he served in campaigns in France and against the Turks.

Hirschhorn

In the seventeenth century Friedrich von und zu Hirschhorn died without leaving an heir. In 1770, when work was being carried out on the walls of the castle of Handschuhsheim, there came to light a cavity in which were found the remains of a knight in richly decorated armour bearing the marks of sword blows, and though his identity has never been established, there is no doubt at all that he had been walled up alive. Sixty years after this discovery, workmen repairing the castle of Hirschhorn came upon a lady's shoe, and excavating the wall they discovered the standing skeleton of a young woman who had been similarly buried alive within the masonry. The two finds confirmed a strong local tradition that a member of each family had been punished in this barbarous way for an illicit union, and that a Carmelite friar had once told a local hermit that he was sworn to secrecy as to details, but that the hermit, who had been a foundling boy, would find the bones of his mother within the castle of Hirschhorn.

Leonard, the foundling, had in fact been brought up by the Carmelites, who had taught him to read and write and also trained him as a joiner, and connecting his own existence with the tradition of the pair of lovers walled up in the two castles (and whose remains had not then come to light), he repeatedly wandered both to Hirschhorn and to Handschuhsheim, begging permission to carve memorials to his mother and his father. His entreaties were not well received – perhaps because to have granted his wish would have been an admission that there was more than mere legend in the tale of the victims – and both Friedrich von Hirschhorn and his relative Johann von Handschuhsheim turned the man away from their gates.

Of Leonard the hermit little more is known, except that he is said to have built the six coffins for the band of musicians who were drowned with the ferryman when crossing the river by night after playing at Freidrich von Hirschhorn's wedding feast up at the castle. It may of course have been the Hakenmann who was responsible for the disaster, but more probably the ferryman had drunk too freely at the party. So, perhaps, had the minstrels. But whatever the cause, as they crossed the swift passage below the village, playing on their instruments, in the light of the moon, their boat was overset and all were drowned.

This tragedy might well have marked the wedding as ill-starred. And so it proved. Both the Hirschhorns and the Handschuhsheims had already been in danger of dying out for lack of heirs, and it is possible that the walling-up of the lovers had been intended in some way to put matters right, for such a practice was often regarded as favourable to the birth of boys. But however that may be, Freidrich von Hirschhorn, who was to be the last but certainly the greatest member of his family, had tragedy enough hanging over his head. When he was hardly 20 years old he attended a party at Heidelberg with his uncle, the lord of Handschuhsheim, who was about the same age as himself. On this occasion the Elector Friedrich V presented von Handschuhsheim with an ornamental dagger, and for some reason Hirschhorn coveted this gift – and perhaps the special esteem which it implied. The two men became involved in a quarrel, and that same night they drew swords on each other in the marketplace of Heidelberg. Handschuhsheim, the only heir of his line, was slightly wounded, but the cut became gangrenous and three weeks later he died of blood-poisoning. His mother, Hirschhorn's own grandmother, called upon his attacker and cursed his house that he, too, might die without an heir.

Judged by his fellow nobles, Hirschhorn was ordered to expiate his deed with a considerable sum of money to support needy students at Heidelberg, and this he willingly did. In fact, he was so overcome by remorse that he devoted much of his life to charitable works. He was a model landlord for his days, and apart from his own manors and his properties in Bruchsal and Heilbronn he owned more than 100 villages in the Neckar valley. These he managed with such wise political skill that not one of them was destroyed in the wars of religion which raged through the land – for this was the time of the Thirty Years War. Yet the guilt for his uncle's death could never leave him, and it was in vain that he married twice and had a considerable number of children with each wife. Every one of his sons fell a victim either to Tilly's Spanish cavalry, or to sickness. The last of his boys died in infancy in 1632. With resignation Friedrich von Hirschhorn retired to his seat at Heilbronn, drew up a will in which he disposed of his possessions to the benefit of his many subjects, and died within a few weeks.

Neckarsulm

Bad Wimpfen is a resort. On the outskirts it now has saline baths, mud packs, massage, diet, breathing exercises, and everything necessary to attract the sick and the hypochondriac, but tucked away behind the palace of Barbarossa and his successors is the most perfect town of timbered houses to be found anywhere along the Neckar. Most of it dates from after the Thirty Years War, when nine-tenths of the town was destroyed and the place was so impoverished that the wealthy burghers of Nuremberg generously presented the citizens with a new tower for its walls. There was, however, a limit to their magnanimity, for the little Nürnberger Turm with its tiny half-timbered turret has the appearance of having been built several sizes too small. Some of the exquisite houses in the alleys are thin and pinched, as though there was no place to put them, whilst others in the main street reach to seven storeys and perhaps reflect the rich prosperity which was to follow when Wimpfen recovered from fire and plague and poverty.

Opposite Wimpfen the Jagst and the Kocher both add their waters to the Neckar, and a short way further ahead the navigation leaves the river for a while and passes up two or three miles of canal to enter Neckarsulm, a busy manufacturing town but also one of viticulture, for the hills behind it produce as good a wine as the Neckar can furnish. Close behind the quay stands another castle of the Hochmeister of the Teutonic Order, the windows of its square tower decked out with shutters in herringbone stripes. And if the Knights of the Teutonic Order have vanished, their castle is very well worth a visit, for it is now the Two-Wheeler Museum. Once in a year, at Whitsun, its curious inmates are allowed out of their knightly hall to join with other veterans, horseless carriages as well as two-wheelers, in a rally which is Germany's equivalent of the London to Brighton run.

Oldest among the venerable pioneers of the road now stabled in the castle is the machine of the Freiherr von Drais of Karlsruhe, a mere frame and two wheels without anything so elaborate as pedals or brakes, and formed by dismembering a handcart, which also provided the steering handle. In the course of time the notion of having a brake seemed desirable, and the earliest form was worked by the handle of a coffee-grinder borrowed from the kitchen quarters and mounted amidships. Then came the day when a French gentleman whose boy had rickets commissioned a coach-builder to design a two-wheeler for the lad to use, and this model was such a success that Napoleon III also ordered one for his son, and thus the cycle achieved status as something which the top people might ride. In fact it became such a rage at court that a score were built for the families of the top 20, and the first cycle factory of the world came into being.

It was shortly afterwards that the link between sewing-machines and bicycles was forged. Adam Opel, a maker of sewing-machines, ordered five English bicycles as Christmas presents for his five sons. No doubt the boys were thrilled, but their excitement was to be short-lived, for Papa decided to try one of them for himself, and whilst his servants held the

211

machine steady he swung himself over the frame and gave the signal for launching. Alas, he crashed, and deciding that the toys were too dangerous for his youngsters, he ordered all five bicycles to be removed at once and sold.

The Opel boys, however, had seen enough to want to own cycles themselves, and banding together they ordered a five-seater, a model of which is in the Neckarsulm Museum. Although it must have been much more difficult to ride than a single-seater model, the Opel boys became so proficient that even their father saw that cycling was not necessarily a lethal occupation. It was then that his sons pointed out to him that to be a maker of sewing-machines was not without its dangers either. Poor father, when he travelled about the country selling his mechanical stitchers, was he not frequently stoned by textile workers who saw in his inventions a threat to their livelihood? Why, if he made bicycles as well, he could at least sell these safely without a riot. Adam Opel was soon convinced. He started a bicycle department, from which the modern Opel works were eventually to be developed.

Perhaps sewing-machines and cycles are basically more similar than one might think, for one has only to recall the names of several of the world's makers to notice that they have graduated from the one to the other, and thence to automobiles. Daimler was not a sewing-machine man, but Christian Schmidt was one – or, more precisely, he had a workshop on an island in the Danube valley in which he constructed knitting-machines, the power for the machine tools being provided by a water wheel. As trade expanded, the island site was too small to meet his needs, and he moved to Neckarsulm. Penny-farthings were now making their appearance on the streets, and in his new mechanical workshop Schmidt began to manufacture these too. Many years later his establishment was to become famous as the NSU works, the name being merely an abbreviation of Neckarsulm. Chassis for horseless carriages were the next introduction, and these were delivered to Herr Gottlieb Daimler, who fitted them with his ingenious internal combustion engines. Eighty years after Schmidt settled in Neckarsulm, the NSU works was employing 6000 men and women, many of them from the wine-growing villages of the hills around the town.

Lübeck. The Schiffergesellschaft

PART V

THE DORTMUND-EMS CANAL AND CONNECTIONS

The Dortmund-Ems Canal links the Ruhr area with the River Ems, and thus with the sea at Emden. It was constructed largely to supply the Kaiser's warships with coal, but nowadays it serves more general purposes. It is notable for the lift at Henrichenburg, replaced by a new one in recent years, but after great efforts the old one, a splendid model of iron-age engineering, appears to have been saved.

The canal has innumerable connections (see map), the most important of which is the Mittelland Canal, crossing the country from west to east and giving a connection with other waterways on its way to Berlin, and thence to Poland. This canal crosses the Weser (with which it connects by a very deep 'shaft lock' at Minden) on an aqueduct of large proportions. Built in the Hitler years, the canal – which has no locks in 100 kilometres – was drained dry when the aqueduct at Minden was blown up during the Second World War.

The crossing at Minden divides the Weser into the Upper and Middle rivers. The Upper Weser flows through the Weserbergland, and notably by Hamelin. The Middle Weser flows through somewhat uninteresting country, once the homeland of the English Georges, whose arms can be seen in the 'By Appointment' signs of shops in such places as Verden on the Aller. From Bremen to the sea the river is known as the Lower Weser.

The navigation of the Upper Weser is tricky, and the current swift; but it leads to the Fulda, a short stretch of river leading to Kassel.

The Elbe-Trave Canal leads from the Elbe at Lauenburg to Lübeck, and the sea at Travemünde. This is an easy way to reach the Danish islands and Sweden.

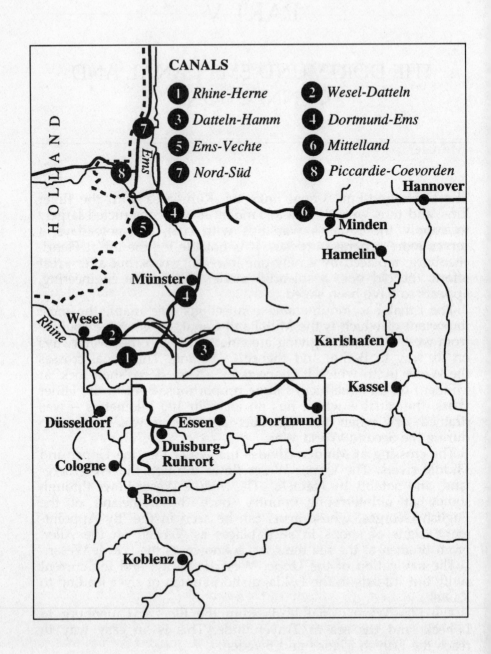

CANALS

1	*Rhine-Herne*	**2**	*Wesel-Datteln*
3	*Datteln-Hamm*	**4**	*Dortmund-Ems*
5	*Ems-Vechte*	**6**	*Mittelland*
7	*Nord-Süd*	**8**	*Piccardie-Coevorden*

13

*Münster, Bodenwerder, Hamelin, Hannoversch Münden,
Kassel, Mölln, and Lübeck*

Münster

John of Leiden rose from tailor's apprentice in the Netherlands to
King of the Realm of Righteousness, the capital of which was to
be Münster (now on the Dortmund–Ems Canal). Even before he
arrived to take up his short reign his chief prophet had been
preaching the new order, and lest any should think that the rule
was to be oppressive, this *Wederdoper* or Anabaptist leader
offered the good people of Münster absolute freedom of choice.
They might choose to be rebaptised or exiled or slaughtered.
Some opted for baptism, but many families were stripped of their
belongings and driven from the city. Those who remained were
soon to find that another baptism had not bought them very
much in the way of freedom, for all valuables and provisions
were forfeited. The last straw was the compulsory polygamy.

The Anabaptist King of Münster was at least a practical man.
His leading theological adviser preached so eloquently against
the monastic system that the nuns streamed from the convents
and were soon found to outnumber the dissident monks and the
bachelors among the townsfolk by three to one. John of Leiden
solved the problem by having a vision in which he saw that
polygamy was not only something for David and Solomon and
other Old Testament heroes, but the immediate will of God for
sixteenth-century Münster. Refusal to renounce a former
marriage and take other wives was promptly made a capital
offence. A smith of the town led a spirited revolt, but he and his
followers were obliged to surrender to the cannon of the king,
and all were beheaded.

John of Leiden certainly did what he could to find a husband
for every surplus spinster, and he inaugurated the new era by
choosing as his own wives the first 16 among Münster's young
beauties. One of them had the courage to suggest to him that he

217

was living on the fat of the land while the poor starved, and he promptly sliced off her head with the special sword which he kept handy 'to wish poor sinners to eternal life'. Then he led his remaining 15 in a dance around the corpse, and after that there was no more trouble in the hen run. Yet the kingdom of Polygamous Righteousness could not last for ever. The city was blockaded, and its skilled defence by John of Leiden – who demolished the church steeples to form artillery platforms – only added to the starvation and misery. The incident ended in the smoke of burning fat which drifted across the market-place of Münster, where the executioners heated their implements at the bellows.

Even more famous than its period of Anabaptism is Münster's Town Hall, and there can be no doubt that it was long the most glorious Gothic building of its kind in the world. Its famous façade collapsed into the street of the Prinzipalmarkt during one of the air raids of the Second World War, and so did the entire market of splendid gabled merchants' houses with their attractive colonnades. All this has since been rebuilt in an imaginative combination of ancient and modern, and the Town Hall itself has been restored in very much of its original form.

The Town Hall is an object of pilgrimage for every Dutchman, for it was there that his country was officially born. During the Thirty Years War Europe was aflame from end to end, but two cities were declared open and neutral. The one was Osnabrück and the other Münster, and it was natural enough that these two places should become the venue for the scores of plenipotentiaries and their retinues, who settled down to the long task of hammering out a stable constitution for Europe. For five years the delegates met in the council chambers at Münster, and as this was before the days of walk-outs and press conferences and shoe-beating on the desks, they succeeded in reaching agreement and the Peace of Westphalia was signed. Master Gerard Terborch attended at Münster to paint the scene, and one of his pictures shows the reading of the preliminary Treaty of Münster, which crowned the 80 years' struggle of the United Provinces of the Netherlands to free themselves from the Spanish yoke.

Bodenwerder

Like any respectable German locality, the shipbuilding town of Bodenwerder is good for you. It has a mineral spring with such an admirable content of iodide, chloride and sulphate that it is said to be excellent for extending the blood vessels, stimulating metabolism, and rejuvenating the cells. Hardening of the arteries is particularly likely to abate after a holiday at Bodenwerder, it is said, and vegetative neuroses (whatever they might be) are as good as finished. I have not tried inhaling cold fog or drinking the water, for any hardening of the heart that I might have been suffering from would have been more radically cured by reading once again the delightful tales of the Lord of Bodenwerder, whose cheery figure, spurred and booted, seated on a flying cannonball and waving his three-cornered hat in a gesture of welcome, looks down upon the ships passing under the town bridge.

The fame of this unrivalled spinner of yarns has for long been almost as great as that of Hamelin's rat-catcher, but in recent years his name has become known in a new and more restricted sense, for it has been attached to the typically twentieth-century disease known as *Münchhausen's Syndrome* – usually incorrectly spelled as Münchausen's by the medical profession, which is not always very literate. Münchhausen patients are not very common, but a mere hundred or two can keep doctors, nurses, anaesthetists, medical superintendents, almoners, surgeons, night porters and hospital visitors remarkably busy. They may be physically healthy, but they will be experts in consciously and subconsciously simulating the symptoms either of some serious condition, or of violent injury.

The typical Münchhausener, male or female, arrives gasping on the hospital doorstep in the middle of the night, doubled up as though wrestling with internal agonies, or even dripping with blood. Nurses rush to assist, the surgeon is called, the theatre prepared, and the doctor on night duty listens to a gasped tale of fits and haemorrhages, or temporary paralysis. If the doctor is very fortunate one of the nurses may recognise the patient as an old hand at the game, or the quantity of scars and slashes already decorating the abdomen may cause him to pause and wonder if there can really be anything left to remove, but if he is less lucky he will swallow the bait and get to work with scalpel and needle.

The sole aim and object is to get into hospital, and for this the Münchhausener is often willing to undergo serious operations, or treatment which others would do much to avoid. It is not just a question of free board and lodging – this can be more easily obtained by a little petty larceny – and probably there are

219

almost as many reasons as there are patients. Hospital is no bad place in which to escape a police search, and there may also be access to drugs. A real or imagined grudge against doctors and nurses in general will cause some people to spend their entire lives trying to cause them extra work and trouble, and a few cranks feel they have been swindled by the Welfare State if they have not had all the most expensive treatments which the money of others can buy for them. Others just like to be the centre of attention, and if they have failed for 20 years to make a mark in any other way, then at least they can become problems.

Some of these curious customers are known to have visited hundreds of hospitals, not always in the same country; and it is this travelling tendency, combined with the extraordinary yarn-spinning talent, which has given them their name, for both these qualities were highly developed in Baron Hieronymus von Münchhausen, Lord of Bodenwerder. And yet the naming after him of this odd condition is particularly unfair to that splendid character, whose charming half-timbered residence lies at the upstream edge of the little town, for he told his tales not to obtain comfort, nor even for publication, but merely to while away the long winter evenings over a round or two of punch or Tokay shared with his friends and neighbours. One of the rooms of the manor is set out as a museum where the usual pathetic relics of a literary man are to be seen, but the scene is enlivened by the fact that an American bullet in the Second World War shattered one of the Baron's vital certificates, and by the murals which recall some of the most famous of his tales – the flight on the cannonball, his adventures in the Turkish campaign, and others.

Münchhausen was only 12 years old when he was appointed page to Prince Anton Ulrich of Brunswick, who was to become the tragic victim of a political marriage into the family of the Czar and was to die in prison after 33 years of captivity. It was through his patron that the young Münchhausen came to know Russia, to fight in campaigns in Finland and Turkey, and to have sufficient experience of Russian court life to prompt his remarkable imagination to such delicious absurdities. He was a born storyteller, and all his life he would relate in the course of conversation the most splendid and apparently serious but nevertheless understandable adventures.

Once when he was at a banquet in Hannover, some of the young aristocrats present were boasting at table of their gallan-tries to the ladies with whom they had been out on a sledging party. Münchhausen remarked that this sort of sledging was a mere nothing. One should just see the way they sledged at the court of St Petersburg. He knew all about it because the Tsarevich had personally invited him, he said, and he went on to describe in detail the royal sledge which was so large that it carried a ballroom and audience chamber, and had so extensive a platform that after a fresh fall of snow the courtiers would take their ladies for promenades upon it in smaller sledges. And when, only a few days before his death, the old woman who looked after him in his final years noticed that he had two toes missing – they had been frostbitten in Russia – he briefly informed her that they had been bitten off by a polar bear he was chasing.

Hamelin (Hameln)

What became of the rats? Much depends upon whether there were any. One must not be misled by the words of a song which, so far as I remember, trickled frequently from the speaker of the steam radio about the 1930s:-

> The mice came out, the rats came out,
> From every belfry bats came out
> To listen to the tune the piper played.

The same song began with the memorable lines:-

> Hamelin town's in Brunswick,
> Brunswick is in Germany,
> Long ago, the mayor said so,
> The town was getting verminy.

The first line was of course a crib from Browning, who further went on to explain that

> Rats!
> They fought the dogs and killed the cats,
> And ate the cheeses out of the vats,
> And licked the soup from the cook's own ladles
> Split open the kegs of salted sprats,
> Made nests inside men's Sunday hats,
> And even spoiled the women's chats,
> By drowning their speaking
> With shrieking and squeaking
> In fifty different sharps and flats.

221

Well, if so, what became of them? Of course we all know the answer, which is traditionally that a piper came and piped them all to their death in the river Weser.

All the same, hidden behind all this nonsense is one of the most curious mysteries of the Middle Ages, and one which has nothing whatsoever to do with rodents of any kind, whatever Goethe and half a dozen other romantics, who presumably had never been to Hamelin, may have imprinted on the memories of the young.

There can hardly be many countries in which the terrible cautionary tale has never been heard, of how the town was reduced to starvation, the sudden arrival of a young man who volunteered to pipe the rats away, the mass drowning of the rodents in the Weser, the refusal of the town council to pay up, the crafty return of the disappointed piper when the grown-ups were in church, and his piping all the children of the town away into a hole in the hillside, a hole which immediately closed up behind them without trace. Few tales have so universally gripped the popular imagination.

And, of course, in summertime Hamelin thrives upon the story as the bus-loads of visitors arrive to watch the tragedy of the ratcatcher and the children acted out in front of them. The usual setting is beside the Hochzeitshaus or wedding-house, a truly beautiful hall built in the early seventeenth century to serve as the scene for marriage feasts and private celebrations of one kind and another, a house built in the magnificent Renaissance style of the Weser area. This happens to be one of the two houses bearing an inscription which bears witness to the tragedy of the year 1284, when on the feast of St John and St Paul (that is, on 26 June) 130 children of the town of Hamelin vanished without leaving any trace behind them.

The second inscription is on the so-called Rattenfängerhaus in the Osterstrasse. But here, as upon the Hochzeitshaus, there is no mention of a Council rodent officer or a ratcatcher, although both inscriptions mention a piper. There is no more than a brief mention of the disaster to the children, and the same is repeated in the medieval stained glass of the Marktkirche, on the beams of other houses in the town, and in the fourteenth-century minutes of the Council. These references are all sufficiently old to be taken at least as some sort of evidence – a distinction that can hardly be accorded to the script of the twentieth-century song or Browning's imaginary rodents.

The earliest non-Hamelin record of whatever may or may not have happened, is so far as I am aware, a manuscript in the library of Lüneburg which relates the incident thus, and says that it is quoting from 'an old volume':

'A most rare and mysterious event is reported to have happened in the town of Hamelin in the diocese of Münden, in the year of our Lord 1284, right upon the day of John and Paul. A young man of 30 years, so handsome and well-dressed that all those who saw him were astonished at his appearance and clothing, walked over the bridge and in at the Weser gate. He then began to pipe the whole town away, blowing upon a silver flute of strange shape. And all the children who heard this flute, to the number of 130, followed him out of the Easter gate to the

223

so-called Calvary and place of execution. There they disappeared, vanishing so completely that no one could discover where any of them had gone. The mothers of the children hurried from one town to another, but could find no trace of them anywhere. And so (as it is said) "A voice was heard in Rama, and every mother lamented her son." And just as one reckoned the date as the year of our Lord, or as 1, 2, 3 after a Jubilee, so in Hamelin was the year reckoned as 1, 2, 3 and so forth after the departure and disappearance of the children. All this I have found in an old book. And the mother of John, deacon of Lude, saw the children depart.'

No rats. Yet that something terrible happened in the town, an event so disastrous that the archives were to be dated by counting the years since the loss of the children, is clear enough. The last sentence in the Lüneburg manuscript is clearly an addition by the compiler, perhaps recalling something that he had heard in his youth, and it has a very straightforward and genuine ring about it. In fact, it is upon this single remark that it has been possible to build a considerable amount of theory, for if – as one may calculate – the woman in question was about 12 years old at the time, it would seem that the exodus of the children did not happen in secret, and also that not every one of the boys and girls of Hamelin was irresistibly drawn away.

There seem to have been no rats to start with and if they later appeared and got mixed up in the mystery that may well have been because the medieval equivalent of the modern Borough Rodent Officer sometimes disposed of rodents not by trapping or by poison, but by conjuration, casting spells or otherwise using magical arts. Added to which, rats and mice were often much more than rats and mice to the medieval mind – *vide* the awful tale of how Bishop Hatto was shut up in the Mouse Tower at Bingen and was eaten by the relentless creatures which swam across from Bingen. No, rats and mice were involved – even if they looked just like rats and mice – with the transmigration of souls and other such mysteries. Even Shakespeare refers (in *As You Like It*) to Irish rats being killed by verses, and Ben Jonson's line about rhyming Irish rats to death is not far removed from piping the rodents out of Hamelin. Yet the ratcatcher addition has done nothing to make the original tale more mysterious than it was already.

What really happened to the children has provided an apparently inexhaustible mine of doctor-theses at German universities. The theories are of several kinds. The literalists like to think that events took place exactly as described. Then there are those who think that the children were lured out to the Children's Crusade, whilst others more inclined to try to extrapolate backwards the local climate have come to the conclusion that the youngsters were piped out right enough but were swallowed up in a bog. Others have pointed out that it is extremely unlikely that if 130 children vanished without trace, and their mothers (according to the Lüneburg manuscript) visited town after town in search of them and could discover no clue at all as to their whereabouts, then they can only have been lost in some sudden and drastic disaster, such as the loss of a ship at sea. A similarity has been traced between the name of the hill in Hamelin, where they are supposed to have vanished, and Kophahn on the Baltic coast – but what on earth the children could have doing aboard a ship off the coast of East Prussia is not easily explained.

Did the children all die of the plague? Was the piping and procession out of the town in the nature of a funeral cortège leading to a mass grave which has never been discovered? Or was perhaps the piper no piper at all, but merely a conventional medieval symbol of death? Or could the piper have been – daring and irreverent thought – merely a piper?

Perhaps the youngsters were worked up (like many in our own day) into a frenzy of ecstasy and excitement; or maybe they had ergot poisoning which manifested itself in a dancing mania. Perhaps there was a sudden attack of an infectious neural disease leading to a mass St Vitus's Dance. Or could it be that there was a battle against one of the traditional enemies of the town, which resulted in all the young men being slain, the 'children' being a term for the 'sons' of the city? Or the children might have been enticed away by some medieval public relations man who was sent to wheedle them away to found a new town, or to resettle an area decimated by the plague. The See of Olmütz has been suspected in this connection, if only because it founded 200 new villages in the Sudetenland, in some of which family names identical with those of Hamelin families have been found. This is indeed plausible, and at least it accounts for the piper, who would have been a sort of recruiting-officer, whose job it was to pipe young people out of their towns; and besides, it is in harmony with the fact that Hamelin's annals are not dated as so-and-so many years after the disaster, but *na user Kinder uthgang* – after the departure of our young people. But if that were so, why is there no similar record of a piper in connection with any other of the couple of hundred villages in the

Sudetenland which were established at the same time?

Of the making of many theories there is no end, and some of them have a rough-and-ready fit to the known facts – that is, if the facts can really be distinguished from fancies. All that can definitely be said is that 130 children vanished out of Hamelin without trace on a particular day in 1284, and that they passed down a particular street toward the Weser. That street was afterwards renamed the Bungenlosestrasse, and it acquired a tabu indicated by its name – Boom-boom-less street. Where once the gay children of Hamelin had flocked down its cobbles at the heels of the gaily dressed piper, the sound of a drum and the happy notes of a flute or recorder were never to be heard again. Not even a wedding party, nor the triumphal marches in the procession after the annual marksmen's festival were ever to be allowed to emit a single boom to break the silence of its sad and mysterious memory. The children had vanished, and with them had disappeared all straightforward explanation of their leaving their homes. But the rats, I think, probably stayed put.

Hannoversch Münden

When Hannoversch Münden is seen at close quarters it is found to be sheer delight. At its edge stands the chestnut tree on the very tip of the promontory where the Fulda and the Werra, the two parent streams of the Weser meet, and there under its bough is the Weser stone with its famous verse:

> *Wo Werra sich und Fulda küssen*
> *Sie ihre Namen büssen müssen*
> *Und hier entsteht durch diesen Kuss*
> *Deutsch bis zum Meer der Weser Fluss.*

Where Werra and Fulda kiss each other, says the stone, they must surrender their names, and out of their kiss is born here the Weser, German to the sea. The Weser is indeed the only river of any size to be German to the sea, for the Rhine washes six countries, the Moselle three without reaching the sea on its own, the Elbe comes from Czechoslovakia, and even the Ems just spoils its chances by having a strip of Dutch water across from Emden. But the rhyme is really something of a cheat, for the river formerly had a single continuous name and was called the *Wisura*, or *Wisuraha*, all the way from its source to the sea.

226

About the ninth century the name seems to have become differently spoken according to whether it was flowing through a high German or a low German language area, and the names Weser and Werra emerged, both of them really one and the same, according to how well one happened to pronounce the *s* and *r* sounds.

But if the name is slightly dubious, the most extraordinary legend of Hannoversch Münden is that of Professor Papin's steamboat, which has become so firmly entrenched that it is contained in every guidebook and displayed in an ambitious mural in the town hall itself. And once the fiction had achieved the distinction of being related as sober truth to the Tenth International Navigation Congress at Milan, by no less a man than the Manager of the Schiffs-und Maschinenbau AG of Mannheim – an expert whose word would obviously carry a considerable tonnage of respectability – this mythical ship has come into history to stay there, complete with its engine, which the same authority confidently stated to have been 'probably of an improved Savory (hydraulic) type'.

The legend began more than a century ago, and since that date many technical journals and historical papers have repeated the same story, the tale that in the summer of 1707 the Frenchman Denis Papin, Professor of Physics at the University of Marburg, set out from Kassel in his steamship, a paddle-wheeler, to voyage to London. He reached Hannoversch Münden, and there the Guild of Shipmen, furious at this possible infringement of their staple rights, attacked the ship and smashed it to pieces. Professor Papin travelled to London by more conventional means, and died there about 1712, so the deed of the wicked men of Münden can be said to have held up the development of the steamship for nearly a century, for it was not until 1803 that the first really successful voyage was made under steam power, by Robert Fulton on the Seine.

It is, of course, very unlikely that any man – especially a Professor of Physics – who had constructed a ship capable of crossing the North Sea under an entirely new and revolutionary form of power, should simply retire into oblivion when his invention was destroyed by Luddite bargees, or that nothing more should be heard of the idea. The legend began because an archivist happened to turn up a brief note about the destruction of Papin's paddle-boat, and he did so in 1843 – just at the time when paddle-streamers were becoming established on the Oberweser, and in the very year that the first such ship to be built in

227

Münden was taking the water. Being a man of no great engineering knowledge, the worthy archivist published an account of the destruction of Papin's *steamship* – no doubt assuming that all paddle-wheelers in every age were steamers such as he could see on the river with his own eyes.

The fact is that drawings of paddle-wheel boats, their wheels turned by hand-cranks, go back as far as the fifteenth century. In the sixteenth, the great fortified paddle-wheeler *Ark van Delft* played a leading role in the relief of Leiden during the struggle of the United Provinces to throw off the hated and cruel rule of Spain. The boat which Papin possessed was certainly a hand-cranked boat of this kind, though much smaller and not very different from the paddle-boats one may find on the boating pond of a park today. Perhaps it even had something of the pedalo principle about it. Papin could not conceivably have expected to cross the North Sea in it – in fact it is known that the craft was no more than a model boat, and that he was arranging to have it shipped with his baggage aboard a sailing vessel. That the Münden shippers destroyed it seems to be true enough, even though the professor tried to bring it through their barrier in the tow of a Münden barge.

In extenuation of the error it must be admitted that Papin, who had been an assistant to the scientist Christian Huyghens, was interested in steam and condensation, and he was actually the first man ever to use steam to move a piston. His mechanism – for it was not really an engine – consisted of a vertical pipe fitted with a piston. The bottom of the tube was sealed and contained a small amount of water, and when it was heated the steam would slowly raise the piston to the top of the tube, where it was held by a catch until the tube had cooled and the steam condensed. When the professor released the catch, the atmospheric pressure would push the piston back to its original position. This device of Papin's certainly contained the elements of a steam engine – boiler, cylinder and condenser, all in one – but it was no more than a laboratory demonstration of the idea which later became the basic principle of engines. Certainly his tube could never have pushed a boat from Kassel to London, and he did not attempt to harness its negligible power, but that has not prevented his becoming the father of all steamers, Kassel's pride and joy, Münden's slight embarrassment and the hero of his native town of Blois on the Loire, where his statue looks out hopefully towards the river.

Kassel

The Fulda at Kassel is surprisingly unspoiled. Down in the harbour area the banks may be black and the bushes dirty, but up in the town the bastions of the old castle fall straight to the river and give an impression of venerable age. Not, of course, that all the ruins are by any means ancient.

Inevitably the foreigner will think of Kassel as a manufacturing city rich in locomotives, machinery, technical colleges and power stations, scientific instrument factories and engineering workshops. It was this face of Kassel, or Chasalla, which attracted the terrible retribution of 1943 that was to reduce it within an hour to such an inferno that the flames robbed the air itself of oxygen and thousands of those not burned alive died of suffocation. On that evening the parish of the great twin-towered church of St Martin, standing in the older part of the city, was one of 12,000 people. After the night, less than 50 remained in the area.

This single tragic, if commonplace, link in the terrible chain reaction of cruelty, suppression, aggression, retaliation and annihilation sent much of the glory that once was Kassel up in smoke and dust – and very glorious it was, for before the city became the royal capital of one of Napoleon's jobs-for-the-brothers kingdoms, in this case Westphalia, it was the seat of the Electors and Landgraves of Hessen in all their magnificence. Yet whatever may have vanished beyond recall, Kassel's most extraordinary piece of romanticism is left, and even if the visitor to the Wilhelmshöhe is quite convinced that the Hercules and all its associated wonders can only prove to be a particularly large-scale folly, when he actually sees them for himself he can hardly fail to sense something of the exuberance of spirit which led the rulers of Hessen to plan and build the outlook from their palace in the way they did.

The Wilhelmshöhe is best taken from the rear, by a tram which winds up and up along a woodland track until nearly at the top of the hill. A short walk to the summit, and one comes round the corner of the extraordinary octagonal Castle of the Giants to look down a long cascade of ornamental basins which leads down to lawns and trees, and finally the Palace. It does not look particularly far off, this Palace, but after one has been walking down the steps and graded slopes for nearly an hour one begins to realise that if things are done at all at Wilhelmshöhe, they are executed on the large scale.

The creator of the cascades was the same Landgraf Karl who founded Karlshafen. He began with the Castle of the Giants and the cascades, fed by reservoirs dug on the nearby hill tops and planted round with conifers to increase the condensation by the large total surface area of their needles. Soon the huge Hercules was added, standing nude on a kind of spire, and leaning on a ragged club as though wondering how on earth he is to come down from such an awkward position. He, too, is supplied with water, a 40-foot fountain spurting out of his gigantic mouth on Sundays, Wednesdays, and Bank Holidays – for even the best designed reservoirs could not be expected to keep up a flow for these ornamental waterworks all the week round. Below him, in a kind of cave in the rugged castle of the giants, are the *Vexier* fountains. Nowadays one must put a coin in the slot if one wishes these hidden jets to shoot out of their tiny holes in the floor and send the ladies screaming for cover, but it is worth it.

On the days when the cascades are to run, people are drawn from all over Hessen to see the waters pour down from basin to basin in a broad flight of steps between two narrower ones. So long is the descent of the main cascade alone, that water is still flooding down the lower steps a quarter of an hour after the upper basins have ceased to flow, but even this is not the end. Through channels and conduits and pools and fountains the water still has far to go. Some runs over the 14 arches of a ruined roman aqueduct, built for the purpose, to spill from the edge of a ruined tower in a waterfall more than 100 feet in height. Another part of the supply collects in a pool above the grotto of Pluto and is led down to the pretty lake by the Temple of Apollo, were it sends a fountain jet 200 feet into the air – by far the highest gravity-fed fountain ever to have been designed. And so it flows on, down and down by waterfalls and pools, grottoes and fountains, by Virgil's grave and Homer's tomb (for the Landgraves had everything) and a full-scale medieval castle and a Chinese pagoda, to the lake below the palace. Napoleon's brother, a vulgar man, is said to have used an island in the waters as a safe place for amorous adventures, but the Landgraves had their eyes on wider vistas, and in the Wilhelmshöhe they have a memorial on a scale worthy of their greatness.

Mölln

The pleasant town of Mölln is reached from the Elbe-Trave Canal by turning across the lake of Mölln and passing under the

railway embankment.

Against the outside of the Cathedral is the tombstone of Mölln's celebrated practical joker whose pranks, legendary or real, infuriated the citizens from one end of Germany to the other. His favourite gambit was to apprentice himself to some worthy tradesman and do exactly what he was told. For instance, a baker into whose employ he had needled himself might tell the honest apprentice to put all the loaves in the oven. This he would do – and burn them to cinders. Or if told by a joiner to stick the table-tops together, he would do precisely that. And when the shoemaker left him alone with the order to cut out as many shoes as he could, he snipped all the leather to miniature footwear so that the number would be greater.

Soon, however, he graduated to more cunning pieces of buf-

231

foonery, by which he could also make some honest (or at least not too dishonest) money. One of his best tricks was played upon the Council of Nürnberg, and it was a device which must appeal to many a modern doctor overburdened by the supply of hypochondriacs through the National Health Service.

It was at the time of the later Crusades, when the soldiers returning from the Middle East frequently brought with them fevers and other strange sicknesses for which at that time no cure was known. These, together with the usual collection of the halt and maimed and chronic sick, so filled the hospital at Nürnberg that there was no room for new cases to be taken in, and the Council were considering the provision of a new hospital wing.

Hearing of this, the joker of Mölln presented himself in the guise of 'Doctor Tillius', an eminent doctor trained in the famed medical school of Bologna. Having secured an audience with the Council, he undertook to cure the whole collection of patients for an agreed and handsome fee. Prudently the Council stipulated that they would pay when they saw the results, but the doctor could hardly expect mere laymen to believe that his cures could be so effective, he said.

So the new doctor went his round of the wards and whispered to each patient separately that in order to cure them it would be necessary to take one of their number, kill him, pound him up, and give the concoction to the rest to drink. This, he said, was an infallible cure. However, he was averse to killing any patient unnecessarily, even in the interest of the others, and so he had decided to select the weakest of the inmates. Shortly he would stand at the end of the ward in the company of the hospital superintendent, and would shout 'All those who are not sick, leave the premises'. The last man out would of course be the weakest, and he was only giving the others fair warning so that there should be no mistake.

So, in the course of time, he brought the superintendent to the ward. 'All those not sick, away, ' he called. And to the astonishment of the official every single patient tumbled out of his bed and raced for the door – even those who had been there for ten years already, and others who limped on crutches or could hardly drag their bodies along. They fell over each other in their hurry to escape, and within a few minutes the ward was empty. The superintendent was amazed to find that all his charges were suddenly healthy, and grateful to the doctor for having cleared the hospital so quickly.

Delighted with the results, the council paid the physician from Bologna his fat fee. He took it and left Nürnberg immediately. And this was only prudent, for on the morrow every one of the patients was back again at the hospital, queuing for the strange medicine which the physician had promised them the day before.

The name of this ingenious hoaxer was, of course, Till Eulenspiegel, whose merry pranks set many another city by the ears. The earliest known account of his ongoings is found in a book printed in 1515, *Ein Kurtzweilig lesen von Dyl Ulenspiegel geboren uss dem land zu Brunsswik*, but no doubt this was only an anthology of comic tales of earlier date which had become woven around a possibly real individual who had a peculiar but often attractive sense of humour. Till was not a Möllner, but as the title suggests he came from the area of Brunswick. Born at Kneitlingen, he had entertaining adventures right from the day of his christening, for the party which followed his baptism was so hilarious that the nurse staggered as she was crossing a plank over a stream on the way home, and fell in. Saved just in time from being smothered in the mud, baby Till was carried triumphantly home to Kneitlingen. A good bath soon brought his pink skin to light again, and as he had now been dipped three times in one afternoon all were sure that his life would be no ordinary one. And so it was to prove.

After many years of moving from one employment and one town to another, usually with great rapidity in order to escape the hue and cry raised by the irate victim of his latest trick, Till was fortunate enough to be taken into the employment of the Bishop of Bremen, who for a while kept him as a jester. The Bishop was a worthy man, and amongst other things he was very distressed by the problem of magic and witchcraft. Till assured him that the subject was nonsense, but the Bishop was not inclined to agree.

Till was one day walking over the market square when he noticed a woman with a stall of crockery. She looked miserably sad, and when she explained that she could not sell her wares and so had no money to take home to her sick husband and their family of small children, the warm-hearted Till was sorry for her. Having just received his wages he was comparatively well-off, and pulling out the money he asked her if she would take the 30 gold crowns for the entire load of crockery on her stall.

The woman could hardly believe her good fortune, and she accepted. She was also very willing to agree to a ruse which he

233

whispered in her ear. He then gave her the money and walked away.

Later that day Till came strolling across the market again, this time in the company of the Bishop of Bremen.

'You know your concern for the evil of witchcraft, Your Reverence,' Till said. 'I can prove to you that any fool can do such things. Even myself. For instance, look at that woman with her stall of crockery. She is calm enough, is she not? But if I were merely to wish it, she would in an instant be made insane.'

The Bishop shook his head. No, the evil art was something infinitely more serious, a secret work involving the Devil, he said. Till, simple soul that he was, could not conceivably bewitch a poor woman and rob her of her sanity just by wishing it.

'What do you bet, your reverence? Shall we say thirty gold crowns?'

This seemed easy money to the bishop, who at once agreed. The wager was made, and hardly had the two men shaken hands upon it when the woman leapt from her seat, picked up a piece of timber, and attacking her display of earthenware with insane ferocity she slashed and smashed at it until not a piece remained.

So Till received his 30 crowns, exactly the amount he had given to the poor woman. The Bishop was somewhat reassured about witchcraft when Till explained that the woman had agreed to attack her crockery the moment he put his hand to the tassel of his cap. Being a kindly man, the Bishop himself challenged all his guests at dinner that night to wager an ox apiece that they could explain the woman's sudden fit of demonic possession correctly, and of the 12 oxen he won in this way he presented the best animal to Eulenspiegel and ordered the remainder to be sold and the proceeds taken to the wife of the sick potter, so that her family should never want again.

Lübeck

At the Baltic end of the Elbe Trave Canal, this one-time Queen of the Hansa is palatial, with its huge Gothic churches in red brick and its magnificent hall of the shippers, the *Schiffergesellschaft*.

The house of the *Schiffergesellschaft* is a typical building of the southern Baltic, plain and rather severe, with its four-stepped gable in red brick topped by a golden ship voyaging under full sail as a weather vane. The house was bought by the Hanseatic Guild in 1535, and somebody later knocked out the Gothic doorway and replaced it by an elegant Rococo entrance. Above the door there is another sailing ship, this time a painted one, and to either side in kinky old-style German lettering some verses. Standing to the sides of the steps and several feet in front of the building are set two tall flat slabs, somewhat like tombstones. These have painted tops which show a water-joust in progress, and across them they carry the legend *Allen zu gefallen ... Ist unmöglich.* One cannot please everybody – for what is a fair wind for one voyager will be a contrary wind for another.

These slabs are called *Beischläge*, and others can be found in Lübeck. They were the outer pew ends of seats which stretched to the wall of the house itself and which could be tipped up out of the way. A pair outside the entrance to the town hall once served as a court of petty sessions where citizens might bring their charges against each other, and there was also a pleasant custom that any bridegroom from one of the patrician families of this Hansa city was obliged to go there for one week before his wedding and stand by the seat for an hour, decked out in his best suit. During that time any citizen might lodge a complaint against his character or integrity, and if it were upheld the young man was banished from the city and might not renew his addresses to his beloved until he had satisfied any claims against himself.

Inside the house one steps down into as extraordinary a restaurant as can be found anywhere; and curiously enough the *Schiffergesellschaft* has served the double function of livery hall and public eating place from its earliest days. The walls are painted with age darkened pictures of Old Testament scenes – the flood, with a very seaworthy Ark, Lot's daughters making their father drunk enough to set about a bit of incest, Solomon and the disputed maternity case, and others. Magnificent model ships hang from the ceiling, and beneath them the hall itself is laid out with three long rows of tables, for all the world like an Oxbridge dining-hall. Here one may eat and drink among the clerks and typists from offices in the city, who take their lunch sitting in the same elegant pew-like seats where the shipmen themselves would once take their meals when, at the height of winter, the Trave was frozen over or the Baltic itself icebound. The pew ends are carved with the arms of the various companies or divisions of the guild, and one can identify those of the

Riga shippers, the Bergen shippers and the Reval shippers. There were other divisions of the Guild, whose pews have gone, such as the Novgorod and Skåne voyagers. And no doubt the Stecknitz boatmen used to look in for an evening of wine and gossip when the ice made the locks of their salt route unusable.

At the end of the hall is the raised 'confessional', so called because it is hidden away behind a fretted screen. Here the wardens and court of assistants would sit, spying out over the others in the body of the hall, and when the bell was struck within this sanctum all had to hearken. The word of the court went as unchallenged as did the order of a captain on his ship, but as those who resisted it could not very well be keel-hauled under the building there was a blackboard on which their names were written so that they might be subject to the general scorn and contempt of their fellows and the public. At first a name would be added in chalk, but if the man still proved unwilling to accept the ruling of the court of the Guild the chalk was rubbed out and the name replaced in paint. And there the board still hangs, although two centuries have passed since the city forbade the use of such a sensible device in any house of meeting. The inscription, in a somewhat ancient and perhaps Wendish form of German, says that the undermentioned have gone against the brotherhood of the Hansa, and as they are unwilling to do without question as they are told their names are written up and will stay there until they have done the bidding of the company. Meanwhile they are not to be served with beer.

236

Gripsholm

PART VI

SWEDEN

To reach Sweden one can cross Schleswig-Holstein by the Kiel Canal, or take the Elbe-Trave Canal through Hamburg. Both are easy routes. Then after threading the Danish Isles one may head for Göteborg (Gothenburg), where the Göta Canal begins.

The side routes from the Göta Canal are fascinating, penetrating far into the hinterland. They consist mainly of short connections cut between lakes of considerable length. They are:-

The Dalslands Canal, entered at Köpmannebro on the western side of Lake Vännern. This passes over the astonishing aqueduct built by Nils Ericson when faced with the difficult problem of how to get past the violent falls at Håverud, and leads into Norway.

The Kinda Canal, from the southern side of Lake Roxen, leading southward to Linköping, Rimforsa and Horn, through a land of stately manors.

The Strömsholms Canal, recently entirely refurbished, and passing through an area of well-preserved industrial monuments on the way to Fagersta. The entrance is on Lake Mälaren, west of Västerås.

The Hjälmare Canal, leading off the Arboga river at the western end of Lake Mälaren. This leads across the divide to Lake Hjälmaren, with the city of Örebro at the end.

All these waterways are in excellent condition, and are popular cruising grounds.

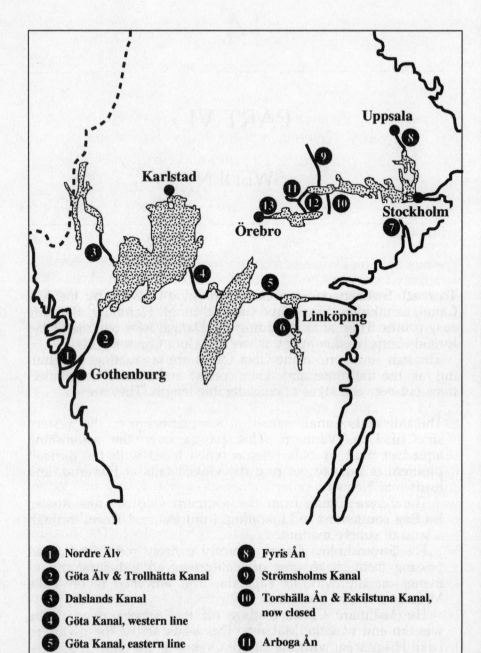

Uppsala

Karlstad

Örebro

Linköping

Stockholm

Gothenburg

1. Nordre Älv
2. Göta Älv & Trollhätta Kanal
3. Dalslands Kanal
4. Göta Kanal, western line
5. Göta Kanal, eastern line
6. Kinda Kanal
7. Södertälje Kanal
8. Fyris Ån
9. Strömsholms Kanal
10. Torshälla Ån & Eskilstuna Kanal, now closed
11. Arboga Ån
12. Hjälmare Kanal
13. Örebro Kanal

14

Trollhättan, Vadstena, Sundbyholm, Gripsholm, Birka, Sigtuna, Hammarby, Stockholm, Eskilstuna, Drottningholm, Uppsala and Strängnäs

Trollhättan

The one apparently insuperable obstacle in the way of a possible waterway from coast to coast of Sweden was the fall of the Göta river at Trollhättan. The Göta Canal, surveyed by Thomas Telford and energetically brought into being by Baltsar von Platen, is a triumph of engineering, and became possible after several unsuccessful attempts to bypass the great cataract of Trollhättan. It is one of the most impressive sights in Sweden, and as the falls are diverted for hydro-electric purposes on weekdays, it is only on Sundays that the full majesty of the tamed river can be appreciated as it is released to cascade down the hillside with a mighty roar.

Dr Clarke, a Fellow of King's College, visited Trollhättan shortly after the end of the Napoleonic wars, and he recorded in his journal that a few years previously 'to gratify his Majesty's curiosity, and by his order, two pigs, a house, and two geese, were sent down the principal fall. The pigs had the precedence upon this occasion; after a headlong roll they were landed very safely and proceeded quietly back to their stye. The floating house followed next; it was dashed to pieces. The geese came afterwards, and shared the same fate. The original possessor of the pigs had previously sold them to his Majesty, but he disposed of them afterwards again, at a very advanced price, because they had been down a cascade.'

The Sunday waterfall is by no means the only sight, and if a hydraulic engineer were to have a vision of paradise it would probably bear a very close resemblance to Trollhättan, where the roar of the water as it leaps down a gorge of such beauty provides a continual background of sound to a scene in which

241

sluice gates and overflows and conduits are interspersed with no less than four distinct systems of locks, large and small, ancient and modern.

From the swing-bridge by the steamer-quay a path leads across the lawns towards the forlorn but very imposing remains of Polhem's unfinished lock, a stone-hewn pen so deep that he designed the lower entrance in the form of a tunnel in order to overcome the difficulty of making wooden gates stout enough to hold up unaided the weight of the entire 53-foot head of water. Beyond it the track winds down the steep side of the gorge and passes the cavity of the Elvius lock, the lowest of the three designed by Polhem in his ambitious plans, but it is more than a mile further downstream that the now derelict but once successful lines of locks are to be found. Here is von Platen's famous line of 1800, with its three deep locks leading up to a basin from which a further five run up the hillside to the small Åkerssjö lake, emerging into it immediately opposite the upper entrance jetty of the topmost of the modern ship-locks. This flight is known as the 'old' staircase, to distinguish it from the 'new' flight, built by Nils Ericson in 1844 in order to accommodate the somewhat longer vessels capable of passing through the locks of the Göta Canal, which had at last been completed. For technical reasons Ericson considered it better to make the locks less deep than those of the old flight, and so he used four to reach the original basin, from which his new line then crossed the old one to climb in four steps to a second pool. The final leap to the Åkerssjö, which is now made by the fourth ship-lock, was overcome by Ericson with three chambers which run parallel to it and emerge close beside the top of von Platen's flight.

The newest flight, which since 1916 has served the needs of modern shipping, starts still further round the base of the Åkersberg hill, which was cut through with a deep gash to accommodate it. The four great chambers are now the only ones in use out of a total of twenty-five locks at the side of the cataract – except for one of the older ones which may still occasionally be brought into service as a dry dock for trading schooners – and, in common with the rest, they are blasted out of the solid granite.

Vadstena

The convent of Vadstena, on the eastern shore of Lake Vättern, and on the Göta Canal route across Sweden, is inseparable from the memory of St Birgitta, or Bridget, whose intervention in the

affairs of her country has been regarded by some historians as inspired and by others as mischievous interference.

It was in a June night of 1303, according to the chronicles of Sweden, that a parish priest was at his prayers when he saw a bright cloud from which a virgin spoke to him. 'A daughter has been born to Sir Birger,' his visitor declared. 'Her wondrous voice shall be heard all over the world.' And if the first years did not seem to bear out what the vision of the priest foretold, because the seventh child of Sir Birger Persson and the Lady Ingeborg was dumb until three years old, Birgitta was certainly experiencing ecstasies at the age of eleven, and her voice was eventually to resound as far away as Rome.

Birgitta was a Folkung, an aristocrat of the most powerful ruling class of her day. Married at the age of 13 to Sir Ulf Gudmarsson, she begged him not to consummate their marriage for two years, that she might come to love him even more deeply, and then she settled down to raise a family of eight, one of whom was to become St Katherine. It was not until after the death of her husband, when she was forty, that she blossomed into the greatest mystic and visionary the North has ever known.

Her visions were sometimes ecstatic, at others devotional, or concerned with the practical affairs of the politics of her time, and she either wrote them down by her own hand or dictated them to others such as Master Mattias, the learned canon of Linköping, who rendered them into Latin, which she subsequently checked word for word. As a relative of the King, Magnus Eriksson, she obtained the position of mistress to the royal household, where she sought to instruct her royal master in proper behaviour through the detailed revelations contained in her *Liber Coelestis Imperatoris ad Reges*, a book of divine instructions to kings of the earth. Indeed, Sweden's foreign policy was very greatly influenced by her, and the reputations of many rulers of the period were permanently coloured by her spirited denunciations of them.

Birgitta ordered Magnus and his queen to make amends for their sins of greed and lust and pride by building a convent on the royal estate of Vadstena (or *vatn stenar* – the stones by the water), and in 1346 the royal pair executed a deed presenting the land and a considerable endowment for the building, which was to be erected to the very precise architectural specification vouchsafed to her in yet another vision. She next had to obtain Papal sanction, and setting off for Rome, she spent 20 years there denouncing the many sins of the Church and priests, and castigating a succession of Popes, who at that time were in Avignon, for their pusillanimity in abandoning Rome. In 1367 Urban V came back to Rome, but after only three years he left for Avignon again, followed by Birgitta, who confronted him with a vision in which he was severely reprimanded. As a result, Urban sanctioned her order as an Augustinian institution, and Birgitta's victory was won. An English offshoot of Vadstena, a Bridgittine convent in Devonshire, still survives, and of the original building of her convent on the shores of Vättern the church is still there in very much its original state as defined in her vision.

If the voice of Birgitta of Sweden was a much-needed blast of reproof in the age in which she lived, her power and forthrightness as a visionary with unchallenged influence at court made her a number of enemies, upon whom vengeance was not always long delayed. The King's own cousin was bold enough to jostle her during a court function, and he died within three days of the insult. Sir Knut Folkesson poured water on her from his window – and he expired too, choked by a nose-bleed in bed, just as she foretold. Then there was the matter of the priest of Örebro who, at her insistence, had been dismissed by Magnus from his post as tax-collector, an occupation which Birgitta felt to be incompatible with the priesthood. Shortly after his dismissal the priest, meeting Birgitta in the forest, took the opportunity to tell her briefly and forcefully just what he thought of her interference, and Birgitta answered him that if he did not withdraw his words he would not long escape divine punishment. Unrepentant, the man went to watch the casting of a new bell – and if the mould burst and he was engulfed in the molten metal, had he not been warned?

It is hardly surprising that many intriguing stories should have become woven about the reputation and memory of such a revolutionary and reforming figure, but of her genuine piety of a very practical nature there could never be any doubt – as, for instance, when she stormed into the house of a notorious Stockholm harlot and drove the Devil out of her. Even today Birgitta is much more than a pious memory in Sweden, for although those who felt the lash of her denunciations regarded her as a meddlesome witch, her reputation as a mystic of the North has never been rivalled.

A delightful story is told of Birgitta's grandmother, Sigrid, and if modern research has cast the gravest doubt on its authenticity, the same might equally well be said of many other tales of the Middle Ages and earlier; yet if all the records of the past were stripped of their embroidery, there might be little left of beauty and of chivalry and charm. However that may be, the tale relates that Bengt, the lawman of Östergötland who lived at Ulfåsa (later the marriage home of Birgitta), fell in love with a young girl of no great class, a maiden so uncommonly beautiful that she was known as Sigrid the Fair. There followed a secret marriage which, when it was discovered, so enraged the bridegroom's brother, the proud and powerful Birger Jarl, that he sent to the bride a present of a cloak, half of which was made of the finest cloth of gold but the other half of coarse woollen cloth – a plain and practical hint that the union of an aristocrat and a common girl was quite improper. Sigrid's husband took the cloak and had the woollen portion embroidered and sewn with gold and pearls and jewels so that it became far richer and finer than the half which was only of gold cloth, and then he returned it to Birger Jarl with his compliments. Beside himself with rage, Birger came to Ulfåsa to vent his fury upon the loyal Bengt, but it was Sigrid herself who received him. So lovely was she that Birger's anger melted before her charms, and he embraced her and kissed her, offering her his profound apologies. A great scene of reconciliation between the brothers took place, and Bengt and Sigrid the Fair were accepted into the family circle. Their daughter was the Lady Ingeborg, the mother of St Birgitta.

245

Sundbyholm

A short way inland of the southern shore of Lake Mälaren, beyond the manor house of Sundbyholm, is a broad and smooth surface of rock, upon which is cut a runic memorial, the largest and most remarkable not merely of the many hundreds in Södermanland, but in all Scandinavia. Nor is it a mere inscription with a statement of the person in whose memory it had been raised, for although the outer frame is composed of three serpents, the largest of which contains the traditional dedication, within the 15-foot space enclosed by their sinuous bodies is a picture story showing the legend of Sigurd the Volsung.

The Sigurdsristning on the Ramsundsberg is probably the largest and oldest strip cartoon in the world, and it sets out the adventures of Sigurd, son of Sigmund, who had as his foster-father the crafty dwarf Regin, whose two brothers were Otter and Fafnir. Otter had the habit of assuming the form of an otter and going to fish for salmon in a waterfall, where on one of these innocent expeditions he was killed by that evil genius of northern mythology, the crafty Loki. The crime of Otter's murder had to be expiated by the gods in covering the skin of the Otter-otter with gold, and Fafnir kept guard over the treasure by sitting upon it in the form of a huge and formidable serpent. Regin was determined to get the gold for himself, and so he persuaded Sigurd to slay Fafnir, for which dangerous deed he forged for him a mighty sword.

It so happened that Fafnir in his serpent form was accustomed to crawl down from his seat on Gnita heath, where he guarded the gold of the gods, to drink at the edge of the lake, and Sigurd dug himself a pit in the path along which Fafnir habitually came. Hiding in this, he waited until the serpent slithered overhead and then plunged his sharp sword right through Fafnir's body – and on the stone at Sundbyholm Sigurd can be seen beneath the body of the serpent, his weapon forcefully driven through it between the words 'for' and 'soul' of the runic inscription.

The next incident shows Sigurd sitting by a fire, roasting Fafnir's heart over the flames to prepare a tasty dish for Regin. Anxious to make sure that it is done to a turn he touches it and burns his thumb, which he very naturally sticks in his mouth. But the thumb has on it some of the blood from Fafnir's heart, and in this way Sigurd unintentionally gets it on his tongue, with the surprising result that he can now hear what the birds

246

Till Eulenspiegel's statue, Mölln.

Medieval cranes, Trier.

Roman wine ship, Neumagen.

Stuben.

Kues.

Burial mounds, Uppsala.

Sigtuna.

Sète.

Carcassonne.

are saying as they twitter to each other in the trees.

It is no wonder that he should look up in such astonishment towards the branches of the tree to which he has tethered his good horse Grani with the gold laden on his back, for two little birds which, for all their appearance of giant parrots in the drawing are really a couple of tits, are chattering away to him with the news that Regin has planned to double-cross him and get the gold for himself. They strongly advise Sigurd to take the opportunity of killing the dwarf while he is still asleep, and in the final sketch it is clear enough that Sigurd acted with decision, for Regin's body is lying on the ground with the head neatly severed, and his hammer and anvil, bellows and tongs on either side of him. And there the story-sculptor leaves the tale, space not permitting to tell of how the treasure which Sigurd had thus acquired was to bring disaster upon himself and his family.

The Sigurdsristning at the foot of the Ramsundsberg is remarkable not only for its size and its drawings. It is clear that the Sigrid for whom it was executed was a Christian, for although the tale is concerned with the mythology of the ancient North, she prays for the soul of her husband and seeks to ease its passage by building such a useful public utility as a bridge. 'Sigrid, Alrik's mother and daughter of Orm, raised this bridge for the soul of her husband Holmger, father of Sigröd' run the runes on Fafnir's body, and the abutment of her bridge is still to be seen at the foot of the drawing. But the water no longer washes its foot, for during the nine centuries since Holmger died the shifting of the levels of land and water has caused a drop of at least ten feet in the bed of the brook over which the bridge once stood.

Gripsholm

The magnificent pink brick castle of Gripsholm stands at the head of a bay on the southern side of Mälaren, opposite the charming little town of Mariefred.

Gripsholm was originally one of the medieval strongholds of that almost legendary character Bo Jonsson *Grip* (or Griffin, from his coat of arms), Lord Chancellor of Sweden and a man of such power and wealth and energy that he personally owned about two-thirds of the entire country and was so rich and mighty that he was not deterred from declaring war personally on

247

Danzig, with the immediate result that it prudently came to terms with him. When he died in 1386 he owned more land than any private individual has ever been possessed of in any country or any age, and he left a fabulous fortune in gold and silver – quite apart from the long list of castles, of which Gripsholm was only one.

Some of his means of enriching himself were original, as for instance on the occasion when his first wife died in pregnancy and he immediately had her dissected in front of witnesses to prove that the child was alive, so that by Swedish law he could inherit her property through her child. For this he was sharply criticised by the bishop of Linköping, and had to appease the anger of the Church by considerable gifts of cash and property to the Vadstena foundation. The Church also profited well from the occasion when he wrongly suspected a young nobleman of trifling with a beautiful girl whom the Chancellor had successfully demanded in marriage when the young man himself, who was betrothed to her, had been sent away on some convenient pretext. This knight had given his word not to draw his sword against Jonsson, and, true to his promise, he fled into the Greyfriars church in Stockholm and took refuge at the altar, where the frenzied Jonsson promptly murdered him.

Although Grip was the originator of Gripsholm, the building now standing on its little promontory in the Mälar lake was mainly the work of Gustav Vasa and his three kingly sons, two of whom (John III and Erik XIV) imprisoned each other within its solid fortress towers.

Today Gripsholm is the historical portrait gallery of Sweden, and those who like to stop and stare at one royal face after another, often rather indifferently painted, can see all the top people, from Oliver Cromwell to the English Georges, or from Gustav Vasa to Swedenborg, as well as the horses and dogs of Charles XI. One of the most interesting pictures is that of Erik XIV, said to have been painted for him by van der Meulen so that it might be sent to Elizabeth I of England to add weight to the proposal of marriage which he made to her by letter, just as a modern young man might enclose a suitable photograph. Inevitably one wonders what she thought of it, but whatever her opinion the picture remained in England until 1930, when it was returned to Gripsholm to keep company with the portrait of the Virgin Queen, which she herself is said to have given to Erik.

But perhaps of greater interest at Gripsholm is exploring its corridors and chambers of painted wood, and visiting the theatre of that strange Rococo monarch Gustav III, whose French inclinations led him to scrap the chapel and convert it into a playhouse. This monarch extended his passion for theatricals, in which he usually played the leads himself, to designing the market square of Mariefred with a town hall which would serve as a backcloth for such open-air battle scenes as could not properly be enacted in the castle playhouse itself, and the result was to leave the little township in possession of a most charming and elegant building of ochre boarding which looks precisely like the stage set that it is, but yet is solid enough to house the local administration. Looking at the doorway between the two wrought-iron lamps at the top of the double flight of steps, one can almost imagine that once more would emerge the wigged and elegant figure of that aesthetic monarch whose whole life was itself a piece of high drama, right up to the final act which was to culminate in nothing less than a genuine assassination at a masked ball before his curtain fell.

The former Carthusian monastery of Pax Mariae, the only one in Sweden, gave the town its name of Mariefred (Peace of Mary), and the town – a quiet country village by English standards – is a pretty place, remarkably free from artificial old-worldliness and dominated by the white church standing on a knoll among the trees, built by two of the royal queens. In the time of Charles XI, when towns and districts were required to furnish specific supplies of arms and men for the defence of the realm, Mariefred was obliged to perform the relatively pleasant service of maintaining four bosuns for the royal fleet. Their little cottages with the diminutive gardens so beloved of sailors are still there, even if Mariefred's naval prowess has now declined to its being the end of the run for the steamboat *Mariefred* from Stockholm and a port of call for occasional trading ships.

With portraits and tapestries, gilded chairs and the sumptuous bedsteads of gentle queens, Gripsholm has everything one expects of a royal castle, and like Windsor it has its giant oaks in the park. There are rune-stones too, and a couple of queer Russian cannon from the battles of Narva and Ivanovgorod, and of course a herd of deer grazing outside the walls. Yet the unforgettable feature of Gripsholm is the majestic bulk of its pink towers rising from Mälaren's edge, and no view of the castle can compare with that which is to be had from a boat approaching from the bay beyond. And indeed it was by boat that the monarchs and their consorts came and went in spring and summer between Stockholm and their castle 30 miles out, whilst in wintertime Gustav Vasa himself would indulge in exhilarating races against his companions during the journey, the horses galloping foaming over the crisp ice and the sled-runners creaking and jolting over the frozen ripples of the lake.

Birka

Although some scholars maintain that it is a case of mistaken identity, there can be little doubt that the remains of a Viking settlement on Björkön, the Isle of Birches, in Mälaren are those of the great Viking trading station of Birka. Fifteen thousand men are believed to have lived there, but of its wooden houses nothing was left after the abandonment of the site, about 1,000 AD.

Here and there among the grave mounds elegant cypresses give an almost Mediterranean air to the scene, standing upright and smoothly symmetrical as though clipped by a head gardener well practised in the art of topiary. They add a strange sense of reality to the life of the people buried beneath the hundreds of grave mounds.

From the crest of the fortress hill one can imagine these earlier people as they stood to listen to the strange words of the man to whom a plain granite cross was erected in 1834, right on the summit of the ancient camp. It carries an inscription from John 12. 46, and the name of Ansgar, the Frankish monk who became the Apostle to the North.

Ansgar came from the Somme valley, and as a boy he entered a monastery near Amiens. Later he moved to Mainz, and it was while he was there that King Harald of Jutland came on a visit and was baptised. When eventually Harald asked for a teacher to be sent to his own land, there was only one of the brethren who was prepared to undertake the formidable task of carrying the gospel to the fierce men of the north, and that man was Ansgar. Yet at the last moment Autbert, the steward of the monastery at Mainz, volunteered to accompany the young monk, and when Bishop Hadebold presented the two men with a small but sturdy vessel they set off from Cologne – the stretch of the Rhine between there and Mainz being impossible of navigation by any ship with draught enough to make a voyage on the open sea.

Ansgar's first missionary voyage took him down the Rhine,

and he must have reached the North Sea through the channels of Zeeland. He was bound for the trading and portage centre of Haithabu near the site of the more modern city of Schleswig, and there he founded a school for twelve boys, the first school ever established in Jutland. Yet the efforts of Ansgar and his companions to train the lads as missioners were frustrated by the well-intentioned enthusiasm of Harald himself, who attempted to introduce Christianity by the more direct means of destroying the temples and sacred groves of the northern deities. Hatred of the Christians became quickly inflamed, and although Ansgar stuck to his post for twelve years after Autbert had been obliged to return to France, a sick man, he himself was finally driven out of the country by a popular rising. Greatly disappointed, he fled to France.

The lands still further to the north were then comparatively unknown, but Ansgar had now heard enough of them to be determined to go there if he could, and in 829 his chance came when messengers reported to the Frankish court that a Christian mission would not be unwelcome in Svea. On this occasion Ansgar did not have his own ship, but he and his new companion Vithmar set out from the southern shore of the Baltic as passengers in a trading vessel. Probably the traders intended to follow the eastern coast of Sweden and enter the Mälaren archipelago by one or other of the two approaches which today are supplied with locks – for Mälaren was then still continuous with the sea – but as they were sailing across the lower part of the Öresund their ship was attacked by a Viking raider. At the first encounter the merchants drove off their attackers, but the Vikings returned to the onslaught and succeeded in boarding the vessel. Ansgar and Vithmar only managed to escape with their lives by leaping overboard, but fortunately they were good swimmers and they reached the Swedish shore, though they had lost their priceless possession of the 40 books with which they had set out.

Striking northward through the marshes and forests, the two Benedictines marched onward day after day, and according to the account of Rimbert, Ansgar's friend and biographer, they were ferried across many of the lakes in boats – a clear indication that their reception by the people living on the lake shores cannot have been unfriendly.

This journey of hundreds of miles through a rough and unmapped country was an astonishing feat, and not unlike that of David Livingstone a thousand years later. And even though the gifts which they carried from the Frankish Emperor to the men of the trading centre of Birka had been lost in the fight on the Baltic, Ansgar and Vithmar were well received by King Björn when at last they disembarked from their final voyage at the quay below the fort of Birka. A little more than a year after their arrival, Herigar, the headman of the community, presented the two monks with a plot of land and helped them to build a church – the first church ever raised in Sweden. The mission to the remote and mysterious North was established.

There can be no doubt that the difficulties of language were somewhat eased by the fact that there were people from other lands in Birka when Ansgar arrived. Men and women from England and Scotland and France were there, not of their own free will but as slaves dragged from their homes by the far-roving raiders of Birka. And certainly many of these were Christians, so that enough of the new teaching was already known in the settlement for Ansgar's preaching to be not altogether strange in the ears of the Northmen. Yet, when Ansgar left to become Bishop of Hamburg, the old forces soon reasserted themselves and the Birka church was extinguished. Gauzbert, another Frankish missionary, undertook the attempt to revive it, but he was seized and driven out. For seven years the Christian Church in Svea appeared to be dead, and then, as no other man could be found to face the fierce obstinacy of the Northmen with their deep-rooted cult of Thor and Odin, Ansgar himself returned to Mälaren to restore it.

The reception which Ansgar received when he arrived at Birka for the second time was not very encouraging, yet he was friend enough of the people for them to allow him to land, and he treated the King to rich presents and sought his backing for the revival of the mission. But this time the King was more cautious, and he insisted that he must first ask the people, and also consult their gods – to whom the doctrine of a rival might not be particularly welcome. Summoned to meet in council, the chief men very reasonably decided to enquire of their deities by lot, and the upshot was that the gods graciously gave their permission for the emissary of their opponent to be given a hearing. The next stage in the negotiations was to call all the people of Birka together, and to put to the gathering the acceptance or rejection of the new faith.

Argument raged to and fro, and the prospects for Ansgar's mission were not very favourable until an old man rose up and testified that the Christian God had saved him and others from

252

pirates and from storms at sea. It would be much wiser to adopt the new God too, he pointed out with true Scandinavian reasoning, since the existing ones had not always proved themselves successful and reliable protectors. To this sensible suggestion the gathering readily agreed, and Ansgar was permitted to resume his work.

Even then, the mission had no spectacular success, for the traditions of their forefathers were too strongly rooted for the men of Birka to adopt Christianity very readily. When Ansgar died in Bremen at the age of 64, the little church in Birka had been reduced to a faint-hearted handful, and as one new missionary after another was murdered or driven out, the enterprise seemed doomed to failure. Yet Ansgar's personal courage and perseverance had in fact laid the foundation on which eventually the Church in Sweden was to be founded, and 300 years after his first visit to Birka there were half a dozen episcopal sees in Sweden, and four of them were in the port settlements on the Mälaren shores to which he had been willing to venture – Sigtuna, Västerås, Strängnas and Eskilstuna.

Sigtuna

On an inlet on Lake Mälaren, north of Stockholm, Sigtuna is the site of the second most prestigious Swedish public school, which counts King Carl Gustaf XIV among its alumni. Sigtuna is by English standards no more than a village, and even the Swedes would hardly consider it to be a large town, yet once it was the capital of the country. Originally that position was held by Birka, but about AD 1000 the centre of gravity shifted to Sigtuna, which became the official capital of Olof Skötkonung, ruler of the united *Svea Rike* or (as it is now called) Sverige. And as Olof had contacts with Britain which led to his bringing over Sigfred of York as a missionary, so too he employed English mint-masters at the first Swedish mint at Sigtuna, and the remains of the churches in the little town clearly show the influence of English church builders. The oldest, St Peter's, was the first cathedral of all Sweden, and its rough stone ruin shows by the solidity and design of its walls that considerations of defence were not unimportant. St Peter's was built about 1100, and St Olof's and St Lars' are certainly of not much later date, whilst the monastery church of St Mary dates from the middle of the thirteenth century and is still in use as a parish church.

Between the founding of St Peter's and that of St Mary's

disaster overtook Sigtuna, for in 1187 it was attacked and burned by pirates from Estonia, and it never again rose to the rank of capital of the country. In the following century the Dominicans established themselves in the ruined town, and built St Mary's, but Sigtuna's second burst of life came to an abrupt end with the Reformation. Today it is a little town in which are concentrated a number of important educational and religious institutions, including the Sigtuna foundation, which serves as a People's High School and has its own co-educational boarding school among its range of buildings, which in part are so like those of the French or Italian Riviera that one might imagine the blue water at the foot of the pines to be the Mediterranean itself. The Foundation has rooms for any who want a place in which to settle down to some undisturbed work, and it has a very fine library, but it also opens its doors to those who have no other object than a rest in its particularly pleasant surroundings.

Following the lane back from the waterfront it soon metamorphoses into the main street, a narrow alley of village shops and red or greenish-yellow boarded houses. In the middle of the village is a little square with a delightful miniature town hall of ochreous-painted wood, a survivor from the mid-eighteenth century and such a gem of municipal architecture that if ever its life were in danger it would easily find a new home in Skansen. Behind the Town Hall lies the straggling row of ruined churches which tell of Sigtuna's ecclesiastical past, and still further up the hillside among the trees is a smooth expanse of bare rock, crowned by the most handsome little squat bell-tower daubed in the usual tar and Falun red, and with a pointed shingle hat pulled well down over its ears. The view over the Sigtuna inlet from this point is a fine one, but the sight which holds one even more than the panorama of lakes and woods and fields is the glow of violet which filters through from a clearing just beyond the edge of the wood. There, so thick upon the ground that one has to pick one's steps carefully between them, the magnificent deep velvet bells of the pasque flower open their pointed petals to the sun and their golden centres wink a gay invitation to the bees to carry the pollen from one cluster to another.

In Britain this beautiful flower is sufficiently rare for one to be decidedly cautious about mentioning where it might be seen, whilst here, and elsewhere on the islands and shores of Mälaren, it grows so thickly that no amount of uprooting by visitors from towns would do more than free a patch of soil ready to receive a fresh contingent of the feathery seeds when the early autumn comes and the breeze drifts them hopping and rolling along the ground.

Hammarby

Not on the water, but easily reached from Uppsala, Hammarby is the former home of Sweden's greatest scientist, Linnaeus. His parents intended the young Carl to become a priest, but even when a child he was absorbed in studying flowers, and when at last he persuaded his father to allow him to study medicine and botany, the news had to be concealed from his mother for fear that the shock would be too much for her. Yet study these subjects he did, and the extent to which he used Aristotle's *Historia Animalium* as a basis of his ideas is suggested by the way in which some of the curious errors of the classical author are repeated in the works of Linnaeus. It was also from Aristotle that he took his concise and detailed method of describing living things and their habits, though upon this he grafted a particular imaginative bent of his own, which was not altogether without humour. *Linnea borealis*, the only plant named after him (by the botanist Gronovius), he described as being 'a plant in Lappland, of short growth, insignificant, overlooked, flowering only a very short time; the plant is called after Linnaeus, who is similar to it.'

Returning from Holland, Linnaeus was given the appointment of Physician to the Fleet, and he became Curator of the royal natural history collections. At last he was made Professor of Medicine at Uppsala, but his ambition was the Chair of Botany and Professor Rosen, who at that time held it, was persuaded to exchange professorships with him. It was then that Linnaeus took over the botanical garden, and in six years he raised the number of its exotic species from 40 to 1,100 – a remarkable achievement in view of the not very favourable climate of Sweden. This garden still exists, for in 1917 the Swedish Linnean Society undertook the task of restoring it to its proper Linnean state, with annuals on the right and perennials on the left, and the species set out in the narrow-beds according to his own classification, which was based on their reproductive organs. Neat little slates carry the names of each type, and plants which are garden specimens stand side by side with weeds and wild flowers to which they happen to be related.

'The *genitalia* of plants we regard with delight, of animals with abomination, and of ourselves with strange thoughts,' wrote Linnaeus in his *Philosophia Humana*, and his first and most famous attempt to classify by structure was in a work on the sexuality of plants, in which he examined the 'floral nuptials'. Here too he wrote with a sense of beauty and dignity of how the petals 'contribute nothing to generation, serving only as Bridal Beds which the Creator has so gloriously arranged, adorned with such noble bed curtains and perfumed with so many sweet scents that the bridegroom there may celebrate his nuptials with his bride with all the greater solemnity.' But if he classified the plants according to the structure of their reproductive organs, and saw both among the plants and the animals a certain similarity of structure and a degree of relationship between species, he did not see in these similarities any hint of a common primordial ancestor, but certain brilliantly conceived ideas of structure which existed in the mind of God before the creation was begun at all. Yet, whatever his own conception of the plan of nature may have been, it was on the work of Carl Linnaeus that Darwin and Wallace built and all modern evolutionary knowledge was ultimately founded.

Linnaeus was primarily a field naturalist, and his influence on authors such as Gilbert White of *The Natural History of Selborne* was very great. And because he observed creatures as they lived, he was able to make some shrewd judgements. In his *Migrationes Avium* he outlined the main migration routes over the Mediterranean, and this represented an astonishing amount of careful study at a time when there was no ringing system, and no worldwide network of ornithological observatories.

Carl Linnaeus (or Carl von Linné, as he became after his ennoblement in 1756) was not devoid of a certain conceit, and among his autobiographical notes one finds such self-laudatory statements as the following:

> God has permitted him to see more of his created work than any man before him.
>
> None before him has pursued his profession with greater energy and more listeners.
>
> None before him has been a greater botanist or zoologist.
>
> None before him has become more renowned throughout the world.

At times he could be rude and boorish, and it is said that when attending the village church of Danmark, near his manor-

house at Hammarby, he had the habit of taking his dog with him. After some time Linnaeus himself no longer went, and the only member of his family who attended the service was then the dog, which annoyed the congregation by barking during the sermon. When at last the rector complained, Linnaeus merely told him that he ought to know that the dog was only barking because the sermon had gone on too long already.

It does not reflect much credit on the contemporaries of Linnaeus in the academic and cultural life of Sweden that his papers and books and specimens were soon to be lost for ever from the country of his birth. When in 1778 he died, he left them to his widow, who was a somewhat shrewish and complaining woman but not altogether devoid of financial acuteness. There seems little doubt that she would have sold them to foreign purchasers had not Linné the younger, who succeeded his father in the professorial chair at Uppsala, persuaded the executors to allow him to hold the collections for his personal use if he renounced his share in the remainder of the family property. But only five years later, the son died, and Linné's widow at once asked the executor to dispose of her husband's specimens and library.

The news reached a young medical student in London, J. E. Smith. This young man wrote to his father and suggested to him that at the executor's price of 1,000 guineas the collection might well be worth having, and the money was provided. Even then Smith can have had no idea of the priceless possession which was to be his, for he had not even seen the list of items, but when he received the catalogue from the executor he speedily deposited half the purchase price to the credit of the executor's account in Amsterdam. The agreement of sale was quickly completed, and so it came about that 19,000 sheets of mounted plant specimens, several thousands each of shells, insects and minerals, a library of 2,500 scientific works and all the correspondence of Linnaeus were packed up and shipped aboard an English merchant ship in Stockholm harbour. It is said that a belated recognition of what was being lost to their country caused the Swedes to send a vessel out into the North Sea in pursuit, but the collection arrived safely in London, and when Smith had completed his studies he became president of the Linnéan Society, which he himself founded at the age of 26 with the assistance of a number of influential men. The young man then put all his energies into sorting the collections and editing and publishing the manuscripts which had come into his possession, and it was in London and not in Stockholm or Uppsala that such items as Linnaeus' journal of his travels in Lappland appeared.

However much it may since have been regretted in Sweden that Linnaeus' collections were allowed so easily to leave the country, the incident may have been a fortunate one. Smith himself proved to be an admirable owner for the material, and it was probably very much better cared for than would have been the case if it had been split up and sold in Sweden. The Linnean Society soon achieved the highest reputation among scientific institutions, and provided a fine and permanent home for the work of the man who had justly been called the prince of botanists.

Though entirely bereft of its specimens, the home of Linnaeus at Hammarby, a few miles outside Uppsala, is a delightful place. A two-storied house of Falun red wood, it looks out over a little garden with a circular bed, in the centre of which are sown the same 24 plants which were his continual favourites. To the right is the barn and to the left the low building of his workshop, with its thick roof of gaily flowering meadow sitting on top of the layers of birch bark. Behind the house, in the wild wood where once Linnaeus grew his exotics, is the little museum house on a knoll, built by the botanist to protect his specimens from fire, and around it grow the columbines, the *Lilium martagon*, and other flowers introduced by Linnaeus himself. Another of his introductions was the edible snail (*Helix pomatia*) which is thoroughly at home in the copse, but the glass bells, which he used to hang on the branches so that he might hear the music as the wind stirred among the trees, have long since vanished.

Stockholm

Situated where the water of Lake Mälaren pours out into the salt water of the Baltic, Stockholm is the most beautiful capital city of Europe. It is accessible by way of the skerries on the eastern coast, or through the Södertälje Canal and Lake Mälaren, which is the route taken by the Göta Canal steamers. Access to and from salt water is by Slussen – the lock – at the southern side of the old town. Stockholm has innumerable sights; but first and foremost comes the *Wasa*, an absolute must for all visitors to the city. It is a model of what a museum should be, and all the explanations are in English as well as Swedish.

During the last five centuries more than 2,000 travellers have written of their journeyings in Sweden, and almost every one of them has given some sort of description of Stockholm. Its sights, with the Nordic Museum, the Royal Palace on the salt-water side of the little island of the old city and the view of the Town Hall from the freshwater edge of the same isle, are so justly famous that I shall not attempt to describe them at all. Yet there are two cities which to me are more beautiful than all others, and neither Paris nor Copenhagen, for all their charm, is a member of that pair. To myself, Amsterdam is the one charmer and Stockholm the other, and each has a loveliness of its own. Stockholm is tritely referred to as the 'Venice of the North', but it needs no such excuse for its existence. Once seen, the mellow colouring of the somewhat severe houses tightly packed on the Riddarholmen can never be forgotten, and, just as in the case of Amsterdam, the way to explore Stockholm is by boat, for it is only from the water that the beauty of either city can be seen in all its fullness.

The upheave of Mälaren during the retreat of the ice caused the step in the water-level which led to the growth of Stockholm around the site of the slight fall, and where once the ships would sail straight inland to the archipelago which now forms the islands of the Mälar Lake, the freshwater is joined to the salt by four passages. Two of these are the pair of swift streams by which the water of Mälaren surges out at the Norrström, racing shallow past either side of the islet of Helgeandsholmen immediately opposite the steps of the Royal Palace, to unite below the bridge where hopeful Swedes are always to be seen fishing for whatever it may be that lurks at that particular spot. Most of them have resin-reinforced rod and nylon line and plastic spinner, but there are old-fashioned drop-nets too, worked from clumsy little boats.

For ships there are two passes, and the large vessels bound for the lake ports use the Danviks Canal which leaves the main fairway a mile to seaward of the palace and passes round the back of the southern suburb and through the Hammarby lock to emerge into Mälaren further west. Smaller craft, however, can burrow under the raised clover-leaf crossing at Slussen, beside the foot of the Katarina lift-tower.

The story of the *Wasa* is one of the strangest in marine discovery. Launched in 1628, this 50-metre warship, armed with 64 cannon and manned by 133 sailors and 300 soldiers, cast off her moorings on an August day of that same year and headed down towards the Halvkakssund. She had not sailed half a mile before a squall caught her sails, and the largest and most magnificent warship of the fleet of Gustavus Adolphus heeled over. Her stone ballast shifted, and she tipped further, capsized, and sank in fifteen fathoms of water.

> *Toll for the brave –*
> *The brave! that are no more:*
> *All sunk beneath the wave,*
> *Fast by their native shore.*

Cowper's lines on the *Loss of the Royal George* might have applied to the *Wasa*, for both vessels were 'overset' in much the same way, but whereas the *Royal George* was lost a century and a half later and no longer exists except in Cowper's poem, the *Wasa* is still very much in existence. When she sank she was left untouched for 35 years, but in 1663 divers were sent down – a very remarkable feat in that era – and they succeeded in salvaging most of the guns. This was particularly fortunate, for had they not been removed their weight would almost certainly have crushed the decks in the course of the following centuries.

Once her valuable gun-metal had been recovered the *Wasa* lay forgotten in the harbour for nearly 300 years, and it was only in 1956 that she was found again by Anders Franzén, an amateur and an enthusiast for the history of shipping. That he succeeded in tracing her was the result of careful study of the original accounts of her loss and of contemporary charts, supplemented by echo-soundings in the area where, as he correctly calculated, she must have gone down. And when her hull was found lying in a mound of mud, divers were able to report the astonishing fact that she was excellently preserved and quite intact.

The next stage was to recover as much as possible of the loose tackle and ornamentation, and beside a few more canon the beautifully carved mermaids and beasts and warriors with which her master-designer and artist Henrik Hybertsson had decked her out were brought to the surface. Then, at last, in August 1959 it proved possible to lift the hull intact, and twelve cables were passed under her hull and fastened to a pair of salvage pontoons.

The pumping began, and when by degrees the lifting power had been raised to 700 tons the stern of the *Wasa* began to rise a few inches from the mud. Soon she was clear of the bottom, and after being lifted a few fathoms from her bed she was towed cautiously towards the shore and beached under water, so that further work could be undertaken. Her final destination was to be a dry dock where, all ship-shape and Stockholm fashion, she would be permanently on view, the only warship of her period in existence, and more than a century and a half senior to Nelson's *Victory*. And if the honour of her discovery belonged to Mr Franzén, the *Wasa's* excellent preservation throughout the centuries was the work of the fine and sterile silt brought down the Norrström in the swift flow of fresh water from Mälaren.

Every detail of the *Wasa* Museum is perfect, and quite apart from the astonishing sight of this huge vessel preserved in a sort of annexe to a dry dock, there are plenty of minor sideshows which demonstrate what the men wore, how they ate, how they lived aboard ship – all illustrated with authentic materials brought to the surface with the wreck.

Eskilstuna

Close to the southern shore of the Mälar lake, Eskilstuna was originally reached by a canal, now abandoned. Its name is derived from that of Eskil, the monk of Canterbury, who was murdered there.

Eskil was one of that long line of English missionaries who came to the Mälar shores, and according to the legend he took it upon himself to visit Strängnäs at the time when the local king was carrying out one of the great periodic sacrifices to Freyr. Very much after the style of Elijah, the monk from Canterbury called down upon the proceedings the wrath of heaven – though not in the form of fire to consume the water, but in the shape of a violent thunderstorm which extinguished the sacrificial flames yet left Eskil himself dry and untouched. Far from rounding upon their own priests, however, the angry people turned upon Eskil and a man named Spåbodder struck him on the head with an axe. He was dragged away and stoned to death, and later a spring was said to have gushed from the ground at the spot. Eskil's disciples took up the body of their teacher and carried it away, but after they had proceeded for some miles and had crossed the Torshälla river, the bier became unaccountably heavy and they had to set it down, taking the incident to be a sign that this was where Eskil was to be buried. The site of his grave is generally believed to have been that on which the pretty riverside Fors Kyrka of Eskiltuna was afterwards built, and in which one of the ancient wooden figures on the wall is almost certainly that of Eskil himself, holding in his hand three stones as the symbol of his fate.

Drottningholm

The royal palace of Drottningholm suffers from being known in guide books as 'the Versailles of Sweden'. This great residence, built by Tessin the elder as a summer home for the dowager queen Hedvig Eleonora in the second half of the seventeenth century, was given to Louisa Ulrika, the mother of Gustav III, as a betrothal present, and it was her obsession with everything in French culture, together with the passion of her aesthetically-minded son for theatricals, that made Drottningholm what it was to become.

The Palace is on the edge of the large Mälar island of Lovö, looking out across a hundred yards of sound toward the smaller islet of Kärsö and half a mile or more from the mainland shore. Originally it was reached only by water. 'The voyage is made in small sailing boats, there being no access but from the lake, which is here very narrow, at most not above a quarter of a league in breadth,' recorded the Dutch officer Johan Drevon, when he visited the place in 1785. 'This short navigation, however, in windy or rainy weather, excites a great deal of discontent among the foreign ministers, and others who are obliged to pay their attendance at court two days in a week. In order, therefore, to spare them this inconvenience, a bridge is constructing at immense expense and trouble.' Since then the approach has been by the causeway, yet Drottningholm, like Gripsholm, is at its most impressive when reached by water.

Drottningholm has everything that eighteenth-century kings and queens and twentieth-century travel agencies could desire. Avenues of limes leading to shady bowers, lawns and box hedges, terraces of steps, balustrades set with all the best statuary on which the Swedish armies could lay their hands in their thrust towards the heart of Europe, fountains and ponds and ornamental sheets of water. There is the *Théâtre de verdure* of Gustav III, too, with stage and auditorium laid out in clipped hedging, the goddess Flora on her hill, the *kina slott* or Chinese residence, complete with the Canton village where King Adolf Frederick, the most skilled locksmith of his day, amused himself in working at the forge.

The thunder machinery, like all the other accessories of the Drottningholm stage, is as simple as it is ingenious, and yet no thunder of a radio effects studio could be more realistic. In fact there are two thunders, home and away, the nearer peals being manufactured within a heavy wooden trough or thunderbox balanced at its centre, with ropes at the ends so that it can be tilted on its fulcrum. Inside it at the downhill end is a heap of cobbles ranging from shingle to heavy rounded stones, and when the tilting begins it is the smaller pieces which first start to move, accelerating along the sloping floor of the box to rustle and strike the opposite end with just the proper preliminary crackling. Then come the heavy thumps of the main flash of ionisation and discharge as the heaviest of the stones race forward to rumble and crash against the end of the trough. A quick tilt, with a more concentrated and faster landslide gives a fine illusion of a storm right overhead.

The distant thunder – at Gripsholm perhaps, or over Sigtuna –

is even simpler. A stone ball like that of a skittle alley has merely to be rolled along the entire length of the stage, stotting and thumping over the floor boards, and the theatre echoes with a long drawn-out grumble which becomes either fainter or louder according to the direction in which the ball is rolled.

The wave machine consists of a series of enormous wooden rollers cut to the shape of Archimedes screws and painted blue with a foam-flecked edge to the thread, and these extend right across the back of the stage, ranged up so that the upper part of each roller can be seen over the one in front of it. Each wave-roller has a crank on its end, and when they are turned the wooden spirals run past each other, the waves apparently flowing in from one side of the stage to vanish into the park beyond. Looking at the rollers themselves, it seems impossible that their rotation could produce any other effect than that of rotating wooden screws, yet from the auditorium the appearance is so exactly that of wind-driven waves that a timid theatre-goer might be excused for fumbling for his packet of sedatives.

Uppsala

A short way outside the modern town, at the end of the Fyris River – as far north as one can penetrate by inland waterways – is a row of artificial hills where nine males of various species were sacrificed on each of eight successive days, a different creature being selected every day. Nine men would be slain, nine dogs, nine horses, and nine of any other suitable creatures which might come to hand, and when their blood had been drunk or used for propitiation ceremonies the bodies were strung up to hang from the trees of the sacred grove. One Chris-tian mentioned having seen 72 corpses dangling from the branches of Uppsala. Even now there is a copse close to the church, and its trees are probably the lineal descendants of those of the sacred grove from which the carcases hung until decay and putrefaction, aided by the birds and animals, had disposed of them.

In spite of the roar of the jet planes as they take off from the nearby military airfield and sweep low over the fire-cracked tower of the church which was once a cathedral, Old Uppsala gives one an extraordinary sense of the past, for running almost to the gate of the church itself is the line of the three huge tumuli which were formerly said to be the grave-mounds of the three great deities of the temple. In the nineteenth century the central mound was excavated, and the English traveller George Atkinson wrote in his *Pictures from the North* (1848) that 'in the centre of a large mass of bone-ash formed from horses, dogs, and perhaps a hecatomb of men, stands a potter's vessel, containing the mortal ashes of some once notorious thief of the fourth or fifth century'. Archaeologists are now convinced that the hillocks are the burial mounds of three Yngling kings of the fifth and sixth centuries, Aun, Egil and Adils, but whatever the identity of the men who were buried in them the mounds themselves give a remarkable sense of the power and grandeur of the warrior-people of those far-off times, and as one stands on their summits one looks far down upon the hundreds of humbler hummocks of many other men of lesser rank, and on the grove where the annual victims were slaughtered.

There is a fourth hill too, a little way from the royal tombs, and this one is not as high but rises steeply to a broad and flat top. This, the Tingshög, was the scene of the judgement gatherings, and even as late as the sixteenth century Sweden's first monarch of the Vasa dynasty, Gustav I, sometimes addressed the peasants from its summit, but in the heyday of Old Uppsala the local king, more important than other neighbouring chiefs on account of the revenue received from the temple rites, would sit there to judge disputes and his decisions were approved by a clashing of swords and shields.

Built into the wall are fragments of rune-stones with their curious characters outlined in red or black, some of them pagan and others pieces of memorials to early Christians. The custom of raising such monuments lived on beyond the introduction of Christianity so that one may sometimes see the cross, cut very much to the Maltese shape, mingled with the traditional dragon or serpent, along which the inscription is carved in the curious characters which, for ease of cutting, consist entirely of straight lines. Usually the runes tell a simple message such as 'A and B raised this stone to C their father', but sometimes the inscription is longer and tells where the person commemorated died – for it was the custom when a rover died away from his native parts to erect such a stone in his memory. From these one may well be astonished at the enterprising voyages which were undertaken, for the memorials mention places not only in Russia, but far away in the Eastern Mediterranean. One of those in the wall of the church at Old Uppsala records that the man met his death in England. He, too, was a Christian, and his memorial carries not only a cross, but the words 'Gold help his soul' – in runes.

New Uppsala, on the Fyris River, is a most attractive town. Splashing over a mill weir, the stream runs fast and shallow in a channel cut down the centre of the main street, and but for the gurgle of its swift rippling the visitor might think that he was in one of the water-cities of the Netherlands. The stone quays, the steps, the trees along either bank of the watercourse, and the little bridges all give the place an air of Delft or Utrecht, and like those cities Uppsala has many sights – from the giant wrought-iron pumps set at intervals along the riverside, with which the citizens drew their water before the days of reservoirs and piping, to the great bulk of the Castle hill, upon which the students throng to celebrate the night of Walpurgis. And behind the hill is the handsome yellowish building of the Carolina Rediviva, the name of which commemorates the fact that it replaces the Academia Carolina of earlier days. It now contains the very fine collection of books and manuscripts of the university library and some half-million doctoral theses.

The Uppsala library does not conceal its treasures, but with admirable openness displays a fine selection to the public. There are manuscripts of Hans Andersen, Mozart's draft of part of *The Magic Flute*, early works printed by Caxton and by the Gutenberg workshop, and some of the books which belonged to Vadstena and to Birgitta herself. Even the letter of proposal sent by poor mad Erik XIV to Queen Elizabeth I is there, and a Bible annotated in the margin by Luther. Yet nothing can really compare with the famous *Codex Argenteus*, which has belonged to the university library since 1669. Even in Georgian times visitors from Britain would make the journey to Uppsala in order to see it.

This codex is one of the most remarkable manuscripts in the world, and far from being a collection of yellowing leaves with faded writing, its startling lettering of bright silver and gold on parchment sheets of royal purple appears so fresh that one might think it to be a new work. It dates from the early years of the sixth century, and before reaching the library of the University of Uppsala it had a very adventurous history.

During the third century the Goths from the North invaded the lands of the Danube, and it was there that they came in contact with Christianity. One of them, Wulfilas, set about the task of translating the Bible into the Gothic language, but before he could do so he had to prepare a suitable alphabet, just as modern missionaries may be obliged to do when undertaking to translate the scriptures into a language of New Guinea or the South Seas, where there is no indigenous literature. For his Gothic version Wulfilas used a mixture of Greek characters with Roman letters and runes from the North.

At the end of the fifth century the Ostrogothic leader Didrik marched into Italy, and the version of Wulfilas which his Christian people took with them was copied again and again, and blended with the Latin texts of the land to which they came. One of these copies was the magnificently executed *Codex Argenteus*, and the fact that it was done in imperial purple is thought by scholars to indicate that it was made for the personal use of the great Emperor Didrik himself.

The Ostrogoths were not long in Italy before they were overwhelmed, and those who survived left the country. Such Gothic literature as had been produced quickly vanished, and it seems that most of the manuscripts were either destroyed or had their writing erased so that the parchments could be used for works in Latin. Of all that there must have been, the single volume of the imperial copy of the scriptures of Wulfilas alone survived, and it is the only written work in the Gothic language which has ever been found.

The story of how the codex came to reach the land from which the Goths are believed originally to have come is known only in its later stages, for it was not until the sixteenth century that the codex came to light again in the monastery of Werden in the Ruhr. It is generally thought that it was taken there by the founder of the monastery, Ljudger the apostle to the Frisians, who was sent by Charlemagne to found the monastery of Werden. That he brought to it the *Codex Argenteus* is sufficiently probable because the people in that part of Europe spoke the Gothic language. As to how and where he might have obtained the manuscript, it is known that in the interval between his Frisian and Gothic missions Ljudger spent some years in the monastery of Monte Cassino, which was famous for its unrivalled collection of early manuscripts.

Before two Flemish scholars rediscovered the codex at Werden, many centuries had passed, and the book had lost nearly half of its original pages, probably in the fires which overtook the monastery. But they copied the remainder, and their release of a Gothic manuscript caused such a stir that the Emperor Rudolf II quickly acquired the original and added it to his own priceless library in the Hradzcin in Prague. During the

Thirty Years War the Swedish armies advancing through central Europe sacked the city, and, as was their custom, they looted such works of art as they could transport to embellish Sweden in its age of national awakening. The statues which ornament the Palace of Drottningholm in Mälaren were among the booty from Prague, and so was a section of the library of the Emperor Rudolf. In this way the codex passed into the library of Queen Christina, and it was no doubt there when the Lord Commissioner Whitelocke paid her his formal visits and reproved her for allowing dancing at the court on Sundays.

Then Christina abdicated, and she took with her to Rome a quantity of the finest treasures of her library, which eventually passed to the Vatican. Yet by good fortune the codex was not among the volumes she selected, perhaps because it was written in a strange language which she could not herself read. But she left behind her a number of servants and creditors who had to be paid, and as money was short their claims were partly settled with gifts in kind. Thus it was that the codex, along with other manuscripts, was used to pay off her Dutch librarian Vossius, who took it home with him to the Netherlands. There, his uncle Francis Junius, who was particularly interested in the old Germanic languages, was delighted to find such an unlikely treasure as a Gothic codex among his nephew's goods, and he promptly copied it and published it in a printed edition, but even before it had been printed the news that Junius was at work upon it came to the ears of Queen Christina's former noble courtier Magnus de la Gardie, now Lord Chancellor of Sweden. He at once began negotiations for the purchase of the original, and Vossius was persuaded to part with it for the sum of 500 dalers (about £125). Thus the codex was finally returned to Sweden, where the Lord Chancellor provided it with a magnificent binding of wrought silver, and then presented it to the library of the University of Uppsala. And there it has remained ever since, its brilliant parchment leaves containing the greater part of the four Gospels in a language which elsewhere survives only in its influence upon others.

Strängnäs

In the days of the Vikings, Strängnäs was the place at which the people of the Södermanland area gathered for their markets and councils, and for the periodic sacrifices which led to Eskil's denunciation of the rites and his death at the hands of the crowd. Eskil was by no means the only Englishman to come as a missionary to Mälaren, and if he himself was the 'apostle to Södermanland', so David was his counterpart in Västmanland across the water. David was buried at Munketorp, near Ströms-holm, and one of the legends about him tells the delightful tale of how, when he was an old man and his eyesight was failing, he entered his room and drew off his gloves to hang them up, and placed them by mistake on a shaft of sunlight streaming in through the slit of window, which he mistook for his peg. Some while afterwards he sent a pupil to fetch them, and to the young man's astonishment the gloves were still there, supported obligingly by the shaft of light. David, when told of this, took it for a sign that his sins were forgiven. He gave thanks – and ever afterwards the sunbeam appeared when its assistance was needed. But one day David was shocked to find that the kindly light was no longer willing to hold his gloves for him; and taking this for an indication that he was unworthy and was guilty of some moral lapse, he recalled that he had trodden on some ears of corn which, however little grain they may have contained, were nevertheless part of the divine gift to mankind and should have been given to the poor.

An old hymn, sung in Södermanland on the eve of the day of St Botvid, ran 'Hail, O Sweden! A lily from your bosom springs. Hallelujah England sings, that the holy Botvid is born upon her shore.' Whether or not medieval England sang Hallelujahs in remembrance of Botvid, or had indeed heard of him at all, he was the son of an English trader at Birka and was sent to England by his father to train for the life of a merchant. When he returned to Sweden, however, he came not so much as a trader but as a missionary. He happened to purchase a slave, and when he had baptised him he decided to set him at liberty, and the story relates that he set out with him by boat for Visby, from where the man might easily obtain a passage home. When night fell, Botvid and his companion landed on the Mälar islet of Rogö, and when the master was asleep the slave murdered him and went off alone in the boat.

Months passed before the news was received that Botvid had never reached Visby, and the priest Henrik then set out to discover what had become of him. As the priest and his companions were sailing over Mälaren a bird flew beside the ship, keeping them company, and when the sailors wished to catch it Henrik restrained them, thinking from its unusual beha-

269

viour that it had been sent to guide the party. Sure enough, the faithful bird continually showed them their course among the islets of Mälaren, and when at last they were passing Rogö it left the vessel and flew ashore to perch on a tree, where 'it broke forth into such sweet song that the men left their rowing for sheer delight at so beautiful a melody'. Beneath the trees the searchers found the body of the murdered man, and having at last drawn them to it the bird finally took off in flight and steered toward the stars. Botvidskirka was built at the spring which gushed from the spot, and probably it was visited by St Birgitta, for St Botvid was one of the saints whose conversations with her are recorded in her revelations. 'I and other saints have obtained for you the grace of God that you may see and hear things spiritual, and the spirit of God shall fire your soul' – it was Botvid, one of the trio of English saints of the Mälar lakeland, who thus spoke to her a few years before the death of her husband.

Strängnäs became an episcopal see within a century of the death of Eskil, and it was there that the last of the Roman Catholic bishops of Västerås consecrated Laurentius Petri as his first Protestant successor, thereby preserving the apostolic succession. The Cathedral in which this act was performed is a sheer delight, and its tall square tower of pink brick with plain whitewashed decoration of cut-out design has the expanse of its walls cleverly broken by the simple expedient of leaving unfilled the hundreds of scaffold-pole holes which were necessary for its building and repair. From the railings at the top of the cupola there is a magnificent view over Mälaren for those who can bring themselves to climb the wooden ladders to such a height; from no other place can the visitor have a better glimpse of the maze of woods and fields, rocks and islands, sounds and creeks and buoys which make up the Mälar landscape. Away to the horizon the land looks continuous until one notices here and there in the distance a glint of blue shining from one of the innumerable channels and inlets.

Down below in the nave are the memorials of the Dukes of Södermanland, including the great vault of the canal-builder Charles XI, and in a side chapel the magnificent tomb of Carl Gyllenhielm with the same fetters hanging on the wall which he wore during his years in the fortress of Rava. He was buried in great pomp and splendour, and so vast was his funeral cortège, with horsemen riding five abreast at the head of a procession which included – as one can see from a contemporary engraving

270

– the royal ice-sleds of Queen Christina and the queen mother, that the street leading up to the cathedral had to be widened for the occasion, and even the artist, who drew the procession sinuously coiled to save space in the picture, found that he had no room left to sketch in behind the sleds of the royal ladies the 45 *slädar medh Fruentimber*, and contented himself with noting that they were just off the edge of the drawing.

Strängnäs Cathedral may have suffered at the Reformation, but it was fortunate in its benefactors, and the fact that it was at the bishop's castle of Strängnäs that Gustav Vasa was chosen as the first hereditary monarch of Sweden in 1523, brought it into royal patronage. It was here that he came under the influence of the preaching of Olaus Petri of Örebro, who at that time was warden of the Cathedral school, and who was later to introduce the Reformation for his royal master. The wealthy Bishop Rogge was also a great benefactor, and to him the Cathedral owes its magnificent carved tryptich of Flemish workmanship, which is one of the most splendid in the world. Gustavus Adolphus enriched the cathedral too, and so did Queen Christina, who presented it with many rare volumes looted by the Swedish armies in Bohemia and still to be seen ranged on the bookshelves of its famous library. And quite apart from the Cathedral itself and the school where Gustav Vasa sat at the feet of Olaus Petri, there is the splendid Bishop's Palace of the seventeenth century, as pink and white as a bridal cake, looking out down the hillside across its pretty garden to the blue water of the lake. To be Bishop of Strängnäs must be the dream of many a Swedish vicar or dean.

PART VII

SOUTHERN FRANCE

The sole route to the South of France, other than by sea, is by way of the rivers Saône and Rhône. The latter has in recent years been canalised and supplied with locks (including the deepest one in Europe at La Bollène), and its one-time terrors have vanished.

Before the Rhône delta, a canal leads through to the Gulf of Fos and that is the route to Marseille and Provence. But just above Arles the Little Rhône branches off to the right and provides access to the Canal du Rhône a Sète, and so to the Canal du Midi route through to the Atlantic at the Gironde.

The Canal de Fos from Arles is now closed at its lower end, and one no longer has the privilege of passing through the double-bascule bridge made famous by Van Gogh.

The Dordogne, which joins the Garonne just below Bordeaux, is navigable for a limited distance only, but works are in hand to put the Tarn into a navigable condition above Moissac.

The whole Canal du Midi system is now kept in excellent condition as a cruising waterway, but commercial traffic ceased shortly after 1990.

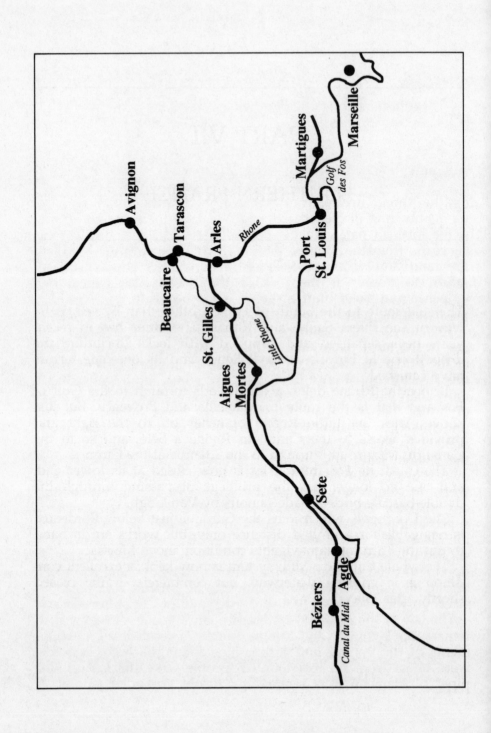

15

Avignon, Tarascon, Beaucaire, Arles and Marseille

Avignon

On the Rhône, upstream of Beaucaire and Arles, Avignon, with its mighty ring of crenellated walls, is a city of treasures. There is the fortified palace of the Popes, who resided in the city for 70 years, from the time of John XXII in 1309 until the Swedish firebrand and visionary St Birgitta persuaded Gregory XI to return to Rome, at the foot of the Rocher des Doms, the immense and sheer bluff of limestone dominating the river and the remaining part of the bridge of St Bénézet.

The story of the construction of the famous Pont d'Avignon is one of the most remarkable of the Middle Ages, and such little of the bridge as still survives gives an impressive idea of what this structure must once have been like when, in all its length of more than half a mile, it crossed the river with low arches each of nearly 100 feet span. Even now the sheer audacity of the undertaking is startling enough, but in its own day it must have seemed to the people of Provence as great an achievement as the Golden Gate and Sydney Harbour bridges appear in our own century. Nowadays we assume that engineers bring their works to completion as a result of proper designing, but almost any sizeable bridge of medieval Europe seemed to demand supernatural navvying. The splendid Pont Valentré at Cahors on the Lot is only one of many which legend declares to have been successfully erected only because a mysterious mason employed upon it proved to be the Devil himself. Yet somehow the great bridge of Avignon was too sublime to be satanic, and the construction was attributed to a direct demand of Christ himself.

The tale of the Avignon bridge is a curious one. Not only is it remarkably complete, but it is recounted in great detail in documents of the period, and testimonies about the hero, Bénézet, were taken from no less than 15 people. Like the tale of the piper of Hamelin it is remarkably firmly grounded, and it is almost impossible to say where reality ends and legend begins. And as though to discourage anyone who should try to do so, the relevant papers end with the blunt injunction: *Fassan totz ensems a notre Seinghor Dieu et a sant Beneset a cui es honor et gloria.* Let us all bless the Lord God and Saint Bénézet, to whom be the honour and glory.

The year was 1177, and there lived near Viviers, close to the site of the modern lock of Châteauneuf, a woman who sent her twelve-year-old boy to watch her sheep, very much in the way Moses watched over the flocks of his father-in-law. Benoît, Benedict, Bénézet or Beneset, as he is variously called, was engaged in this pastoral activity when one day he heard a voice calling him three times from heaven. Samuel-like – for the tale of Eli as well as the boyhood of Moses may have left their mark upon the account – young Ben answered and was astounded to hear the voice announce that the speaker was none other than Jesus Christ himself and that he had an important piece of work for Bénézet to undertake.

'*Ieu vole que tu laisses las fedas que gardas, quar tu mi faras un pont sus lo flumi de Rose.*' So ran the request, as recorded in the language of the day, 'I want you to leave the sheep you are looking after, because you are to make me a bridge over the river Rhône.'

Bénézet quickly protested that he could not leave the sheep, he knew nothing of the Rhône, he had only three farthings to his name, and what with one thing and another he was the last individual to be capable of the work. But the voice insisted that he was to do as he was told, and that an angel would be sent to lead him to the Rhône.

The lad set out, and he had not long been on his way when the angel arrived, disguised as a pilgrim and carrying a staff and scrip. This individual introduced himself as the boy's appointed guide and led him to the bank of the river, the size of which filled Bénézet with such fear that he protested it would be quite impossible to build a bridge over it.

But the angel told him not to worry, and leading him down to a trading ship he told Bénézet to go to Avignon and to show himself to the Bishop. So saying, the pilgrim vanished, leaving Bénézet alone at the gang plank.

The boy then asked the mariners 'for the love of God and the blessed Mary' to give him passage to the town, where he had important business in hand; but the owner of the craft happened to be a Jew, and not at all the kind of man likely to be well

disposed to juvenile hitchhikers. Nor was he impressed by invocations. Marys, he said, were cheap enough. Personally he
would prefer three pence to all the love of the blessed Mary,
and if the shepherd boy could not pay the money he would
have to walk.

Bénézet was not a wealthy lad. To be precise, he had exactly
three farthings to his name. But the Jewish shipowner was not
inclined to see three good farthings go from his grasp, and so he
agreed to accept a compromise fare for that amount and allowed
the boy to come aboard. At Avignon Bénézet landed and,
hurrying into the city, he found the Bishop preaching a sermon.
Obedient to his charge, the lad was tactless enough to interrupt
the discourse and announce to prelate and people that he had
arrived, sent upon the special order of Christ to build a bridge.

The Bishop was not accustomed to having his sermons so
rudely interrupted, and he had the lad seized and conducted to
the provost of the city with the suggestion that he be flayed
alive or have his hands and feet cut off – or perhaps both. Ben
was not in the least dismayed, and in front of the magistrate he
repeated his tale and explained that he had only come to build
the bridge over the Rhône which was so much needed. But the
official was unwilling to take him seriously. How, he asked,
could such a simple, common villain, a penniless good-for-
nothing, hope to bridge the Rhône where neither God, St Peter,
St Paul, nor even the great Charlemagne himself had been able
to succeed? And sarcastically he added that he happened to
have a handy stone in his residence; if Bénézet could carry it
down to the river then he would perhaps believe the lad
capable of building a bridge after all.

The stone in question was part of a Roman column, and
according to local accounts it measured 13 feet by 7 and needed
30 men to lift it. Bénézet does not seem to have been deterred
by its size, and led again before the Bishop he explained that
the provost was supplying him with a good piece of masonry
for the foundations of his bridge, and he would now go and
carry it down to the site as the official had ordered. The Bishop
evidently wished his congregation to share the entertainment,
for he led them out to watch.

Taken to where the stone lay, Bénézet braced himself, lifted
the stone as though it were a cobble, and carried it to the river
bank to set it where the first arch was to be built. Amid the
tumult of astonishment the provost flung himself on the ground
before Bénézet and promptly made the first contribution of 300

277

sous to the bridge fund – which within the day ran up to a total of 5,000. The authorities and people alike took up the cause of the bridge with enthusiasm, working so energetically under the guidance of the shepherd lad that within only 11 years the bridge of 19 great arches was complete. As for Bénézet, he was destined never to see the great work brought to completion, for in 1184 he died at the age of only 19. A chapel to hold his remains was built above the fourth arch, and it naturally became a place of considerable pilgrimage. Within it Bénézet remained buried for nearly five centuries, until the arch beneath the chapel was so seriously threatened by ice floes that his remains were removed.

Tarascon

The romantic relationship between love and marriage under the influence of the troubadours obviously raised problems, and Courts of Love became established, of which those held by René of Anjou at his castle of Tarascon are among the most famous. And it was to them, and to the brilliant and romantic women who formed the bench of judges, that lovers brought their problems for adjudication. Their proceedings were as confidential as those of a modern consulting room, and for this reason there is more rumour than certainty about their sessions, but sufficient references can be found in the literature of the troubadour period to suggest at least that the cases they advised upon involved matters of principle in which romantic love was supreme.

Not that the verdict of the women was always in line with that which a modern consultant might give. For instance, a *seigneur* fell in love with a single lady who already had a lover, and although this was in accordance with rule 34 (*Nothing should prevent a lady having two lovers at the same time*), the lady had relied upon the rather contradictory rule 3 (*No person can genuinely love two at the same time*) and had turned him down, but she had generously promised him the right of succession in case of the demise of her original hero. Eventually she married this first lover, and the claimant asked for implementation of his rights on the basis of rule 1 (*The married state is no reason for refusing love*) and the general principle that love and marriage were normally irreconcilable.

The lady refused him, and this was the situation when, in all

278

fairness, he brought the matter before a Court of Love. The experienced women listened to the arguments on either side and then considered their verdict. The decision upheld the claim of the *seigneur* and decreed that the lady who had married should accept him as she had promised. Which no doubt she did – unless she invoked rule 5 (*Favours unwillingly given are tasteless*).

Of the troubadour nobility, René of Anjou in his castle of Tarascon was perhaps the last. Married in real romantic style at the age of twelve – and to a bride of ten – he lived in that Provence which acquired from the crusaders and by trade with eastern countries an exotic flavour, a tang of love and a zest for life as gay as the scent of the flowers which decked its hills. The troubadours sang and dreamed of beauty, of valiant fights, of chivalry and self-sacrifice, but above all of love. And this ideal of love was such as would send shivers down the spine of any marriage guidance counsellor, for it had nothing to do with marriage. One might well be married, and this was very necessary to preserve the line and raise children, but it had little to do with love.

Ermengarde of Narbonne stated explicitly that a husband could only really begin to be the true lover of his wife when she had divorced him and married another. Love was secret, dangerous. It drove men to great deeds of chivalry and daring, it made them strive to win the right to be the lover of another man's wife, and it impelled women to take immense risks – for the double standard had already been invented, and a woman whose chastity and honour were suspect could be ejected, and even murdered by her husband. Clandestine, undiscovered love was the ideal, and this meant a mutual trust between lovers as complete as might be the deception of the spouse.

The good René of Anjou, at whose castle of Tarascon such proceedings were often said to be held, was a kindly man, well read and generous, a, linguist and a mathematician, a poet and painter, a lover of good wine, a ruler simple and philosophical, a peaceful man in an era of violence, and above all a troubadour. His subjects loved him – a thing rare enough in those days – and it was for their amusement and gaiety that he commissioned the re-construction of the Tarasque, the fearful monster which gives its name to the town.

During the first persecution of the Christians in the Holy Land a boatload of refugees escaped to Provence. According to some, they were forced into a leaking boat without food, water or sail, and pushed out to await their fate, whilst others suggest they

fled by sea of their own free will. The passengers were Mary
Magdalene with her brother Lazarus and sister Martha, Mary
the mother of James and John, Mary Salome, and two servants.
The people of·Provence are quite convinced that this is so, and
that the boat reached their shores.

St Martha is remembered at Tarascon. The tenth-century
church where she is buried stands close to the end of the bridge,
and even though it was rebuilt in the twelfth and heavily
damaged by British and American bombardment of the bridge
in the twentieth, it is very well worth a visit if only because
there is really no serious reason to doubt that the lady who lies
in a renaissance tomb of marble in the ancient crypt is indeed
Martha of Bethany.

The good Gervais of Tilbury – who, being English, would
never lie and could not conceivably be fallible – also mentions
Martha, and the legend of Provence attributes to her power the
saving of Tarascon. She was making her way up the valley of
the Rhône when she came upon a crowd of people weeping and
wailing. On her enquiry the people told her about the Tarasque,
and said that their high priests and magicians had failed to
persuade it to depart, the warriors had blown their trumpets in
vain and clashed their shields to no effect. Armed knights had
courageously sought to fight the beast, and many were those
who had not returned. Meanwhile, the Tarasque continued to
sink the ships and ravage the countryside just as before.

'Ne pleurez pas,' said Martha. 'Pray to the only God who can
vanquish dragons.' And with cross in hand she followed the
trail of bones (for the Tarasque was a messy eater) until she
came upon the beast in a wood. It was still engaged in its
horrid meal, 'mengeant ung homme en sa bouche.'

The beast reared, flapped its wings, cracked its tail, and
uttered such a cry that the whole countryside shook. Martha
held up the cross and the Tarasque at once became so docile
that she could put her girdle round its neck and lead it, meek as
a kitten, into the town. There the people in their fury despatched
the beast with lances and stones.

And that might have been the end of the terrible monster
which lived in the hole under the rock and roamed the forest in
search of prey. But it was to be reborn, made of wood and cloth
and with eight young men inside it to propel its fearsome body
through the streets. It survived until the Revolution when the
National Guard was sent to hew the dragon to pieces and burn
it in the street, so that the happy people of Tarascon might not

have their attention diverted from the more strenuous business of class hatred.

Since then the Tarasque has been once more reincarnated, but for many years she no longer roamed the streets at Whitsun, knocking people down with great flicks of her powerful tail. Instead she lived in a little house near the church of St Martha, and was shown to visitors on request. Now she has returned to activity once more, and on the last Sunday of June she comes out of her lair as large as life, and brings back to Tarascon something of the gaiety that it knew under René, Count of Provence and Duke of Anjou, King of Sicily and Aragon, Hungary and Jerusalem.

Beaucaire

Across the river from Tarascon is Beaucaire, with its mighty keep of white limestone standing majestically on a rocky hill at the edge of the town. This castle is inseparable from the great tale of Aucassin, son of the Count of Beaucaire, and of the captive slave girl Nicolette, a prisoner taken in battle against the Saracens. Who she was, none knew, for she had been taken from home as a child. But she was beautiful in the eyes of Aucassin, her hair curling and golden (somewhat surprising in an Arab, perhaps), her eyes blue-grey and full of laughter, her lips of vermilion richer than ever rose or summer cherry wore, her form so slender that one might clasp her round with one's two hands. So white were her feet, for all their colour, that the daisy blossoms broken by her gentle tread seemed black beside them. No wonder that Aucassin should have loved her so deeply that his only joy was in waiting upon her, or thinking of her. This he much preferred to joining in the wars, and fighting his father's mortal enemy, the Count of Valence from further up the Rhône.

But this notion of making love not war so angered Aucassin's father that he forbade his son ever to see the lovely Nicolette again, and to make sure that his wishes should be obeyed he ordered the girl to be shut away in a lonely tower with only a slit for a window. There she was to stay with none but an old woman to watch her, and if Aucassin should try to reach her or to speak to her she was to be burned alive.

When Aucassin learned of the fate of his beloved he retired to his room and wept without ceasing. Meanwhile the terrible

Count of Valence came to lay siege to the palace, and Beaucaire was under bombardment with stones flung by every possible engine of war available at that period of time. At the height of the attack, Count Garin ran to summon his son to defend the family castle but all Aucassin could do was to weep. He would never bear arms again, he said, unless his father allowed him to come to his beloved Nicolette and to marry her.

Never, never would he be allowed to see the girl, his father declared in his fury. But the sound of the onslaught made some sort of compromise seem desirable, and with the enemy thundering terribly at the gates a formula was agreed upon. Aucassin would fight to defend Beaucaire, and if he returned alive from the encounter he would be allowed to see Nicolette, but once only, and for long enough merely to exchange a few words of love and to share a single kiss.

So great was the joy of even that limited expectation that Aucassin began to daydream of his love even in the thick of the battle, and he was being led away captive from the battlefield, stripped of his shield and lance, when he most fortunately came to his senses, ran down furiously upon the Count of Valence and gave him so lusty a clout with his sword that he stunned him and could lift him up and carry him off as a prisoner. The battle was won, and Aucassin rode home triumphant to claim his prize of the single kiss upon Nicolette's lips.

But the Count of Beaucaire had no intention of keeping his part of the bargain. He would never allow his son to see the wretched, low-born, worthless Nicolette, he stormed. And Aucassin, helpless before his blank refusal, promptly freed his prisoner the Count of Valence and retired to his chamber to give himself up to weeping.

This everlasting crying seems to have worked on the nerves of the Count of Beaucaire, for soon it was Aucassin's turn to be dragged away and thrown into a dungeon. Nicolette came to hear of how he wept and suffered for her still, and one warm night of May, as the nightingales sang sadly outside her tower, she could bear it no longer. She waited until the woman set to watch her was asleep, then swiftly knotted together her bedclothes and coverings to make a rope down which she could glide. Being so slim she could squeeze through the narrow window, and so find her freedom.

Fleeing through the moonlit alleys of Beaucaire, Nicolette came at last to discover the dungeon where her true love lay imprisoned. She managed to squeeze her head through a hole, and sure enough she could hear her beloved Aucassin weeping the night away, still sobbing helplessly in his love for her. But already her escape was discovered, and the guards were out looking for her. Warned by the kindly night watchman she hid behind a pillar, then fled barefoot from the town and out to the forest. And there it was that Aucassin came to her when his father, thinking Nicolette dead, at last released him.

Now the joy of the lovers was complete. Together they reached the coast and sailed away to a castle where they were received with kindness and sympathy. But alas, one day the ships of the terrible Saracens appeared, the castle was overrun, and many of its defenders slaughtered. Aucassin and Nicolette were seized and carried away to slavery, each on a different ship. The two craft were driven asunder in a swift and dangerous storm, and Aucassin came to the coast of Provence. Free at last, he reached Beaucaire and discovered that he had succeeded to the title. As for Nicolette, she was taken to Carthage. And there, to the great joy of all the people, she was identified as their long-lost princess. She had no lack of rich suitors; but no, Nicolette would not stay. Once more she set out on her travels, and with blackened face and in the guise of a troubadour she crossed the sea to Beaucaire.

Troubadours were always welcome, so in the castle of the new young Count she sang to him the true tale of Nicolette and of the Aucassin she had lost and to whom she would for ever be faithful. And of course her song brought back the tears to Aucassin's cheeks, but when the troubadour threw off the disguise and her tears of happiness began to wash away the blackening, his own weeping also changed to tears of joy unbounded. The next day the two young lovers were married, to live for many years in such a state of ecstatic love as only a troubadour could sing – even if they seem to have been an exception to the rule that love could never be found in marriage.

Arles

Arles is a city of wonders of which the Roman arena is the most impressive. Capable of holding more than 20,000 spectators, it is like some vast Olympic stadium, and the three towers added to it in the twelfth century are a reminder that after the fall of Rome it became a fortified town in itself. Even nowadays it is used for entertainments and (I am sorry to say) even for blood-

Arles

thirsty bullfights in the Spanish style. There is the Roman theatre
too, the remains of which have a strange and melancholy beauty
of their own, and are still used during the summer for concerts
or classical plays. The church and cloister of St Trophime recall
that Arles was one of the very earliest bishoprics of Roman
Gaul, Trophimus having been a companion of Paul on his last
journey (2 Timothy, iv) and personally consecrated bishop by
the apostle. Believed to have been a cousin of Stephen, Trophimus was sent to Arles in AD 45 and is said to have brought
with him the skull of Stephen. *The Pilgrim's Guide* to St James of
Compostella, a detailed Baedeker of the routes thither published
in 1140, states that Trophimus died in 94 and was buried in the
Alyscamps, which the author recommended as a place that no
pilgrim should miss. I can only confirm that recommendation,
even for non-pilgrims.

Although much of this great ancient cemetery was boorishly
destroyed to provide a railway cutting to the locomotive repair
workshops, that which remains is strangely beautiful, nostalgic,
haunted by many centuries of loving and of dying. Les Alyscamps (or the Champs Elysées, the Elysian fields) was an important burial ground as far back as the time of the Roman
occupation, and it achieved such prestige that three separate

284

layers of sarcophagi came to lie one above the other as the centuries passed. More than a dozen chapels served it, and their remains are still to be seen, bordering the quiet avenue that runs between the tombs.

The Alsycamps burial ground, originally pagan, seems to have achieved renown through St Genest, a local Roman clerk to the court who refused to write out an edict ordering the persecution of the Christians. Condemned to death, he fled over the Rhône to the marshes of the Camargue but was overtaken and beheaded under a tree, which quickly became an object of pilgrimage. However, the continual plucking of the leaves and bark as souvenirs eventually killed the tree and it was replaced first by a column, then by a chapel of pilgrimage. It was the continual threat of attacks by the moors which led to the body of the saint, and the pilgrimage also, being transferred across the Rhône again to the greater safety of Les Alyscamps.

The cult of Les Alyscamps became so popular that Christians as far upriver as Vienne and Lyon wished to be buried there, and their bodies made the journey by water. A corpse would be placed in a coffin on a raft, or in a barrel sealed with pitch, and the float bore oil lamps at each corner so that its arrival would be noticed if it should happen to approach Arles at night. The cemetery staff and the Guild of Boatmen at Trinquetaille on the opposite shore had the duty of bringing the bodies to land, and for this service they were paid by means of a gold piece inserted between the teeth of the deceased and held there by the rigor, or with a purse hung round the neck.

One of the chapels is that of the Porcelets, an Arlesian family dating back to the Crusades. Their peculiar name is said to derive from a curse laid upon one of them by an aged hag, who swore that the lady would have as many children at one birth as a sow would have in its litter. The sow in question turned up nine piglets, and the lady is alleged to have had nonetuplets (if that is the right word) the very same day. Naturally, the family came to be nicknamed The Piglets, and eventually took the name instead of their original title, which later was forgotten.

A place such as the Alsycamps cannot fail to have its own legends. One of them tells of a wealthy man of Lyon who was dangerously ill. Certain of his approaching death, he gave away all he possessed to his family, took leave of his wife and rode off down the towpath toward Arles so that he might die in the city and be sure of burial in the Alyscamps. Yet when he at last reached the place he found Arles so enchanting that he felt continually better and better, and as the weeks and months went by he began to live in some style. At last his money was all gone, and yet he had never felt better than now. Mounting his faithful steed he rode back up the towpath, living on the generosity of the bargees and monks whom he met on his way.

Arriving at Lyon, he found that his wife was now remarried and his family were generally embarrassed by his return alive and well. Deprived of the welcome he had expected, he wisely but sadly set off once again for Arles to enter the abbey of Montmajour, set on a rocky knoll outside the town. And there eventually he died.

An earlier tale is that of the lovely Arcella, a girl of 17 whose actual sarcophagus was found in one of the chapels. She was so famous as a dancer in the Roman theatre that crowds would attend the performances in which she was to take part. On one occasion a young Roman officer was so overcome with passion for this graceful girl that he rushed up the steps which led to the stage and lifted her up in his arms to carry her before the statue of Venus, where he vowed to love her eternally.

Wonderful to relate, Arcella's heart was stirred by his bold action, and faced with the choice before her, she eventually decided to abandon the theatre and become the wife of her gallant admirer. But a few days before her marriage the lure of the dance became so strong that she decided to dance just once more, not before the adoring crowd in the theatre but alone, under the clear moonlit sky, and in the solitude of Les Alyscamps. There she danced the night away, swept up in the delirium of her own grace and motion. She danced until she could no longer stand, then collapsed against a stone sarcophagus and fell gently to the ground, where next morning the attendants found her dead.

Arles has long been renowned as a place for female beauty, the dark handsome faces of the girls being said to come from their Greek forebears 2,000 and more years ago. So far as I am aware, none has ever alleged that the male inhabitants of Arles are particularly handsome, but *l'Arlésienne* is of great repute and not only because of Bizet. Indeed, Charles Wood wrote enthusiastically about them when he visited the city in 1899.

'Fair women? They are indeed fair women. We had long heard of the charm of the *Arlésiennes*, but our imagination fell short of the truth. We never anticipated such a galaxy of beauty – beauty of a noble and splendid type ... Their forms are magnificent; they hold themselves like queens, walk like queens, their heads are set upon their shoulders as though they were mistresses of the world.' He went on for two more pages, so impressed was he with Arlesian beauty. Indeed, he went to the arena not to see the *course de cocarde*, at which he apparently never cast a glance, but merely to watch spellbound the graceful ladies of Arles.

It is not easy to imagine that Arles was once a seaport. In fact, it originally had two ports. One was on both sides of the Rhône, much where the small amount of river traffic draws in nowadays, but the silting of the river mouth meant that Arles was only accessible to ships drawing less than three feet, and already in the seventeenth century the great engineer Vauban declared that the mouths of the Rhône would always be *incorrigibles*. Long before that the merchants of Arles had solved the problem by constructing a second port on the other side of the town, connected by a channel to the lagoons. This, as Petrarch related, made it possible for fully laden vessels to come and go between the city and the Grau de Galejon, a deep-water, sheltered inlet on the coast.

Originally the waterway, which is now closed, had two intermediate locks along its 30 miles of straight and somewhat uninteresting cuts. The first one, a mere mile and a half down from the entrance, has the double bascule of Van Gogh's famous painting *Canal en Provence*.

It may seem strange to have a small canal running parallel to a broad and navigable river, but its origin goes back to Roman times, when Arles was a port not too far from the sea, which has moved back about 15 miles since the days of Constantine. Roger de Howeden described in his travelogue of 1191 how, on their way to join King Richard in the Holy Land, the English vessels followed the Mediterranean coast as far as Marseille, touching successively at the ports of St Gilles and the episcopal city of Arles.

In the days of the Romans the whole area was one of marsh and shallow lagoons, and it was the commander Marius who undertook the work of cutting a new channel through the soft and partly waterlogged ground. Three factors were against the shipping coming up the Rhône. First, the bar at the mouth. Second, the adverse current, especially in time of flood. Thirdly, there was the mistral. The Roman cargo-ships were somewhat clumsy and had no more than a lugsail, and if the full force of the mistral was added to the current of the Rhône the upstream journey was impossible.

Marius hit on the very sensible idea of cutting a canal through the flat land to the nearest point on the coast, so that the ships could be bank-hauled in still water.

The canal of Marius consisted of cuts (*fossae*) which joined the meres, and channels through shallows. There were of course no locks, but the present canal is a direct descendant of the Roman waterway – a fact that is hinted by the name of its destination, Fos, where the Fossae Marianae reached open water. Marius later ceded the canal and its upkeep to the Greek shippers in Marseille as a reward for their help in supplying his army in his initial campaign against the barbarians who were intending to march along the littoral to Rome itself. It was on the flat hilltop at the end of the Alpilles hills, only three miles from Tarascon, that he encamped during that fateful camping in AD 101, and it was a good position. His forces were safe on the hilltop, the plain of Arles was an excellent source of provisions, and he could watch for the enemy arriving in the Rhône valley. When the barbarians appeared, he followed them eastward toward Aix and then descended upon them with such success that the name of *campi putridi* (now Pourrières) attached to a locality in the plain of the small river Arc is a fearful reminder of the massacre. According to Roman authors, who may well have exaggerated, 200,000 were killed and 86,000 taken as slaves in the battle, and the weary legionaries had to drink water from streams red with blood.

Marseille

Marseille has nothing to do with the French national anthem, beyond the fact that when Captain Rouget de Lisle had knocked up his song for a banquet in Strasbourg, the tune was a catchy one and, when first sung by soldiers on the march, those troops happened to be Marseillaises. It is obviously a very ancient town, and if Greeks from Phocis found and settled in the excellent natural harbour which is now the old port, they later found it also to be an ideal place for producing salt by evaporation of sea water. It became known later as Salt Farm, Mas Salia. Marseille has long been celebrated for its dark-eyed female beauties, and some like to trace the origin of so much feminine grace back to the beginnings of the city itself as told in the romantic story of Gyptis, the lovely daughter of Senannus, King of the Segobrigi.

It was in 599 BC that a small flotilla of Ionian ships from Phocis arrived in the bay which nowadays is the Vieux Port, under the command of a young adventurer named Protis. As soon as they had landed in the bay the Phoceans very wisely decided to place themselves under the protection of the local tribe, and Protis set off with suitable gifts to Arles, where the King had his headquarters. By good fortune Protis arrived there on the day when Senannus had invited all his redoubtable chieftains to a feast. During the dinner his graceful daughter Gyptis was to select one of them as her husband, and according to custom she would advance toward her chosen man and hold out to him the goblet of wine from which – if able to stand – he was to drink. Protis arrived at Arles unexpected, a complete stranger, but Senannus had the goodwill to invite him to the banquet. His courtesy, his elegance and charm, his good manners and no doubt his behaviour at table too, were so much in contrast to the tough vulgarity and coarse boasting of his companions at the feast that the girl, passionate and determined and perhaps lured by the attraction of something so unusual and exotic, and an escape from a less attractive fate, advanced straight toward him and, in spite of the protests and belchings of the warriors, proudly held out to Protis the goblet which was the symbol of union. He took it from her, looked into her eyes and drank the cup to the bottom. The betrothal was sealed.

When they saw the courteous treatment Protis showed to his bride, a number of the friends of Gyptis were quick to escape and seek out other young men among the Phoceans at Massalia. The happy couples quickly put up a few houses and some sort of stockade. This was a wise precaution, for more and more of the wives and daughters of the tough Segobrigi defected to the civilised ways of the new community. Naturally, their former menfolk became worked up into a state of fury. Craftily the warriors from the surrounding country came in great numbers to one of the festivals in the new town. They arrived smiling and friendly and obviously unarmed – for they had sent all their weapons ahead of them in market wagons covered with foliage.

Yet the romantic charm of the men from Ionia was to save the infant city, for a daughter of one of the warriors who was about to take part in the slaughter revealed the plot to a young Phocean with whose mere appearance she had instantly fallen in love. Swiftly his companions raided the wagons, seized the

289

arms, and, inviting the rough and hardened Segobrigi to enter
the gate, they inflicted such a slaughter upon them that they
never again attempted to conquer Massalia. More and more
Ionians arrived by sea to swell the population, and we may
assume that fresh waves of beautiful girls managed to escape
over the arid country to join them. In this happy way, if we can
believe the legend, Marseille was established, a city founded on
brains and beauty.

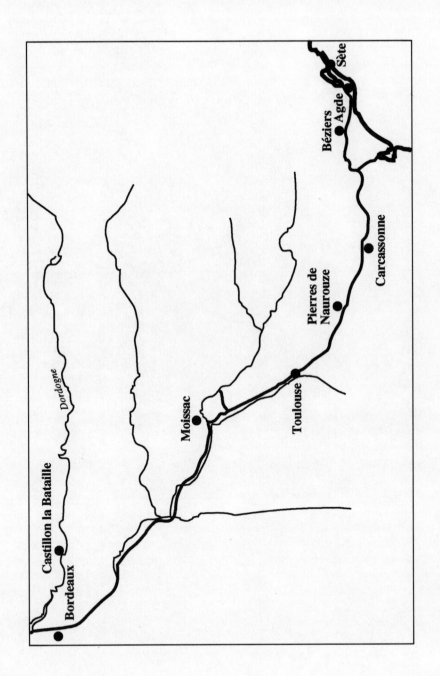

16

The Canal du Midi, St Gilles, Aigues Mortes, Maguelone,
Sète, Agde; Béziers, Carcassonne, Naurouze, Toulouse,
Castillon-la-Bataille and Moissac

The line of the Canal du Midi is that of the earliest interseas
canal in the world. Constructed by a collector of taxes, Pierre
Paul Riquet, it is a triumph of engineering carried out without
modern machinery, and with little experience to go on. It has
the world's first canal tunnel, and its course is lined with plane
trees which gave shade from the southern sun to the horses
which hauled the ships. Louis XIV declared the work worthy of
his patronage and 'capable of perpetuating through the centuries
to come the memory of its author and reflecting the grandeur,
liberality and happiness of his reign.' (By author he meant
himself.)

The canal being in one of the driest areas of France, Riquet cut
a feeder 65kms long to bring water from the Montagne Noire to
the summit level at Naurouze, an amazing achievement.

Much of the canal follows a contour – as in the 53km pound
west of Béziers. Various works were later added by Vauban,
and in the nineteenth century a branch leading to Narbonne was
added. At the same time, the Garonne (into which the canal ran
at Toulouse) was becoming unnavigable through shoaling, and
it was by-passed most of the way to Bordeaux by a new line,
the Canal Latéral à la Garonne.

The Dordogne is nowadays only navigable on the tide as far
as Castillon, with difficulty.

St Gilles

It was here halfway along the Canal du Rhône à Sète that the
papal legate Pierre de Castelnau was murdered, giving an
excuse for the Albigensian Crusade. The Abbey still has a few

items of great beauty, but the ignorant Revolutionaries thought the saints to be members of the royalty, and cut off the heads of most of them.

St Gilles is a good starting point for a visit to Les Saintes Maries de la Mer. In summertime this small town on the coast is high on the list of tourist traps, with stalls selling cowboy hats and bags made of horsehair, but I personally think it worth wearing blinkers and making straight for the ancient fortified church, for the memory contained within it is believed very possibly to be that of the first Christian community in France. According to legend it was here that the boat landed which carried St Martha and her companions, and it is where the two Marys settled after Lazarus had gone to Marseille, Mary Magdalene to the Massif of the Sainte Baume (Holy Cave) behind the coastal hills towards La Ciotat, and Martha to Tarascon. The Marys in question were the mothers respectively of St James the Major (of Compostella) and of St John, and of St James the Less and St Jude. They are said to have erected here the first Christian altar in the whole of France about the year AD 42, but to have lived a quiet and secluded life, unrecognised and undisturbed, pondering the amazing events which they had witnessed at the Crucifixion and immediately after.

The two women are also said to have had a girl servant named Sara, who later became the great patroness of the gypsies. None are quite sure whether they took to her because her statue had a black face, or whether the Sara in the church was given the black face later to please them. But she is there as large as life, in the crypt. Not being a saint she is not allowed upstairs, only emerging on 24 May for the two days of celebration and pilgrimage attended by the Camargue *guardiens* (or cowboys), by gypsies from all over Europe, and of course a great crowd of visitors. The reliquaries of the Marys are brought out, the charming statues of the two women in their little boat are carried round the town and out into the water, where priests wading out to their armpits (provided the sea is calm) bless the sea and the fishermen. It is a most extraordinary and exuberant Camargue occasion, and perhaps most easily witnessed if wearing a swimsuit.

Even if Les Saintes Maries in summertime seems ready to sink into the sand under the weight of junk – for tourism is its only trade – it is worth turning a blind eye to all the trading just to enter the cool, dark vault of the fortified church, which rises up like a castle among the houses. It can be a most moving experience, for an air of age-old devotion pervades the building. On the left of the nave are the figures of the two Marys, waiting in their little boat for the next blessing of the sea, and under the east end a few steps lead down to where the figure of Sara stands arrayed in one of her glittery dresses, illuminated by the flickering light of the hundreds of candles provided by her devotees. Indeed, the whole church is blackened on the ceiling by centuries of waxy smoke, yet there is something about the place which is not just tawdry and superstitious but sincere and not easily forgotten.

Much research has gone into the matter of the Marys. It has even been suggested that they have been derived from Marius the Roman canal builder, who was said by Plutarch to have had a female Syrian soothsayer in attendance upon him, named Martha. This is the disadvantage of living in a hypercritical and sceptical age. Much that is beautiful and romantic is missed, and in this book I unblushingly tell the tales and legends that have been handed down, for very often they have a charm and poignancy of their own. It is possible to explain the colours of a sunset over the Camargue entirely in terms of refraction and absorption of various wavelengths – to say nothing of retinal pigments and optic nerves. But I like the sunset all the same for its glory of colour. And the same is true of Les Saintes Maries. Besides, I suspect that the tale may well be founded on fact.

The Abbey of St Gilles was a place to which pilgrims in their thousands would come on their way to St James of Compostella, or if taking ship at Aigues Mortes on their way to the Holy Land. They would file past the tomb of St Gilles himself, the same whose Cathedral of St Giles in Edinburgh takes him half way to being a national saint of Scotland. Not that St Gilles himself had any connection with that country, for he began his life in Greece and ended it in the abbey which bears his name. Between these two events he lived the life of a hermit, and he has a permanent place in the legends of Provence.

Aegidius, Gilles or Giles, set out on his wanderings in the sixth century, and leaving his native Greece he eventually reached the forest near the mouth of the Rhône. It was there that he was to become one of the many European saints associated with deer. He did not hunt a stag as Hubert did, nor was he saved from an untimely and involuntary marriage, as was Notburga of the Neckar. But he has this in common with the rest, that his deer was an albino. It is said that he lived alone with it in the forest, and that in return for the hospitality of his

295

rough shelter the doe nourished him with her milk. News of the white doe – which by reason of its albino genes could hardly escape being seen – eventually reached the King of Provence, who at once decided that he must hunt it down. A party was got together consisting of seven score dogs and an even greater number of huntsmen, and as this immense force accompanied the king through the forest a white flash among the trees showed that they were on the right trail.

Fleeing before the hunt, the doe led the chase further and further into the forest, and as she drew near to where Gilles lived beneath the trees, the din of the pursuit roused him from his prayers. He hurried out to see that his faithful friend and provider should come to no harm, and saw the doe cornered, cowering in terror behind a tree. At this moment one of the royal huntsmen drew his bow and shot, but Gilles stretched out his leg and the arrow lodged in his knee. He pulled it out, the tale says, and prayed that the wound might never heal, so that he should always be reminded of the sufferings of Christ.

This curious incident so surprised the king that he asked his attending bishop to enquire of Gilles who he was, and how and where he lived. The hermit told his tale and the king immediately offered to subsidise him, and to give him a position where he could live in comfort and honour. Gilles preferred to return to his lair with only the doe as company, but now that his secret was out he was continually sought out by the poor and needy. At last he accepted the repeated offer of the king to build him an abbey, and the institution was erected on the spot where he had been pierced by the hunter's arrow. Gilles still slept on the ground rather than in a bed, but he accepted the role of Abbot. So good and saintly was he that the great Charlemagne is said to have been willing to confess only to Gilles, and in Chartres a window shows him doing so; but as Gilles lived in the sixth century and Charlemagne in the ninth the tale is not altogether convincing.

The magnificent front of the abbey was wrecked by the French Revolutionaries, who chopped off the heads of most of the statues, thinking that they were the kings and queens of France. This was iconoclasm at its most stupid. Nevertheless, enough remains for one to realise that it was one of the greatest works of medieval art.

The legends of Gilles do not stop even with Charlemagne. When his abbey was to be founded he naturally betook himself to Rome to have the Pope approve the scheme, and it is said that the Pope not only gave his sanction but a pair of fine carved wooden doors as well. Gilles had somehow to take them back to Provence, so he threw the doors into the Tiber – presumably when the Pope was not watching – and sure enough, he had only just reached home when they were washed ashore on the bank of the Petit Rhône close to the abbey.

In the year 1207 the Cathar heresy was by no means new, but it was in that year that St Gilles was the scene of an event which was to have the most terrible consequences for the Languedoc. At that time Pierre de Castelnau was Legate to the Languedoc, and his particular charge was to contain or put down the heresy which was growing so alarmingly in the domains of the Count of Toulouse. Count Raymond VI openly gave shelter and encouragement to those who did not agree with the dogma and practices of the Church of Rome which, within his realm, had reached an almost unbelievable state of corruption. Pierre de Castelnau set about inciting the lords of Provence to rebel against Raymond, and as this was not successful, he publicly excommunicated him and outlawed his territories, pronouncing in advance a blessing on any who should strike the Count dead. Either from real fear for the fate of his soul, or more probably to make an appearance of subservience and so avoid the worst result of the interdict for his people, the Count came to St Gilles to make formal submission to the authority of Rome. The scene in the abbey was a victory for the Legate, and certainly it was his day of triumph. But it was also his last, for as he left the town to cross the Petit Rhône, one of the Count's officers ran him through with a sword. That was too much for Pope Innocent III, and he gave the signal for the forces of Europe to be launched against the Albigensians in a war of extermination.

The final destruction of the last strongholds of the Albigensians was not to be achieved for nearly 40 years, but only two years after the murder of the Legate the crowds were gathered again at St Gilles to see Count Raymond VI humiliated a second time. He was forced to submit in public to the supreme religious authority of the Pope. More than a score of bishops had been summoned to see Raymond submit to whatever the new Legate demanded of him.

There was little that the Legate did not require. A collection of relics (which the heretics despised) was set outside the door, and grovelling before them, the Count had to swear obedience to the officials of the Pope. Stripped to the waist, he was then led into the church with a rope round his neck. At each step the clergy beat him on his bare back, and still stripped and bleeding, he was forced to pass through the crypt where not only St Gilles but the Count's own former mortal enemy Pierre de Castelnau lay buried. Even this was only a beginning, for the outward humiliations were no more than the formal seal set upon eight conditions which he had to accept, each of which involved either submission to the clergy of his domains or some restriction of freedom for his subjects – such as that all Jews were to be dismissed from holding office in his territories.

Probably the Count thought that by appearing to accept these indignities he would hold off the storm which threatened his people, but he was mistaken. He was a tolerant man, and there was no place for tolerance in the world of Innocent III. When, 13 years later, Count Raymond lay dying, he was refused the Last Sacrament – a thing that may or may not have been so terrible to his mind but which showed unambiguously the extent to which the Church of Rome knew his submission was not genuine. And not content with that, they refused him burial, and for years his coffin remained above the ground until finally his remains were eaten by rats. Yet even this was as nothing to the fate which was dealt out to those throughout his domains who dared to accept teachings which had not the stamp of Papal approval, and in one locality after another they were slaughtered without mercy and their homes razed to he ground.

So much for the events in the Abbey church of St Gilles. The heretics were duly exterminated, and the *ignorami* of the French Revolution eventually succeeded in smashing most of what was beautiful on the façade of one of the finest medieval buildings in all France. Perhaps it is no accident that the kiss of Judas has remained unscathed as a monument to socialism.

Aigues Mortes

A walled town on the Canal du Rhône à Sète, with an outlet to the sea at le Grau du Roi, Aigues Mortes is in the centre of the Camargue, a large marshy tract extending from near Arles to Sète. North of the canal are the remains of the Abbey of Psalmodi, though it was salt and not plainsong which gave the place its name. The monks who lived entirely on the fish which abounded in the marshes, sold some of their land to Louis IX when he needed a base for his operations against the Infidel. Upon it he built the astonishing town of Aigues Mortes.

When Louis IX assembled his force of 60,000 men, the walls had only just been begun, but planning for a protracted war with the Saracens he had devised a fortified town which could serve as a permanent point of assembly and supply, and the building of it was finished by his son. And while a fleet of Genoese vessels was being assembled in the grau, royal quarter-masters were preparing dumps of supplies in places as far away as Cyprus. No previous crusade had been more carefully con-ceived, or more magnificent. Each involved nation had its encampment around the little town – for the great walls were not yet built – and the various flags showed which they were. There was the Leopard of England, the Lion of Brabant, and the Lion of St Mark for the Venetians. The Genoese vaunted a red cross, the papal contingent a triple crown. Altogether, 60,000 warriors are said to have been assembled, but personally I doubt this estimate, for such a crowd could hardly have found standing room on the ships of that period assembled in the grau. Yet it was certainly a long procession that filed through the little church to receive a blessing upon their undertaking, for the special envoy of the Pope had come to bestow on each knight a particular benediction as the warriors filed and clanked through the chapel which is still there, very much as it was at the time but mellowed by age. The year was 1248, and some of those who received the benediction bore titles newly taken from the heretic lords of the Languedoc whose people they had so recently slaughtered.

Even now one can almost see them embarking, each knight with a chest to serve him as travelling trunk, as a bed, as a coffin if he should be unfortunate enough to die at sea instead of cleft to the waist by a Saracen scimitar on the hot sands. And notable perhaps by his simplicity amid all the pomp and glitter was the rather dreamy figure of Louis IX, the future saint. Thin and fragile, pale and with his refined face framed in locks of long fair hair, he moved about with gentle confidence and an almost unearthly surety in the rightness of his mission. Cheers greeted him, we are told, wherever he was seen, but always he remained humble, the very epitome of gentility. Yet it seems that he had a tougher side too, for a hagiography which I acquired from a *bouquinist* at Aigues Mortes itself mentions that he was so pious that if anyone should blaspheme he had their tongue bored through with a red-hot iron, declaring to the unfortunate victim that he would most willingly suffer the same torture himself if by doing so he could rid his realm of cursing and blasphemy. But now his thoughts were fixed only on wresting the Holy Land from the Infidel, as he stood with his fair hair streaming from below his helmet, beside the queen and her ladies aboard the royal galley to receive a final blessing, and the soldiers, bareheaded, raised the great strain *Come, Holy Ghost, our hearts inspire*, and then the sails unfurled, and the heavy vessels slowly lumbered out to sea – the *Reine*, the *Montjoie*, the *Damoiselle* and their 35 companion ships. The banners streamed in the salty air and after some hours the fleet was hull down on the horizon. The Seventh Crusade was on its way.

Months later, Louis leapt ashore at Damietta and would have attacked the Mussulman host single-handed. Then came the costly victory of Mansourah, and after it the capture of Louis himself. He was ransomed in gold to return to France with such few of his soldiers as survived.

The queen who stood beside Louis as the fleet sailed from Aigues Mortes was the striking and talented Marguerite, eldest of the four remarkable daughters of Raymond-Bérenger V, Count of Provence and of Forcalquier – in which little Provencal town there is a monument with an inscription in English to remind the visitor that the eldest of Marguerite's sisters, Aliénor (that is, Eleanor of Aquitaine, the province she collected through her first marriage), spouse of Henry Plantagenet, was born there. Beside the voluptuous Eleanor, whose funeral journey was one day to be marked by the erection of crosses such as Waltham Cross and Charing Cross where her cortege rested overnight, there was Sanche, who married the brother of the English king, and Béatrice, who espoused the brother of the French monarch.

Maguelone

Outside Palavas on the Canal du Rhône à Sète, Maguelone was formerly an island. Nowadays it is partly a rehabilitation centre, but during the summer it has a music festival.

It is upon this strange and remote place that centres the story of Pierre of Provence, young and handsome and chivalrous, who, having heard of the astounding loveliness of the daughter of the King of Naples, set off to that far-off destination to behold her for himself, and jousted before her in the tournament then taking place. It proved to be a case of mutual love at first sight, but unfortunately the King of Naples had promised the

300

fair princess Maguelone to a prince, so there was nothing for the young couple but to elope, in the full certainty of an undying love. It can be noted here that this was not a case of betrothal with parental approval, so the story is a perfectly proper one for a romantic troubadour to relate.

In the noontide heat Maguelone became tired, so the couple sat in the shade of a tree and she fell asleep on his lap. Pierre noticed a little silken bag in her bosom, and filled with curiosity he quietly drew it out to peer inside. With joy he saw it contained three rings he had sent to her earlier through her nurse (he must have been quite young at the time), and not wishing to wake her, he put down the little purse on a stone. Unfortunately a raven swooped, snatched the bag and flew off with it.

Pierre pushed his coat as a pillow under Maguelone's head, then rushed after the raven, which eventually perched on a rock in the sea. He flung a stone at the bird and gave it such a fright that it opened its beak and dropped the little bag into the water. At this, he hurried off to find a boat and rowed out to collect the purse, which fortunately was still floating. But the wind got up, and while still trying to retrieve the jewels, Pierre was blown out to sea and eventually reached land again at Alexandria, where the Sultan took him on as his private page.

Meanwhile, the poor girl awoke and found herself alone. After a fearful night in the forest she set out for Rome, and so that she would not be detected by her father's men she managed to exchange clothes with a female pilgrim, and disguised herself as an anchorite. Eventually she set out from Genoa on a ship bound for Aigues Mortes. Hearing of a small island which would serve her as a hermitage, she used her remaining jewellery to pay for the building of a church, and a hospital for the pilgrims and the poor. The one woman who became her close friend was the Countess of Melgueil (now Mauguio), who eventually unburdened herself to Maguelone of the great tragedy in her life. Her beloved son had gone off in a fit of romantic dreaming about some girl or other to Naples, and had never been heard of since.

One day a local fisherman netted a tunny and brought it to the count as a present. When it was gutted, the stomach of the fish was found to contain a little bag with three rings. At once the countess recognised them as the ones she had given to her dear son, and, of course, she told her friend Maguelone about this extraordinary incident, and showed her the rings.

The story now moves to Alexandria, where Pierre had become

such a favourite that the Sultan had come to regard him very much as his own son, and eventually allowed him to return to Provence to visit his home. Pierre had amassed a fortune, but to keep it hidden from the skipper and crew of the cargo vessel on which he was to travel, he packed it in 14 barrels topped up with salt. One day the vessel put in for water at an island off the coast of Corsica, and Pierre went ashore to stretch his legs. He walked some way into the interior, lay down in the sun and went sound asleep.

The crew searched for Pierre but were unable to find him, so eventually the captain assumed some awful fate had overtaken him and set sail without him. When the ship reached Provence, the honest skipper felt that he could not keep the belongings of a man lost on the voyage, and hearing of the energetic and saintly young woman who ministered to the sick, he sailed along the shore to a small islet and presented her with the barrels of salt. When one day she needed some more salt and went to dig in one of the barrels she was amazed to find the store of treasure, with which she reconstructed and enlarged the church and hospital.

As for Pierre, he became ill on his small island, and though sick and half-starved he was lucky enough to be rescued by some fishermen who put in there. Having also heard of Maguelone, they delivered him to her care, but he was so transformed through his sufferings that she did not recognise him. And because she was wearing a veil he, of course, did not realise who she was. Then at last came the day when he told her of his life's great sorrow, the loss of his one true love. The rest of the tale can easily be imagined, and as the fair Maguelone was a free agent and had not taken the veil but was only disguised as one who might have done so, the happy ending was just as one could wish. After which the troubadour no doubt passed round the hat.

Another story makes a more obvious connection for the name of Maguelone. Simon the leper is said in this version to have been among the boatload of refugees from the Holy Land, and to have settled on the island, where there was a temple served by Vestal virgins. He preached the Gospel, which so upset them that the women murdered him and flung his body into the *étang*. His companion, Mary Magdalene, escaped and transferred herself to the cave of the Sainte Baume in Provence after sheltering for a short while in another cave close to the island, at what is now Villeneuve-les-Maguelone. It is her name that is recalled in that strangely romantic isle.

The eastern terminus of the Canal du Midi, Sète is an important port. The town canals are mostly now crossed by fixed bridges, but there is a way through from the sea to the Bassin de Thau, the large salt lake that leads to the lighthouse of Les Onglous, where the canal proper begins.

Approaching Sète the canal becomes dirty, its banks littered with rubbish. But there is compensation in the fact that this is the part of the route where one comes very close to flamingoes. Incongruously, they stand unconcerned in the shallows over the canal bank beyond the oil storage tanks, busily dredging up food with their inverted scoops. Beyond their marsh the route broadens out and at last opens to the long inland salt lake of the Bassin de Thau.

Traffic rumbles over the cobbled streets and along the quay-sides, much of it tanker lorries but not bearing the familiar house colours of Esso and Shell or BP. Instead they are Cinzano and Dubonnet or Martini and Rossi, or more often nameless carriers from which a tell-tale dripping of dark red into a bucket hung beneath the stop-cock at the rear indicates that this is the produce of the Languedoc on its way to be blended or bottled. A smell of wine borne on the wings of the mistral pervades the whole town, but when the mistral dies and is replaced by a warm wind from the south, then the odour changes too. It changes to fish, for Sète is a major port for the sardine trade. Freezer lorries from as far away as Boulogne and Dunkirk are loaded at the fish quay and driven for a day and a night to deliver fresh fish that has never swum in the North Sea or flopped over the Dogger Bank or the Varne.

It is this immense activity of fishing that gives Sète so much of its charm, the big drifters in their sun-faded paint of blue and green and red jostling for position at the unloading quay where the town canal runs toward its end behind the huge protecting mole. And this canal once was spanned by three or four swing bridges, and a strident ringing of bells preceded the clanging of barriers as each span in turn swung to let pass some craft on its way to or from the great salty lake of the Étang de Thau. Nowadays, in the interest of lessening the congestion of road traffic the bridges have been replaced by fixed ones just high enough to pass the one-man oyster boats from the ports on the Étang, but no more.

The Canal du Midi

In 1996 the Canal du Midi was officially recognised by UNESCO as a member of the world heritage of human achievement – along with the Sphinx, the Pyramids, and the Great Wall of China. Undoubtedly it deserves this distinction, for it is the first canal in the world to be built to join two seas (the Atlantic and the Mediterranean), and its construction was a triumph for Pierre Paul Riquet, Baron of Bonrepos, who impoverished himself in the attempt and died shortly before its opening in 1683.

The lowest point between the two seas had for some time been correctly established as the Pierres de Naurouze, some 680 feet above sea level, but this was in a dry district, and vast lengths of feeder streams had to be cut from the Montagne Noire to Naurouze to provide water for lockage in both directions. Not far from Béziers the canal passes through a hill in the *Percée de Malpas*, the first canal tunnel in the world.

The original line began at the port of Sète, passed through the great salty lake of the Bassin de Thau, and at Béziers entered the Neuf Ecluses de Fonseranes, a mighty staircase of nine (but now only seven) locks. Owing to occasional water shortages, this flight has recently been paralleled by an inclined plane, up which boats may be taken with virtually no loss of water.

The canal in its original form only reached Toulouse, where it joined the River Garonne. Later, the shoaling of the river presented too great problems for navigation, and the line was continued in the Canal Latéral à la Garonne to reach the Garonne itself at Castets-en-Dorthe, upstream of Bordeaux. But for all practical purposes the whole route is known as the Canal du Midi, and we shall follow that practice here.

304

Agde

Situated where the Canal du Midi crosses the River Hérault, Agde has that rarity of engineering, a circular lock. The purpose of this is to effect a junction with a short side-branch giving access to the sea, and it is an example of the ingenuity of the designer of the Canal du Midi. Whether it was devised by Andreossy, or young Pierre, or the Royal Commissioners, or by the Baron of Bonrepos himself, the lock was a brilliant solution to a particular problem. The old mill weir which spans the Hérault in Agde itself causes a step in the level, and the Canal du Midi needed access to both parts of the river – the upper section for navigation and the lower reach so that barges could visit the port of Agde itself and ships could sail out to the sea beyond. So the round lock was devised with a gate at each end and another in the side, each at a different level. The roundedness is merely to give space for a ship to pass straight across or out at the side, according to the skipper's intentions.

The lock stands by a group of magnificent plane trees at the end of the curving cut from the upper Hérault, and the deserted tow-path along the quiet and reedy side canal leads to a splendid view of Agde itself. Nothing of the town is seen until at the very last moment, when all of a sudden it is there, straight across the river, its broad stone quay and cramped little houses making one of the prettiest waterfronts in all France. Once Agde used to be on the sea, but that was long ago. The port is now inland, with more than two miles of channel leading down to the salt water. Sitting beside the summer Hérault Agde looks safe enough, but the great iron rings in the walls of the houses across the quay show how high the river may be expected to rise, and no doubt there is sometimes a chance of catching fish in one's own kitchen. Fishing craft, heavy and sun bleached, still lie along either side of the stream, and the humble life of the fishermen and sailors in their waterside houses is emphasised by the enormous black mass of the Cathedral of St Étienne, built eight centuries ago of lava from the nearby hill and so tough and unweathered that it looks as though consecrated only a month ago and made of some new and resistant breeze block.

It is abundantly clear that the Bishop of Agde, back in the days when Infidels were on the prowl by sea, was going to brook no nonsense. This was the Church Militant, even if others might think it the Church Decadent. The Cathedral would stay there, standing fast with all the impregnable rigidity of a dogma. That is why the black building resembles a fort more than a church. There is not so much as an arrow slit or embrasure to let a clink of light penetrate its astonishing black façade. Instead there are machicolations, battlements, and all manner of handy places from which to pour boiling oil or shoot down attackers with arrows. The tower is a fortified keep, with turrets commanding a view of the walls. There is even a means of hauling up supplies from ground level. Naturally, the nave is as dark as a dungeon, and nothing could be more eloquent of the state of affairs in twelfth-century Agde if the church had thus to be protected, not just from possible sea-borne Saracens but from the humble Agathois themselves – *lous bochs* (the madmen) as they are known to their neighbours, on the grounds that they are supposed to spend much of their time in pleasure.

Agde is one of the oldest towns in France, and when the Cathedral was built in the twelfth century the port was already two-thirds of the way along the line of its history leading to today. Like Marseille, it was founded by adventurous seamen from a city state of Greece. Richelieu furnished it with an immense mole, for he intended to make Agde the premier port of the Mediterranean. Whilst he was still alive the States of the Languedoc could only dare accept the idea and foot the bill, but as soon as he died they stopped the works. Then came the plans for the Canal du Midi. Had the port been completed it would certainly have been the terminus of the line, but the royal commissioners chose to build a new harbour at Sète instead. Agde was only allowed the short branch canal as a sort of consolation prize.

Béziers

The second city of the Department of l'Hérault, Béziers spills down the hillside toward the Canal du Midi, which here crosses the River Orb on an aqueduct. Up at the summit the city spreads away behind the fortified Bishop's Palace and the great Cathedral of St Nazaire.

The view from the aqueduct is the finest along the whole length of the Canal du Midi, and it is impossible to look across to that splendid and beautiful city without a pang of realisation that there, on the feast of St Mary Magdalene in the year 1209, a terrible event occurred which was to put off the Reformation for more than 300 years and seal the destruction of the highest and finest civilisation which Europe then knew.

The very day after the murder of the papal legate Pierre de Castelnau as he left St Gilles, the signal was given for a war against the heretics, a crusade against those who did not accept the authority of the Church of Rome, and in particular upon the Count of Toulouse and his young nephew Raymond-Roger Trencavel, Viscount of Béziers and Carcassonne, in whose territories the heretics were firmly established and tolerated. These heretics were of two distinct kinds; there were the Waldensians – followers of Pierre Waldo of Lyon, a wealthy merchant who had the scriptures translated from the Latin and who then renounced his wealth and position to live in charity with the poor. Shocked by the abuses and pretension of the Roman Church, Waldo and his friends attempted to live like the Apostles in poverty, preaching the Gospel as they wandered from place to place. They recognised no ecclesiastical authority but God, and they not only threw over the Pope and a corrupt priesthood but much of Catholic doctrine and dogma, too. They could not accept the ideas of purgatory or of transubstantiation, and they ruled out praying to saints. Indeed, the Waldensians were the first breath of the Reformation, and a serious menace to the authority, power and revenues of the Church of Rome – which they uncompromisingly identified with the Great Whore of Babylon.

The same identification was made by the Cathars (or Albigensians, after the Languedoc district where they flourished). The Waldensians were more to be found in the Alps, but there were certainly a number at Béziers, even if the vast majority of those who opposed the Church of Rome where the Cathars, the 'pure ones'. Some of the beliefs of the Cathars have been lost forever, because the crusade against them endeavoured to destroy every trace of their Church, but certainly they emphasised the wisdom of Christ rather than sufferings, and they abhorred reverence for the Cross. If one's son was slain, they logically demanded, would one revere his memory for what he was, or would one worship whatever weapon or accident had killed him?

There was more to the Albigensian heresy than just a revolt against the abuses of the Catholic clergy, great though they were. The movement came from the Bogomils (or beloved of God) who flourished in Bulgaria in the tenth century and spread across to the Languedoc a theology which contained various elements from the East. The chief 'heretical' point was the

307

Cathar insistence that the world was under a sort of dual control, everything physical being the work of Satan, alias Jehovah. The good God sent Christ as a mediator, but because it was unthinkable that he could have had a genuine or satanic body, Christ was not 'really real'. From this it followed that he could not genuinely have suffered or died, but the Devil cleverly founded the Roman Church to make believers think that he had done so.

The notion that everything physical was created by the evil deity led the Cathars to abhor anything associated with reproduction. Eggs and meat were banned, and so was milk. The Cathars themselves had a horror of sexual relations as aiding the Devil in his creative activity. How far these notions were understood and accepted by the *credentes*, the rank and file of adherents, is another matter. Probably much of the doctrine was above their heads, and certainly the great majority of them were married.

There was a single sacrament, a laying-on of hands which conferred the Holy Spirit. This was only given to a person after he had spent a year or two in study and preparation, and when he had received it he thereupon became a *perfectus*, a *bonhomme*. From that moment he gave away all his goods, he ate no food of animal origin, he lived ascetically, gave his life to prayer and preaching and service, and dressed in a black robe. Whether a man or a woman, he swore never to retract for fear of death by fire or any other means, and amid all the barbarity of their persecution there is only one single recorded case of an initiate recanting.

The *perfecti*, or ministers of the Cathars, thus lived in a state of poverty and purity and dedication which stood in complete contrast to the affluence of many of the Roman clergy. Inevitably they were respected, and their logical and liberal preaching, based on the Gospel of St John, mixed with the romantic ideas of the troubadours to make the Languedoc an area of such freedom that Jews held official posts and professorships, Arabs taught in medical schools, women were largely emancipated, and capital punishment was regarded as barbarous. It was against this splendid flowering of justice and equality and faith that Pope Innocent III, a sincere and fanatically enthusiastic defender of the faith, announced a crusade. He wrote to all bishops, archbishops, counts and barons and knights of France and the North, summoning them to root out the heretics.

For a while nothing happened – nothing, that is, but prepara-

308

tions for launching a murderous assault in the name of the Christian Church. Great forces of knights from France and Germany and Brabant gathered at Lyon for the crusade, their numbers swelled by many thousands of mercenaries – outlaws and brigands and cut-throats who were prepared to fight anybody – and by a horde of pilgrims who hoped to be in at the death and earn the wholesale indulgence granted by Innocent III to any who might strike down a heretic in the lands where the Cathars had taken root. In the same month that Count Raymond made his second and humiliating journey to St Gilles, there to be flayed by the Legates, an armada of lighters began to float down from Lyon. Within a short space of time the largest army Europe had ever seen was camped at the walls of Béziers, its leaders determined to teach these damned barons of the Languedoc a lesson.

Every member of the vast beleaguering force had a reason for enthusiasm. The nobles could have the credit of doing their 40-day crusade service without the dangerous voyage to the Holy Land and the menace of Saracen hordes. The Cathars, abhorring bloodshed, were complete pacifists and – at least in the early stages of the war – would be cleft asunder rather than raise a hand in self-defence. They were hardly a dangerous enemy, and there was freedom to seize their goods and lands for oneself 'in the name of Christ'. The mercenaries were after the loot by which alone they lived. The pilgrims, thousands of them led by a kind of wild mass hysteria, had the chance accorded to them by the Pope of winning salvation and forgiveness by the mere act of murdering a heretic.

Yet in spite of such attractions, the siege of Béziers promised to be a long one. Though hurriedly fortified, the city was well placed and ably defended.

The crusading forces issued an ultimatum. Béziers could hand over some 200 known heretics and their families, and the rest of the population would go free. Otherwise the city would be attacked. This choice was put to the townspeople by their Catholic bishop, and though the burghers must certainly have been predominantly Catholic, they respected the saintliness of the Cathars and burned with indignation at the suggestion that they should hand over their fellow citizens. They would rather be drowned, they said, than submit to such terms.

The details of what happened at Béziers have never been fully known, but it seems that the defenders made a rash sally and the attackers managed to wrest from them the control of one of the gates. Almost at once the fortified city itself was open to the full fury of the mercenaries, and of the frenzied pilgrims pursuing at their heels in the hope of achieving salvation through slaughter. Behind them came the knights in armour, furious that the mercenaries and mob were smashing and wrecking so much of value that might have become their own.

It was not the heretics who were thus cut down, but the whole population, much of it loyal and Catholic. The difficulty of distinguishing heretics, other than the Cathar ministers in their black robes, had already occurred to some of the nobles and, according to the testimony of a German monk who took part in the assault, they posed a question to Arnald-Amalric, the leader of the troops and Abbot of Citeaux.

'Kill the lot,' he replied. 'God will recognise his own.'

It has been suggested that this incident is a Protestant invention, but the fact remains that it is character with what is known of the Abbot of Citeaux, a fanatical defender of the faith. And the instruction was carried out. House after house was broken open, every man, woman and child was clubbed to death or cut down and trampled upon. As the insane fury spread down the streets the citizens fled in panic to the sanctuary of the great Cathedral and the other churches of the town. Priests and monks tolled the bells to summon them, and beyond the clanging and pealing the din of destruction and the screams of the victims filled the air.

But the crusaders had no intentions of respecting sanctuary. The prize was too rich for them to be robbed of it so simply, and battering in the doors of the churches, they slaughtered the people where they prayed and the priests at the altar. Seven thousand were said by a contemporary report to have been murdered in the Church of the Madeleine alone, and the Abbot of Citeaux was able to write to Innocent III to report on his success. 'Some twenty thousand citizens were killed by the sword, without regard to age or sex,' he announced.

The wholesale destruction in the city infuriated the French knights. They cared little for the citizens, but they could not abide seeing the rough mercenaries plundering the wealth of so fine a city. So, among the score of thousand corpses, they turned on the unarmored mercenaries and stripped them of their ill-gotten gains. Furious, these men were steeled to destroy everything in sight, and rather than let the riches of Béziers fall into the hands of the lords and barons, they fired the houses. Quickly the city was swept by the flames, and the Cathedral itself cracked, trembled, and crashed to the ground to bury the dead and dying under a heap of rubble and hot masonry.

For three days the crusaders rested from their exertions, taking their ease in the meadow beside the Orb in the good conscience of a worthy deed well done. Then they moved on, and ahead of them travelled the news of their ruthlessness with such effect that the people of the country fled from their path and many of them took to the forests, or the mountain fastnesses of the Pyrenees.

Carcassonne

The capital city of the Department of Aude, Carcassonne is on the Canal du Midi, east of the summit level. The sight of its magnificently restored girdles of walls is unforgettable, and a particularly good view is to be had from the lay-by on the Autoroute l'Aquitaine. It is easy to see that a fortress city of such a kind was virtually impregnable before the age of gunpowder. Except, of course, by treachery. It is from the troubadours that details of the fate of the city have been handed down, and of how the second hammer blow was dealt to the cause of reformation (or heresy) and thereby to freedom of religion, by the rapacious northern knights under the leadership of the unscrupulous legate Arnald-Amalric.

Only ten days after the slaughter at Béziers the fearful army of the Albigesian crusade was stopped before the intimidating walls of Carcassonne. The fortress was held by a strong garrison, commanded by Raymond-Roger de Trencavel, Viscount of Béziers and Carcassonne, a young man of only 24, strong, handsome, utterly fearless and chivalrous, the ideal not only of the troubadours but of all the people of the Midi and of those who had flocked to Carcassonne to fight or die at his side. Not many weeks had passed since he had been summoned to Montpellier, where the authorities of the Church of Rome ordered him to give up the heretics, the refugees and the Jews who enjoyed freedom in his domains. Alone of all the nobles of Europe, he faced them with the challenge that would offer home and food, shelter and clothing and the defence of his own sword to all who had cause to flee, or were in want. No wonder that the young Raymond-Roger was the object of the hatred of the Legates, nor that his stand caught the imagination of the threatened people of the Languedoc.

311

But the Viscount was a skilled warrior as well as a hero, and when war was unleashed upon him without warning he swiftly and rightly decided that, whether or not Béziers could withstand an attack, it was Carcassonne that could hold up the floodtide of the invasion. Had he been at Béziers on the day of the terrible assault, things might have turned out differently for that unfortunate city, but there can be no doubt that his decision to lead in person the defence of Carcassonne was the right one. He had only been there a few days when news of the fate of Béziers began to sweep across the land ahead of the invaders, and the country people fled to the stronghold, bringing with them their families but also driving their stock and hauling in great quantities of provisions.

In spite of deep wells bored in the hill, water was a serious problem for the crowd of tens of thousands of refugees which now supplemented the garrison, but of other supplies there seems to have been plenty. It soon became clear to the Crusaders that there was no chance of taking the city by assault. Nor could they attempt a protracted siege, for the crusading knights were only bound to serve for 40 days. And besides, Raymond-Roger himself led the most destructive sorties, laying about him with his axe to deadly effect. His troops loved him and they would have died for him, yet the prospect of their having to do so must have seemed to the attackers to be somewhat remote. Carcassonne was as secure a stronghold as any heretic could have.

Yet attack the crusaders did, and for two weeks without ceasing the onslaught continued. Raymond-Roger was always to be found where danger threatened, and as assault towers and ladders were laid against the walls he himself would counterattack and hurl the besiegers down to the ground below. Taking off his helmet he was there for all he people of Carcassonne to see, and many a woman would have died to save such a hero.

At the end of two weeks it was clearer than ever that the fortress was not going to be taken. The invaders had suffered heavy losses, and if many of the townspeople had been crushed or maimed by the stones hurled from catapults, the number of mercenaries and knights whose corpses lay in the moat, or who were dying from the terrible burns of boiling oil must have been immense. The time had come to try other means, and the Legate Arnald-Amalric now invoked his moral principle that it was not necessary to keep an oath to the enemy of God. What could be easier than to ask for a parley, guarantee the young viscount safe conduct, and then seize him as a heretic?

312

And so the knights were persuaded to invite Raymond-Roger de Trencavel to their camp. Certainly the heroic young viscount could not have been duped by the Legate himself, and probably some of his fellow nobles were deceived into inviting him in all good faith. However that may be he was seized, and loaded with chains. Bereft of its valiant leader, the city surrendered.

Raymond-Roger was taken into the fortress and shut away in a dungeon. A few months later he 'died', as imprisoned enemies so frequently do. His wide possessions in the Languedoc were forfeited, and awarded to a eager new owner in the person of Simon de Montfort, the most brutal if sincere leader the occupying forces could have had. The great Crusade had won a victory which disposed of the most dynamic leader among its opponents, and set the seal on its future success as a war of extermination.

Carcassonne is not just a double town but a triple one. There is the new one stretching from the canal port to the Aude, a place of streets laid out geometrically, a bustling centre of business and boutiques, a favourite overnight stop for buses heading for distant Lourdes. Then there is the rather scruffy area across the river, a jumble of town built after the destruction wrought by the Black Prince, and finally the ancient walled Cité, founded in Gallo-Roman days, developed into a mighty fortress which was only taken by treachery and eventually restored by that prince of expert architects Viollet le Duc.

This walled town is still lived in much as in the old days, except that there is no Count in the castle and the shops sell the rubbishy sort of souvenirs one would expect. It is undoubtedly one of the most visited sights in France, and in high summer its streets are thronged with coach-loads from all over Western Europe. For this reason it is difficult to see the place in its full austerity of might, but late in the evening the crowds miraculously vanish and that is the time to take the flight of steps near the castle and pass under an arch in the inner ring wall to the wide grassy expanse of the lists. One can walk most of the way round the fortress in this space and climb up steps or ramps to the outer walls, too. It is quite likely that the area will be absolutely deserted, and one can think oneself back without difficulty into the medieval centuries of love and chivalry, of siege and starvation, of gallant knights jousting for the smile of their favoured ladies, and of a troubadour in the great hall of the Castle of the Counts bowing graciously before striking up to tell the story of some great deed of longer ago, perhaps even that of the brave woman who, in legend, held at bay the formidable forces of the mighty Charlemagne.

That the Cité is ancient one cannot fail to notice. There are indeed Gallo-Roman sections in the walls, and there are towers from the era of the Visigoths, those Dark Age characters who flit in and out of history books, broadsword in hand. There was a fortress on the hill in the days of Charlemagne, and one of the troubadour tales explains how the city came by its name. The great monarch invested the citadel, which was in the hands of the Infidel, and when the Saracen king fell into his hands and refused to become a Christian, Charlemagne very properly had him strangled. The Emperor imagined that this removal of their leader would be a deadly blow to the defenders, but the Saracen Queen Carcas took her husband's place and stirred the men to withstand the onslaught of the forces of Charlemagne.

Five long years the army encircled the beleaguered city, and five long years the defenders held out against spear and arrow, famine and lack of water. Or so it appeared, but in fact by this time only the Queen was alive. She had made dummies out of straw and, dressing them in the clothes of the dead defenders, she propped them in the embrasures. She herself ran round the walls from one position to another, hurling darts and spears in the guise of a soldier, but changing hats between appearances. The soldiers of Charlemagne – simple fellows, no doubt – were thus deceived into believing that the citadel was still held by a formidable force of Saracens, and had it not been for their belief that the provisions would run out they would have packed up and gone home. In fact, the brave and no doubt beautiful queen had almost come to the end of the rations, but not of her stratagems. The very last bucket of grain she gave to a surviving piglet, and when she had made it gorge itself to the gullet she tipped it over the battlements so that the poor creature burst asunder before the eyes of the Emperor's troops. Again the poor fellows believed what they saw, and when it was reported to Charlemagne that the garrison was so well supplied that good grain could be used for rearing pigs, he ordered the siege to be raised. Soon the army was ready to start back toward Paris. This same tale of a corn-fed piglet occurs in connection with many medieval sieges, but that we have to overlook. Perhaps it was standard practice.

Carcas was no doubt relieved to see the enemy go. And then, all of a sudden, she felt terribly, frighteningly alone. Everyone

314

else in Carcassonne had long been dead, and the Emperor's men were the only people she knew. Running out from the fortress, she called after the troops, blowing a trumpet or perhaps (as some say) ringing a bell. One of the officers heard the call and hurried to tell Charlemagne.

'Your majesty,' he said, 'Carcas is calling.' That is, in the original, 'Carcas sonne.'

With his customary generosity Charlemagne forgave her for tying down his forces so long and in vain, and as Carcas was willing to surrender the fortress and be baptised he turned back and entered the dead city. Then, as a mark of his esteem, and so that she might for ever be mistress of the city she had held so bravely, immediately after her christening he presented her with one of his most chivalrous officers as a new husband, to become the first Count of Carcassonne.

Thus the troubadours would tell the story of the naming of the city, with minstrel's licence that conveniently ignored the earlier name of Carcaso which the citadel bore long before Charlemagne. But we must not be too particular for truth, especially in a place which so easily conjures up the days of chivalry and romance.

There was, for instance, the troubadour Geoffrey Rudel, who fell in love with a lady of Carcassonne whom he had never so much as glimpsed, but accounts of whose beauty and grace had reached his ears in a far country, so that the love-lorn minstrel had no other desire than to come to her, and after terrible journeyings he reached the city and fell at her feet. So great was his love for her that he could not even frame a single word of speech or song to tell her and, gazing up at her, he died of sheer adoration. That was romance at its highest. But there was also Pierre Vidal, another troubadour, whose lovesickness took a different form. His lady love was named Louve, the she-wolf, a strange name for such a beautiful creature. To her he wrote his songs of adoration, ballads which dealt with her virtues and grace, yet in spite of his lyrical attentions the fair Louve gave herself to another. In a final demonstration of his eternal devotion to the only lady he could ever love, Vidal became a wolf. Dressing in fresh wolf skins procured from the hunters, he let himself be chased through the woods by the wolfhounds of the Count of Carcassonne and when the dogs caught him and practically tore him to pieces, he had the huntsmen carry his mutilated body and lay it at the feet of the one he adored. Louve was not at all moved, and one cannot help thinking she

315

may have been lucky not to have an attachment to one so unbalanced.

Naurouze

At Naurouze, a hamlet at the summit level of the Canal du Midi, everything that could show off the Canal du Midi to the glory of the alleged genius of Louis XIV is there, or used to be. At the lowest point between the Mediterranean and the Atlantic Pierre-Paul Riquet is said to have observed that the water of a small spring struck a stone and divided, part flowing east, and part flowing west. This is said to have inspired him to achieve the canal by bringing a much greater supply of water to that point, all the way from the Montagne Noire.

The waters of the Montagne Noire run in fresh and clear after tripping through a mill to work the machinery and pausing to move more slowly through a stately basin, which was to serve as a port for the small ships of Revel, which never came. There are alleys and seats, specimen trees, sluices and walks, and everywhere the crystal water rippling in its bed, splashing and laughing at its achievements in having found its way through so many miles of trough to the summit of the Canal Royal.

To see the basin of Naurouze as it should have been, but never was, one has to turn to the *Proceedings of the Royal Society* for 1670, where a description is given of the plan for 'a great basin octagonal oval-wise, 200 fathoms long and 150 fathoms large, which shall be surrounded with 72 houses to be raised on arches. This basin shall receive all the waters which the deriving channel is to convey thither from the Black Mountain, to be distributed by the Royal Channel to both seas. In the middle of this basin shall be a Colosse, representing the King standing in a triumphant chariot drawn by four sea-horses, holding one foot upon a globe, and a trident in his hand, as marks of his greatness by both sea and land. And then a stream of water, issuing as from a source under the chariot, shall as 'twere be beaten back, and disgorge itself through the throats of serpents toward the four parts of the world, represented by as many rivers, which shall also pour out of their urns a prodigious quantity of water, to show that the graces which the liberality of the King plentifully diffuses to all his people, do pass through the hands of the Lord Colbert.'

Alas, this statuary was never built, but there is still plenty to see. Behind the basin and across the meadow are the Stones of Naurouze, a pile of blocks so unexpected that it is hardly surprising that they should have been regarded as of mysterious origin. It is said that Naurouze was a giant, way back in prehistoric days, and that he was engaged in carrying a load of stones out of which it was hoped to build Toulouse, but the long ascent to the top of the pass so exhausted him that he dropped his burden. The stones were broken in pieces, and the debris has remained there ever since, with the result that Toulouse had subsequently to be built of brick instead. And very beautiful that result has been.

So striking is the pile of giant boulders standing alone upon an open landscape, that it has always been associated with legend and prophecy. Even the sixteenth-century astrologer Nostradamus brought them into his catalogue, predicting that when they should piece themselves together the end of the world would be at hand. More curiously, it was to this place that Marshal Soult was summoned to sign an armistice, and the ceasefire was signed by the Duke of Wellington at the table in the lengthmans cottage near the spillway. That was before the obelisk to Riquet was erected, for it was not until after the Napoleonic Wars that the site was acquired for a memorial by those descendants of Riquet fortunate enough to have escaped the guillotine. Ambassadors, officers, counts and gentlewomen, their names are all there on the monument, and on one face is a handsome medallion of the Baron de Bonrepos himself.

The descent from Naurouze to Toulouse is a run of less than one day, and on the whole it is not interesting. A motorway runs close to the canal, and the day-and-night hum and smell of the traffic has done much to rob the countryside of its former gentle peace. Not that it has always been free from trouble, for however mellowed the land may appear it has twice been ravaged by the English. In the nineteenth century came the Iron Duke. In the fourteenth it was the Black Prince, who marched past the Stones of Naurouze to pillage the hamlets and sack Castelnaudary whilst the Black Death was wiping out one third of his subjects back home.

Océan lock marks the beginning of the western descent. At the first double lock beyond it a minor road crosses the canal and the nearby motorway to the village of Avignonet-Lauragais, not in itself notable but a fateful place in history, as is commemorated on a tablet in the church. For followers are not always like their leaders. The mission of Dominic began as one of preaching,

317

but he had not long been dead before two of the Brothers
Dominican at Toulouse were appointed as the Inquisitors. There
was to be no more of the gentle Dominic, *Au dieu, pauvré,
chantant* had had its day, and the Dominicans Arnald and Seila
were sent out to interrogate, to root out heresy by threat of
sword and stake without reference to any authority of law, civil
or ecclesiastical, and the area around Toulouse and Castelnaudary was one of the earliest to experience the system of terrorisa-
tion by informers, by interrogation under solitary confinement,
and by every means which in our own day we would associate
with brainwashing and the torture techniques of a police state.

Toulouse

Toulouse stands at the western end of Riquet's Canal des Deux
Mers en Languedoc – that is, the Canal du Midi. Where it
reaches its end in the Port de l'Embouchure it is separated from
the Canal Latéral à la Garonne by a fine monument in Carrara
marble, shipped to the spot directly from Italy. This reminds us
that, in spite of its small size, it was really a ship canal, built for
sea-going ships, which by modern standards were remarkably
small. It avoided the long haul around the Iberian Peninsula,
and the danger of passing the strait of Gibraltar, outside which
the Atlantic was infested with Moorish pirates.

Toulouse is known as the Rose City. The buildings appear at
first sight to be built of a very fine red sandstone, but it is brick.
All those from before the skyscraper era are of the same
material, and the mere colour of the place gives it a real beauty.
But to the boatman, Toulouse is first of all the city where Riquet
is remembered. The canalside road near the station is the Boule-
vard de Bonrepos. In cafés the *croque-monsieur* open sandwich of
the rest of France is called a *Croque Riquet*. A statue of the baron
is at the head of the Allées Jean Jaurés, one bridge east of the
railway station at Matabiau, and his tomb is at the foot of the
massive central pillar of the Cathedral of St Étienne, where a
plaque of black marble describes him as 'the beneficent genius
who created the prosperity of the Languedoc'.

Riquet's greatest memorial, however, is the canal itself.
Toulouse was already a large city when he laid out his
waterway, and he intended to connect the canal with the city
moats so that the ships could load or deliver at many points.
But the city fathers obliged him to keep his works outside the

confines of their great Tolosa, and he had to skirt its perimeter to reach the Garonne below the city. One and a half centuries later Toulouse was threatened by the allied armies, and the canal became the defensive line which served successfully to hold at bay for a while the English forces under Wellington. But the city continued to spread, with the result that Riquet's canal now courses through an outer and decidedly dingy part of Toulouse, an area of motor repair shops and small factories.

Castillon-la-Bataille

On the Dordogne, about 50 miles up from the Gironde estuary, and about as far as the river is navigable, with care, on the tide, this little town is little known to the English, because it was purposely omitted from their school history books. In fact it is the site of the great battle which ended the Hundred Years War. There are two notable memorials to the great defeat suffered by the English. One marks the actual site of the battle, the other right by the overgrown towpath, is on the spot where were slain the Great Earl of Washford, Waterford and Valence; Lord Talbot of Gooding and Urchinfield; Lord Strange of Blackmere; Lord Verdun of Alton; Lord Cromwell of Winfield; Lord Furnival of Sheffield; the thrice-crowned Lord of Falconbridge, Knight of the noble order of Saint George, Saint Michael and the Golden Fleece, and the Great Marshal to Henry VI. Curiously enough, these were all one man, for they were the various other titles of the aged John Talbot, Earl of Shrewsbury, who had been governor of Guyenne for an astonishing span of 53 years.

Talbot had an interesting and unusual dominant gene which caused phalangeal synostosis, which means that the joints of his fingers were fused so that they could not bend like those of most people. This is known because his corpse was returned to England to be buried in the parish church at Whitchurch in Shropshire. The tomb bears one of those fashionable effigies of a knight recumbent, and whether from observation or personal knowledge or hearsay, the sculptor faithfully portrayed him with unbending fingers. The same effect can be noticed in some of his descendants 14 generations later, a fascinating testimony to the faithfulness of chromosome copying at cell divisions, for a little calculation of the kind in which geneticists like to indulge would indicate that the gene must have been reproduced more than 700 consecutive times between the days of the thrice-victorious Lord of Falconbridge and his descendants in our own time.

It is interesting also that when the tomb was renovated in 1874 the coffin was opened for reconstruction – or maybe just out of that morbid curiosity which drives people to peep at the remains of the dead – and the fingers were found indeed to have the peculiarity I have described. Another fascinating discovery was that a church mouse had penetrated the hole made in Talbot's skull by a French battle-axe and had built a nest out of leaves torn from the *Book of Common Prayer*.

As to the battle which put an end to the Hundred Years War and sealed the fate of the English dominions in France, it was notable for two other reasons, the complete success of French strategy and the fact that here for the first time, the day was decided by a new-fangled weapon, artillery. Guyenne had by then been largely reconquered by France, but knowing that the inhabitants were restive under the oppressions of Charles VII, King Henry VI of England instructed the Earl of Shrewsbury to recapture it. Swiftly Bordeaux was retaken, and Castillon also, but the commander of the opposing French forces, Jean Bureau, decided to settle the matter once and for all in a single engagement. The plan was to construct a well protected camp, and lure Talbot to attack.

The French army of 10,000 men was rapidly installed in a camp protected at the rear by the small river Lidoire and its cliffs. The front and sides were contained by about a mile of ditch hastily dug and filled from the river, and so designed that its zigzags gave the possibility of crossfire. Trees were felled along it to obstruct any leaping by English cavalry, and in the centre was a deep nick which appeared to the English (as was intended) to be a gateway.

The English advanced and rushed into this funnel, unaware that no less than 300 pieces of artillery were concealed along the banks on either side. Fired at from both flanks, the English were forced back on each other, yet in spite of their terrible losses they endeavoured to storm the supposed gate. But it was too late. A few more salvos, and they turned to flee. And at that moment a force of Breton horsemen, cunningly concealed at a distance, descended at full gallop and attacked them with their lances.

The English left 4,000 dead upon the restricted field, their commander Talbot among them, and those that escaped were quickly overtaken at Castillon itself and elsewhere. The day of the heavily armoured knight on his war horse was over, and so was the English hegemony over all French territory except for

Calais, even if the local inhabitants may have regretted it. As Charles the Dauphin says in *King Henry VI*, 'All will be ours, now bloody Talbot's slain.'

Moissac

The Garonne lateral canal at Moissac

If it had not been for a storm which felled a number of trees across the Canal latéral à la Garonne, so that I had to wait for a day or two while the engineers winched them out of the way, I would probably never have seen the Abbey of Moissac. And there are certain things which one may come upon unexpectedly but which hit one so violently that life is never quite the same again. It is illumined with a new light, a greater understanding, fresh certainty, an increased wonder, and awe, and thankfulness. Two such things have burst upon my awareness, and curiously enough I discovered both of them by canal and have returned to each of them more than once. The first is the polyptych painted by Matthias Grünewald, which is now in the Unterlinden Museum, not far from the canal basin in Colmar. The other is over the doorway of the abbey at Moissac.

321

The Abbey of Moissac is alleged to date back to the time of Clovis in the sixth century. Legend relates that when he had beaten the Visigoths in battle there appeared to him three angels, bearing with them the architectural drawings for an abbey that he was to build in Quercy and was to dedicate to St Peter. Unfortunately the three heavenly messengers disappeared without identifying the building site any further so Clovis climbed to the top of the hill behind Moissac and, summoning all his strength, he cast his javelin straight ahead. Fortunately his throw fell rather short, otherwise the spear might have vanished in the Garonne or the Tarn. But it landed in a marsh. There Clovis dutifully built the abbey.

Whatever we may make of that story, the Abbey was certainly there in the year 847, when enterprising Viking raiders reached the Gironde, and sailed ahead up the Garonne as far as Toulouse, laying waste, sacking and pillaging as they went. It is known that they destroyed the Abbey of Moissac on their way up the river, but it was later rebuilt and affiliated to the famous foundation of Cluny. This second building with its famous cloisters has survived for nine centuries, in spite of the attacks on the town by Simon de Montfort, the occupation by the English, their expulsion a few years later by the Duke of Anjou, and finally the violence of the French Revolution, when it became in turn a barracks, a gunpowder factory and a forage store. Later still, the great court of the cloisters was to be pulled down to make way for the Bordeaux-Sète railway when reason began to return once more and the Fine Arts Commission intervened to preserve from destruction the finest work of Romanesque architecture in France. And there it still is.

I make no apology at all for saying that to stand before the door of the Abbey and be confronted by the Christ of the second Coming can be a tremendous spiritual experience. He and his whole vibrant entourage of seraphims and angels and evangelists come from a century before the Inquisition burned alive 200 Albigensian Christians in the town. He is not a Christ of hatred, nor is he a sad figure of passion, a man of sorrows and acquainted with grief exalted to wear a saintly dressing gown. He is a person of complete authority and of such power that it would be terrifying, if it were not for the complete calm and serenity with which he is opening the new era of justice and right. There is a halo behind his head, made up of a formal cross and a dozen thistles, but it is not the halo which makes the Christ truly and invincibly royal. Nor is it the grandeur of the kingly robe. It is the face, the face of a Christ who is infinitely great. The 24 Elders of Revelation are almost breaking their necks in the suddenness of their amazement at his appearance, and the rebecs upon which they were to play a well-rehearsed song of welcome dangle unplucked from their hands. Only the two angels in attendance have a smiling air of superior knowledge, as though they have known all along that it will be like this when time has come to an end and existence runs into a new dimension.

There is no anger in the face of the Christ regnant, nor humility, nor pride. He stares one straight in the face, just as he has done to others since 1130. He is a Christ who cannot be deceived, but who understands what it is to be human and bound for the time being within four dimensions. He forgives, but he will have no compromise with evil. Absolute justice and glory are portrayed above the doorway of the Abbey church in Moissac, yet the work was done by a man unknown. More important than his identity is the certainty that this central figure of the parousia is not one that any man could have thought up. I am absolutely certain that it is authentic, that it can only have come from a genuine vision of the truth of eternity. Like Grünewald's Crucifixion in Colmar, it is the work of a man who had seen it, who had been allowed to travel through the dimensions of time and space to glimpse the ultimate reality and to record it for others for all time. And to record it in just such a way that its dynamic power is never forgotten, never lost, and can survive the worst an iconoclastic human revolution can do.